DATE DUE

JOSEPH CONRAD

Modern Critical Views

Henry Adams
Edward Albee
A. R. Ammons
Matthew Arnold
John Ashbery
W. H. Auden
Jane Austen
James Baldwin
Charles Baudelaire
Samuel Beckett
Saul Bellow
The Bible
Elizabeth Bishop
William Blake
Jorge Luis Borges
Elizabeth Bowen
Bertolt Brecht
The Brontës
Robert Browning
Anthony Burgess
George Gordon, Lord
 Byron
Thomas Carlyle
Lewis Carroll
Willa Cather
Cervantes
Geoffrey Chaucer
Kate Chopin
Samuel Taylor Coleridge
Joseph Conrad
Contemporary Poets
Hart Crane
Stephen Crane
Dante
Charles Dickens
Emily Dickinson
John Donne & the Seven-
 teenth-Century Meta-
 physical Poets
Elizabethan Dramatists
Theodore Dreiser
John Dryden
George Eliot
T. S. Eliot
Ralph Ellison
Ralph Waldo Emerson
William Faulkner
Henry Fielding
F. Scott Fitzgerald
Gustave Flaubert
E. M. Forster
Sigmund Freud
Robert Frost

Robert Graves
Graham Greene
Thomas Hardy
Nathaniel Hawthorne
William Hazlitt
Seamus Heaney
Ernest Hemingway
Geoffrey Hill
Friedrich Hölderlin
Homer
Gerard Manley Hopkins
William Dean Howells
Zora Neale Hurston
Henry James
Samuel Johnson and
 James Boswell
Ben Jonson
James Joyce
Franz Kafka
John Keats
Rudyard Kipling
D. H. Lawrence
John Le Carré
Ursula K. Le Guin
Doris Lessing
Sinclair Lewis
Robert Lowell
Norman Mailer
Bernard Malamud
Thomas Mann
Christopher Marlowe
Carson McCullers
Herman Melville
James Merrill
Arthur Miller
John Milton
Eugenio Montale
Marianne Moore
Iris Murdoch
Vladimir Nabokov
Joyce Carol Oates
Sean O'Casey
Flannery O'Connor
Eugene O'Neill
George Orwell
Cynthia Ozick
Walter Pater
Walker Percy
Harold Pinter
Plato
Edgar Allan Poe
Poets of Sensibility & the
 Sublime

Alexander Pope
Katherine Ann Porter
Ezra Pound
Pre-Raphaelite Poets
Marcel Proust
Thomas Pynchon
Arthur Rimbaud
Theodore Roethke
Philip Roth
John Ruskin
J. D. Salinger
Gershom Scholem
William Shakespeare
 (3 vols.)
 Histories & Poems
 Comedies
 Tragedies
George Bernard Shaw
Mary Wollstonecraft
 Shelley
Percy Bysshe Shelley
Edmund Spenser
Gertrude Stein
John Steinbeck
Laurence Sterne
Wallace Stevens
Tom Stoppard
Jonathan Swift
Alfred, Lord Tennyson
William Makepeace
 Thackeray
Henry David Thoreau
Leo Tolstoi
Anthony Trollope
Mark Twain
John Updike
Gore Vidal
Virgil
Robert Penn Warren
Evelyn Waugh
Eudora Welty
Nathanael West
Edith Wharton
Walt Whitman
Oscar Wilde
Tennessee Williams
William Carlos Williams
Thomas Wolfe
Virginia Woolf
William Wordsworth
Richard Wright
William Butler Yeats

These and other titles in preparation

Modern Critical Views

JOSEPH CONRAD

Edited and with an introduction by
Harold Bloom
Sterling Professor of the Humanities
Yale University

CHELSEA HOUSE PUBLISHERS
New York ◊ Philadelphia

Library of Congress Cataloging-in-Publication Data
Joseph Conrad.
   (Modern critical views)
   Bibliography: p.
   Includes index.
   1. Conrad, Joseph, 1857–1924—Criticism and interpretation—
Addresses, essays, lectures. I. Bloom, Harold. II. Series.
PR6005.04Z7496   1986   823'.912   86–2331
ISBN 0-87754-642-8 (alk. paper)

Contents

Editor's Note

This volume gathers together a representative selection of the best criticism devoted to the fiction of Joseph Conrad during the past quarter century, arranged in the chronological order of its original publication. I am grateful to David Parker for his aid in selecting these essays.

The introduction centers upon Conrad's mode of impressionism, which is seen as both reflecting the influence of Henry James's middle period, and as swerving away from the strength of that influence. A contrast is made between the relative failure of the language of Conradian impressionism in *Heart of Darkness* and the extraordinary success of that language in *Nostromo*.

Ian Watt begins the chronological sequence with his shrewd survey of Conrad criticism of the 1950s, particularly in regard to *The Nigger of the "Narcissus."* This sets the background for the criticism of the 1960s, starting here with Edward W. Said's exploration of the shorter fiction, with a strong emphasis upon Conrad's insistence that we survive, as writers and as humans, only through and by our eccentricities. The psychoanalytic critic Norman N. Holland follows with a reading of how style determines the eccentric and almost unique ethos of *The Secret Agent*. In a remarkable exegesis of *Victory*, R. W. B. Lewis also confirms Conrad's faithfulness to "the variable and highly unpredictable character of individual human beings."

Ian Watt returns with a strong defense of impressionism in *Heart of Darkness*, making a positive judgment that contrasts forcefully to the editor's dubiety in the introduction. Another short masterwork, "The Secret Sharer," is analyzed by Joan E. Steiner, who emphasizes the dialectical complexities that Conrad exploits in his version of a doubling relationship. Such complexities haunt the imagination of morality in both *Heart of Darkness* and *Nostromo*, a haunting that is investigated here by Daniel Melnick. Moral imagination, in Conrad, always takes us, via "the logic of perverse unreason," to the limits of the absurd, limits traced by Adam Gillon in the narrative patterns of two of Conrad's aesthetic triumphs, *Under Western Eyes* and *Victory*, and the more dubious *Chance*, which was nevertheless a great popular success.

Conrad's women in his early novels, *Almayer's Folly* and *An Outcast of the Islands*, are judged by Ruth Nadelhaft to be emblems of an alternative vision, one deeply set against "the morality of imperialism and colonialism." Two powerful accounts of *Lord Jim*, by J. Hillis Miller and Martin Price, call into question (in very different ways) any judgments made by moral readings of Conrad. Miller employs the resources of a deconstructive rhetorical analysis to show how indeterminate Conrad's meanings are, while Price subtly demonstrates how Conrad, in *Lord Jim* and also in *Nostromo*, drives apart the heroic and the authentic, without abandoning a desire for both.

In the final essay, Aaron Fogel performs a large-scale exegesis of the poetics of *Nostromo*, in order to examine the book's "tensions between force and farce." Fogel synthesizes a number of contemporary critical modes, and arrives at a powerful conception of Gould's fate as the necessarily Oedipal disaster of the man who has evaded "forced dialogue." Though Fogel sees this and Nostromo's similar fate as farce, I myself would call it a mode of tragedy, because of Nostromo's belated vestiges of the natural sublime. Such a debate, between Fogel and myself, returns this volume full circle to its introduction, and so begins again the endless cycle of critical responses that are prompted inevitably by the permanent and enigmatic strength of Conrad's fictions.

Introduction

I

In Conrad's "Youth" (1898), Marlow gives us a brilliant description of the sinking of the *Judea*:

"Between the darkness of earth and heaven she was burning fiercely upon a disc of purple sea shot by the blood-red play of gleams; upon a disc of water glittering and sinister. A high, clear flame, an immense and lonely flame, ascended from the ocean, and from its summit the black smoke poured continuously at the sky. She burned furiously; mournful and imposing like a funeral pile kindled in the night, surrounded by the sea, watched over by the stars. A magnificent death had come like a grace, like a gift, like a reward to that old ship at the end of her laborious day. The surrender of her weary ghost to the keeper of the stars and sea was stirring like the sight of a glorious triumph. The masts fell just before daybreak, and for a moment there was a burst and turmoil of sparks that seemed to fill with flying fire the night patient and watchful, the vast night lying silent upon the sea. At daylight she was only a charred shell, floating still under a cloud of smoke and bearing a glowing mass of coal within.

"Then the oars were got out, and the boats forming in a line moved around her remains as if in procession—the longboat leading. As we pulled across her stern a slim dart of fire shot out viciously at us, and suddenly she went down, head first, in a great hiss of steam. The unconsumed stern was the last to sink; but the paint had gone, had cracked, had peeled off, and there were no letters, there was no word, no stubborn device that was like her soul, to flash at the rising sun her creed and her name.

1

The apocalyptic vividness is enhanced by the visual namelessness of the "unconsumed stern," as though the creed of Christ's people maintained both its traditional refusal to violate the Second Commandment, and its traditional affirmation of its not-to-be-named God. With the *Judea*, Conrad sinks the romance of youth's illusions, but like all losses in Conrad this submersion in the destructive element is curiously dialectical, since only experiential loss allows for the compensation of an imaginative gain in the representation of artistic truth. Originally the ephebe of Flaubert and of Flaubert's "son," Maupassant, Conrad was reborn as the narrative disciple of Henry James, the James of *The Spoils of Poynton* and *What Maisie Knew*, rather than the James of the final phase.

Ian Watt convincingly traces the genesis of Marlow to the way that "James developed the indirect narrative approach through the sensitive central intelligence of one of the characters." Marlow, whom James derided as "that preposterous magic mariner," actually represents Conrad's swerve away from the excessive strength of James's influence upon him. By always "mixing himself up with the narrative," in James's words, Marlow guarantees an enigmatic reserve that increases the distance between the impressionistic techniques of Conrad and James. Though there is little valid comparison that can be made between Conrad's greatest achievements and the hesitant, barely fictional status of Pater's *Marius the Epicurean*, Conrad's impressionism is as extreme and solipsistic as Pater's. There is a definite parallel between the fates of Sebastian Van Storck (in Pater's *Imaginary Portraits*) and Decoud in *Nostromo*.

In his 1897 "Preface" to *The Nigger of the "Narcissus,"* Conrad famously insisted that his creative task was "before all to make you *see*." He presumably was aware that he thus joined himself to a line of prose seers whose latest representatives were Carlyle, Ruskin, and Pater. There is a movement in that group from Carlyle's exuberant "Natural Supernaturalism" through Ruskin's paganization of Evangelical fervor to Pater's evasive and skeptical Epicurean materialism, with its eloquent suggestion that all we can see is the flux of sensations. Conrad exceeds Pater in the reduction of impressionism to a state of consciousness where the seeing narrator is hopelessly mixed up with the seen narrative. James may seem an impressionist when compared to Flaubert, but alongside of Conrad he is clearly shown to be a kind of Platonist, imposing forms and resolutions upon the flux of human relations by an exquisite formal geometry altogether his own.

To observe that Conrad is metaphysically less of an Idealist is hardly to argue that he is necessarily a stronger novelist than his master, James. It may suggest though that Conrad's originality is more disturbing than that of James, and may help explain why Conrad, rather than James, became the dominant

influence upon the generation of American novelists that included Hemingway, Fitzgerald, and Faulkner. The cosmos of *The Sun Also Rises*, *The Great
Gatsby*, and *As I Lay Dying* derives from *Heart of Darkness* and *Nostromo* rather
than from *The Ambassadors* and *The Golden Bowl*. Darl Bundren is the extreme
inheritor of Conrad's quest to carry impressionism into its heart of darkness
in the human awareness that we are only a flux of sensations gazing outwards
upon a flux of impressions.

II

Heart of Darkness may always be a critical battleground between readers
who regard it as an aesthetic triumph, and those like myself who doubt its
ability to rescue us from its own hopeless obscurantism. That Marlow seems,
at moments, not to know what he is talking about, is almost certainly one of
the narrative's deliberate strengths, but if Conrad also seems finally not to
know, then he necessarily loses some of his authority as a storyteller. Perhaps
he loses it to death our death, or our anxiety that he will not sustain the
illusion of his fiction's duration long enough for us to sublimate the frustrations
it brings us.

These frustrations need not be deprecated. Conrad's diction, normally
flawless, is notoriously vague throughout *Heart of Darkness*. E. M. Forster's
wicked comment on Conrad's entire work is justified perhaps only when applied to *Heart of Darkness*:

> Misty in the middle as well as at the edges, the secret cask of his
> genius contains a vapour rather than a jewel. . . . No creed, in
> fact.

Forster's misty vapor seems to inhabit such Conradian recurrent modi-
fiers as "monstrous," "unspeakable," "atrocious," and many more, but these
are minor defects compared to the involuntary self-parody that Conrad inflicts
upon himself. There are moments that sound more like James Thurber lov-
ingly satirizing Conrad than like Conrad:

> "We had carried Kurtz into the pilot house: there was more air
> there. Lying on the couch, he stared through the open shutter.
> There was an eddy in the mass of human bodies, and the woman
> with helmeted head and tawny cheeks rushed out to the very brink
> of the stream. She put out her hands, shouted something, and all
> that wild mob took up the shout in a roaring chorus of articulated,
> rapid, breathless utterance.

" 'Do you understand this?' I asked.

"He kept on looking out past me with fiery, longing eyes, with a mingled expression of wistfulness and hate. He made no answer, but I saw a smile, a smile of indefinable meaning, appear on his colorless lips that a moment after twitched convulsively. 'Do I not?' he said slowly, gasping, as if the words had been torn out of him by a supernatural power.

This cannot be defended as an instance of what Frank Kermode calls a language "needed when Marlow is not equal to the experience described." Has the experience been described here? Smiles of "indefinable meaning" are smiled once too often in a literary text if they are smiled even once. *Heart of Darkness* has taken on some of the power of myth, even if the book is limited by its involuntary obscurantism. It has haunted American literature from T. S. Eliot's poetry through our major novelists of the era 1920 to 1940, on to a line of movies that go from the *Citizen Kane* of Orson Welles (a substitute for an abandoned Welles project to film *Heart of Darkness*) on to Coppola's *Apocalypse Now*. In this instance, Conrad's formlessness seems to have worked as an aid, so diffusing his conception as to have made it available to an almost universal audience.

III

An admirer of Conrad is happiest with his five great novels: *Lord Jim* (1900), *Nostromo* (1904), *The Secret Agent* (1906), *Under Western Eyes* (1910), and *Victory* (1914). Subtle and tormented narratives, they form an extraordinarily varied achievement, and despite their common features they can make a reader wonder that they all should have been composed by the same artist. Endlessly enigmatic as a personality and as a formidable moral character, Conrad pervades his own books, a presence not to be put by, an elusive storyteller who yet seems to write a continuous spiritual autobiography. By the general consent of advanced critics and of common readers, Conrad's masterwork is *Nostromo*, where his perspectives are largest, and where his essential originality in the representation of human blindnesses and consequent human affections is at its strongest. Like all overwhelming originalities, Conrad's ensues in an authentic difficulty, which can be assimilated only very slowly, if at all. Repeated rereadings gradually convince me that *Nostromo* is anything but a Conradian litany to the virtue he liked to call "fidelity." The book is tragedy, of a post-Nietzschean sort, despite Conrad's strong contempt for Nietzsche. Decoud, void of all illusions, is self-destroyed because he cannot sustain solitude. Nos-

tromo, perhaps the only persuasive instance of the natural sublime in a twentieth-century hero of fiction, dies "betrayed he hardly knows by what or by
whom," as Conrad says. But this is Conrad at his most knowing, and the
novel shows us precisely how Nostromo is betrayed, by himself, and by what
in himself.

It is a mystery of an overwhelming fiction why it can sustain virtually
endless rereadings. *Nostromo*, to me, rewards frequent rereadings in something
of the way that *Othello* does; there is always surprise waiting for me. Brilliant
as every aspect of the novel is, Nostromo himself is the imaginative center of
the book, and yet Nostromo is unique among Conrad's personae, and not a
Conradian man whom we could have expected. His creator's description of
this central figure as "the Magnificent Capataz, the Man of the People,"
breathes a writer's love for his most surprising act of the imagination. So does
a crucial paragraph from the same source, the "Author's Note" that Conrad
added as a preface thirteen years after the initial publication:

> In his firm grip on the earth he inherits, in his improvidence and
> generosity, in his lavishness with his gifts, in his manly vanity, in
> the obscure sense of his greatness and in his faithful devotion with
> something despairing as well as desperate in its impulses, he is a
> Man of the People, their very own unenvious force, disdaining to
> lead but ruling from within. Years afterwards, grown older as the
> famous Captain Fidanza, with a stake in the country, going about
> his many affairs followed by respectful glances in the modernized
> streets of Sulaco, calling on the widow of the cargador, attending
> the Lodge, listening in unmoved silence to anarchist speeches at
> the meeting, the enigmatical patron of the new revolutionary ag-
> itation, the trusted, the wealthy comrade Fidanza with the knowl-
> edge of his moral ruin locked up in his breast, he remains
> essentially a man of the People. In his mingled love and scorn of
> life and in the bewildered conviction of having been betrayed, of
> dying betrayed he hardly knows by what or by whom, he is still
> of the People, their undoubted Great Man—with a private history
> of his own.

Despite this "moral ruin," and not because of it, Conrad and his readers
share the conviction of Nostromo's greatness, share in his sublime self-recognition. How many persuasive images of greatness, of a natural sublimity,
exist in modern fiction? Conrad's may be the last enhanced vision of Natural
Man, of the Man of the People, in which anyone has found it possible to
believe. Yet Conrad himself characteristically qualifies his own belief in Nos-

tromo, and critics too easily seduced by ironies have weakly misread the only apparent irony of Conrad's repeated references to Nostromo as "the magnificent Capataz de Cargadores." Magnificent, beyond the reach of all irony, Nostromo manifestly is. It is the magnificence of the natural leader who disdains leadership, yet who loves reputation. Though he is of the People, Nostromo serves no ideal, unlike old Viola the Garibaldino. With the natural genius for command, the charismatic endowment that could make him another Garibaldi, Nostromo nevertheless scorns any such role, in the name of any cause whatsoever. He is a pure Homeric throwback, not wholly unlike Tolstoi's Hadji Murad, except that he acknowledges neither enemies nor friends, except for his displaced father, Viola. And he enchants us even as he enchants the populace of Sulaco, though most of all he enchants the skeptical and enigmatic Conrad, who barely defends himself against the enchantment with some merely rhetorical ironies.

Ethos is the daimon, character is fate, in Conrad as in Heracleitus, and Nostromo's tragic fate is the inevitable fulfillment of his desperate grandeur, which Conrad cannot dismiss as mere vanity, despite all his own skepticism. Only Nostromo saves the novel, and Conrad, from nihilism, the nihilism of Decoud's waste in suicide. Nostromo is betrayed partly by Decoud's act of self-destruction, with its use of four ingots of silver to send his body down, but largely by his own refusal to maintain the careless preference for glory over gain which is more than a gesture or a style, which indeed is the authentic mode of being that marks the hero. Nostromo is only himself when he can say, with perfect truth: "My name is known from one end of Sulaco to the other. What more can you do for me?"

IV

Towards the end of Chapter Ten of Part Third, "The Lighthouse," Conrad renders his own supposed verdict upon both Decoud and Nostromo, in a single page, in two parallel sentences a paragraph apart:

> A victim of the disillusioned weariness which is the retribution meted out to intellectual audacity, the brilliant Don Martin Decoud, weighted by the bars of San Tomé silver, disappeared without a trace, swallowed up in the immense indifference of things.

> The magnificent Capataz de Cargadores, victim of the disenchanted vanity which is the reward of audacious action, sat in the weary pose of a hunted outcast through a night of sleeplessness as

tormenting as any known to Decoud, his companion in the most desperate affair of his life. And he wondered how Decoud had died.

Decoud's last thought, after shooting himself was: "I wonder how that Capataz died." Conrad seems to leave little to choose between being "a victim of the disillusioned weariness which is the retribution meted out to intellectual audacity" or a "victim of the disenchanted vanity which is the reward of audacious action." The brilliant intellectual and the magnificent man of action are victimized alike for their audacity, and it is a fine irony that "retribution" and "reward" become assimilated to one another. Yet the book is Nostromo's and not Decoud's, and a "disenchanted vanity" is a higher fate than a "disillusioned weariness," if only because an initial enchantment is a nobler state than an initial illusion. True that Nostromo's enchantment was only of and with himself, but that is proper for an Achilles or a Hadji Murad. Decoud dies because he cannot bear solitude, and so cannot bear himself. Nostromo finds death-in-life and then death because he has lost the truth of his vanity, its enchanted insouciance, the *sprezzatura* which he, a plebian, nevertheless had made his authentic self.

Nostromo's triumph, though he cannot know it, is that an image of this authenticity survives him, an image so powerful as to persuade both Conrad and the perceptive reader that even the self-betrayed hero retains an aesthetic dignity that renders his death tragic rather than sordid. Poor Decoud, for all his brilliance, dies a nihilistic death, disappearing "without a trace, swallowed up in the immense indifference of things." Nostromo, after his death, receives an aesthetic tribute beyond all irony, in the superb closing paragraph of the novel:

> Dr. Monygham, pulling round in the police-galley, heard the name pass over his head. It was another of Nostromo's triumphs, the greatest, the most enviable, the most sinister of all. In that true cry of undying passion that seemed to ring aloud from Punta Mala to Azuera and away to the bright line of the horizon, overhung by a big white cloud shining like a mass of solid silver, the genius of the magnificent Capataz de Cargadores dominated the dark gulf containing his conquests of treasure and love.

IAN WATT

Conrad Criticism and
The Nigger of the "Narcissus"

So our virtues
Lie in the interpretation of the time
Coriolanus, IV, vii, 49–50

The increasing critical attention of the last decade brought forth in the centenary year of Conrad's birth a tolerably heated literary controversy: Marvin Mudrick's attack on the views of—among others—Robert W. Stallman, in his "Conrad and the Terms of Modern Criticism" (*Hudson Review*, Autumn, 1954), was answered in the Spring, 1957, issue of the *Kenyon Review* ("Fiction and Its Critics . . ."), an answer which provoked a pretty note of injured innocence from Mudrick in the subsequent issue. Their mutual acerbities may, I think, be welcomed, if only as a reminder that Billingsgate has an ancient title to not the least attractive among the foothills of Helicon; my present concern, however, is with the ultimate grounds of their disagreement and this because it involves several problems of some importance both for Conrad and for our literary criticism in general. It also happens that Mudrick amplified his case against Conrad in the March, 1957, issue of *Nineteenth-Century Fiction* with an essay on *The Nigger of the "Narcissus,"* a book which was at the same time the subject of a full-scale essay in the *Kenyon Review* by another of the writers attacked by Mudrick, Albert J. Guerard; and since *The Nigger of the "Narcissus"* has also received considerable attention in the last few years from a representative variety of modern critics, it would seem that our discussion can conveniently be centered on the criticism of Conrad's first masterpiece.

From *Nineteenth-Century Fiction* 12, no. 4 (March 1958). © 1958 by The Regents of the University of California.

I

In "The Artist's Conscience and *The Nigger of the 'Narcissus'*" Mudrick grants Conrad's mastery of "sustained passages of description unsurpassed in English fiction"; the storm, for example, and the early presentation of Wait, are wholly successful, for there Conrad gives us "an extraordinarily close and convincing observation of the outside of things." But—alas!—our verbal photographer does not always "keep his introspection to a respectful minimum"; he has the gall to tell us "what to think about life, death, and the rest"; and there results "gross violation of the point of view" and "unctuous thrilling rhetoric . . . about man's work and the indifferent universe and of course the ubiquitous sea."

The sardonic irony of that last phrase may give one pause; on an ocean voyage the sea is rather ubiquitous—if you can't bear it, *The Nigger of the "Narcissus"* and, indeed, a good deal of Conrad, is best left alone. True, Stallman can show how impatient Conrad was with being considered a writer of "sea stories," but this methodological strategy seems suspect—minimizing the importance of overt subject matter so as to ensure for the critic that amplitude of sea-room to which his proud craft has of late become accustomed. One may, indeed, find Mudrick's contrary assertion in his earlier essay that the sea is "Conrad's only element" less than final and yet salutary in emphasis; in any case his present jaded impatience seems ominously revelatory.

Mudrick's main charges, however, are not easily dismissed. A number of previous critics have drawn attention to the inconsistencies in the point of view of the narration in *The Nigger of the "Narcissus,"* and to the marked strain of somewhat portentous magniloquence in Conrad's work generally. Mudrick has only given old objections new force, partly by his enviable gift for the memorably damaging phrase, and partly by allotting them a much more decisive significance in his final critical assessment. In some form, I take it, the charges are incontrovertible; but a brief analysis of Conrad's practice and of its historical perspective (the book appeared in 1897) may lead both to a more lenient judgment on the technique of *The Nigger of the "Narcissus"* and to a clearer realization of some of the problematic implications of our current critical outlook.

Among the "gross violations of point of view" specified is that whereby the reader directly witnesses the final confrontation of Wait and Donkin, although no one else, of course, was present. Mudrick argues:

> though the violation in itself compels no distressing conclusions,
> it is a more important fact . . . than it would be in other, more

loosely organised fiction. From the outset, and through more than half of the novel, Conrad has made us almost nervously sensitive to the point of view as product and evidence of the stereoscopic accuracy of the account: I, a member of the crew, restricted in my opportunities but thoughtful and observant, tell you all that I see.

A brief historical reflection forces us to recognize that it is not really Conrad who has made us "almost nervously sensitive to the point of view," or at least, not directly; it is a generation of critics who have developed, partly from Conrad's technique, partly from the theory and practice of Henry James, and even more from its formulation in Percy Lubbock's *The Craft of Fiction* (1921), a theory of point of view in narrative which has been tremendously influential in providing both the critic and novelist with an until-then largely unsuspected key to the technique of fiction. But there is a vast difference between welcoming a valuable refinement of formal awareness and accepting as a matter of prescription the rule that all works of fiction should be told from a single and clearly defined point of view. Yet in the last few years something like this seems to have happened, and one of Mudrick's phrases seems even to bestow on the dogma a quasi-ethical sanction: when he speaks of "illicit glimpses of the 'inside,' " doesn't that "illicit" attempt to convict Conrad of some kind of moral turpitude? To be fair we must at least admit that the charge only became criminal a generation after the fact. And, waiving the chronological defense, hasn't the time come to ask whether Dr. Johnson's point about an earlier formal prescription—the unities of time and place— isn't relevant here? "Delusion, if delusion be admitted, has no certain limitation": the reader knows that *The Nigger of the "Narcissus"* can show very convincingly that the changes in point of view serve a number of turns, and yet there are signs of a lingering embarrassment. He writes, unexceptionably, that, in general, "the best narrative technique is the one which, however imperfect logically, enlists the author's creative energies and fully explores his subject"; in the present case he finds "the changes in point-of-view done unobtrusively and with pleasing insouciance," and shows how they mirror the story's "general movement from isolation to solidarity to poignant separation." However, when Guerard comes to another kind of change in Conrad's method of reporting—the shift from objective reporting to lofty generalization—he comments that it is one of the "incorrigible necessities of the early Conrad," and in that "incorrigible" concedes that such variations in narrative strategy are indisputably literary offenses, although he is prepared to be good-tempered about it.

But Guerard's earlier position is surely equally applicable here; for both kinds of change in Conrad's point of view, not only those concerning the identity of the presumed narrator but also those concerning his varying tone and attitude toward what he is narrating, are closely related responses to the rather complicated imperatives of Conrad's subject as it develops. If Conrad had wholly restricted himself to the mind of one individual narrator, he would have had to expend a great deal of mechanical artifice—the kind of dexterous literary engineering later exhibited in *Chance*—in arranging for them to be plausibly visible: but this particularization of the point of view could only have been achieved at the expense of what is probably Conrad's supreme objective in *The Nigger of the "Narcissus"*; the continual and immediate presence of an individualized narrator, sleeping in a certain bunk, member of a certain watch, caught up in a particular set of past and present circumstances, could not but deflect our attention from the book's real protagonist—the ship and its crew. So protean a protagonist could be fully observed only from a shifting point of view: sometimes hovering above the deck, seeing the ship as a whole; sometimes infinitely distant, setting one brief human effort against the widest vistas of time and space, of sea and history; occasionally engaging us in a supreme act of immediate participation, as when the narrator becomes identified with one of the five "we's" who rescue Wait; and finally involving us in the pathos of separation, when the narrator becomes an "I" to pronounce the book's closing valediction to the crew as they disperse.

The terms of this valediction, indeed, seem to emphasize how well advised Conrad was not to make his narrator too immediate a person to the reader. In general, as soon as we feel that the author's reflections are issuing from an individual character we naturally expect them to be expressed in an appropriate personal vernacular; and this either sets severe limits on the range of reflection, or creates an almost insoluble stylistic problem. Both difficulties, and especially the second, obtrude in the last paragraph of *The Nigger of the "Narcissus"*; for example when Conrad writes: "Haven't we, together and upon the immortal sea, wrung out a meaning from our sinful lives?" The particularized individual cannot—in prose, at least, and since the rise of realism—be both microcosm and macrocosm without some kind of apparent inflation; such was the problem which the Irish dramatists, trying to escape from the "joyless and pallid words" of Ibsen and Zola, had to face; and in this momentary anticipation of the very note of Synge, Conrad surely reveals how inappropriate such quasi-colloquial elevation was for his purposes.

The intrusiveness of the "I" narrator, who only becomes evident in the last two paragraphs of *The Nigger of the "Narcissus,"* thus underlines the book's need for a variable narrative angle easily adjustable to different kinds of vision and comment. Until then, I think, we can find many logical contradictions in

Conrad's manipulations of point of view, but not, unless our critical precon-
ceptions are allowed to dominate our literary perceptions, any consequent
failure in narrative command; and we should perhaps conclude that E. M.
Forster was in the main right, when he insisted, in *Aspects of the Novel*, that
"the whole intricate question . . . resolves itself . . . into the power of the
writer to bounce the reader into accepting what he says."

The shifting point of view in *The Nigger of the "Narcissus,"* then, enacts
the varying aspects of its subject; in a wider sense, it may be said to enact
the reasons for Conrad's greatness: the fact that he was a seaman but not only
a seaman, that he was able to convey, not only the immediacies of his subject,
but their perspective in the whole tradition of civilization. The actual prose
in which some of the loftier elements of this perspective are conveyed, however, is a good deal more grandiloquent than we can today happily stomach.
As an example, we may take a well-known passage which Mudrick quotes as
his clinching specimen of Conrad's "unctuous thrilling rhetoric," the opening
of the fourth chapter:

> On men reprieved by its disdainful mercy, the immortal sea con-
> fers in its justice the full privilege of desired unrest. Through the
> perfect wisdom of its grace they are not permitted to meditate at
> ease upon the complicated and acrid savour of existence [, lest they
> should remember and, perchance, regret the reward of a cup of
> inspiring bitterness, tasted so often, and so often withdrawn from
> before their stiffening but reluctant lips]. They must without pause
> justify their life to the external pity that commands toil to be hard
> and unceasing, from sunrise to sunset, from sunset to sunrise: till
> the weary succession of nights and days tainted by the obstinate
> clamor of sages, demanding bliss and an empty heaven, is re-
> deemed at last by the vast silence of pain and labour, by the dumb
> fear and the dumb courage of men obscure, forgetful, and endur-
> ing.

Conrad himself, apparently, was uneasy about some of this, and deleted
the passage in brackets when revising for the collected edition some twenty
years after. He had no doubt become more aware, and more critical, of the
influence of the stylistic aims of French romanticism, the only specific literary
influence on his work which he admitted. The passage is, in part, an attempt
to write "la belle page"—to achieve the grandiose richness of verbal and rhythmic suggestion found, for example, in Victor Hugo's *Les Travailleurs de la Mer*;
and it can, therefore, if we wish, be explained away in terms of a literary
indebtedness which Conrad later outgrew.

But there are other, perhaps more interesting, certainly more contemporary, issues raised by the historical perspective of the passage.

We have today an unprecedented distrust of the purple passage; the color has been banned from the literary spectrum, and "poetic prose" has become a term of abuse in the general critical vocabulary, including Mudrick's. Since T. E. Hulme, at least, we have demanded in poetry—and, *a fortiori*, in prose—tautness of rhythm, hardness of outline, exactness of diction; we have insisted that every work, every rhythmical inflection, every rhetorical device, shall contribute to the organic unity of the whole work, shall not exist for its local effect. Mudrick takes comment on the passage to be superfluous, but the grounds of his objection are, I take it, somewhat along these lines. So, indeed, are mine, I suppose. At least I can hardly read the passage, or others in Conrad like it, without momentary qualms ("Should I let myself go and enjoy it? No, in real life relaxing's fine, but in literature? . . . Think of Leavis . . ."); and yet, if we consider the Hulmean principle seriously, isn't the cost more than we are prepared to pay?

To begin with, a rather large series of literary rejections may be involved; not only Hugo and Pater and much of Flaubert but also a good deal of Proust and Joyce—not only the *Portrait* but much of *Ulysses*—Molly Bloom's reverie, for example. There are countless passages in the greatest literature which, though no doubt related by subject and theme to the rest of the narrative, are essentially set-pieces, developed largely as autonomous rhetorical units; and in a good many of them every device of sound and sense is, as in Conrad, being used mainly to induce feelings of rather vague exaltation. Nor is it only a matter of the illustriousness of the precedents; they may have valid literary justification. For, although we are no doubt right to reject de Musset's romantic certitude that our most beautiful feelings are our saddest, is there any more justification for the antiromantic prescription that our deepest or most complicated feelings—so often vague and penumbral—can and should be expressed through clear images? And why in images at all? How can we reconcile the symbolist rejection of logic and conceptualization with the fact that our minds often work by partial and groping movements toward conceptualization and logical ordering? More specifically, isn't it carrying the demand for imagistic particularity too far to assert that in literature every part of the picture must be in clear focus? Can we not, on the contrary, assert that Conrad, a preeminently pictorial writer, requires, on occasion, a chiaroscuro effect between one series of concretely detailed presentations and another? Such certainly is the way this passage—and many others of a similar kind— are disposed in *The Nigger of the "Narcissus"*: we get a relief from the immediate image, from the particularities of time and space, and this, by contrast, both brings out these particularities more clearly and at the same time reminds us that there are other less definite and yet equally real dimensions of existence.

It is probably because these less definite dimensions cannot be made real visually that Conrad's style changes abruptly and at once evokes analogies that are musical rather than pictorial. In the Preface to *The Nigger of the "Narcissus"* he wrote that one of his aims was to approach "the magic suggestiveness of music"; and though nowadays we are very suspicious of "word music," there may in this case at least be something in Coleridge's apparently outrageous assertion that "a sentence which sounds pleasing always has a meaning which is deep and good." Conrad's particular sentences here certainly suggested a meaning not lacking in depth or goodness to one of the greatest practitioners of the prose poem; for this is one of the passages by which Virginia Woolf, in "Mr. Conrad: A Conversation" (*The Captain's Death Bed*), exemplifies her assertion that in Conrad's prose "the beauty of surface has always a fibre of morality within." She goes on, "I seem to see each of the sentences . . . advancing with resolute bearing and a calm which they have won in strenuous conflict, against the forces of falsehood, sentimentality, and slovenliness"; and so brings us, at long last, away from this rather inconclusive review of some of the theoretical issues raised by the passage by forcing us to ask whether the relation of form and content in the passage is as she suggests.

To make full sense of its content we must, of course, grant Conrad the benefit of the kind of flexible and cooperative interpretation we are accustomed to give poetry, allow him his steady reliance on ironic, elliptical, and para-doxical, personification. We must accept, for example, the dependence of the paradox of "desired unrest" upon an implicit assertion by the narrator that "life," which is what men literally "desire," is in fact always "unrest"; we must also accept the personifications of the sea's "mercy" and "grace" as necessary to prepare for the final modulation of "the eternal pity," where the sea's order is equated with God's; and we must excuse the somewhat obscure quality of the irony at God's supposedly merciful attributes and at the "empty heaven" because it is evident that Conrad wants to achieve his juxtaposition of religious illusions against the only redemptive power which he acknowledges, "the vast silence of pain and labor," without undermining the traditional sort of literary theism on which the passage's elevation of tone in part depends.

The gnomic compression, the largeness of reference, the latent irony, all suggest a familiar literary analogue, the Greek chorus: and the formal qualities of the passage offer striking confirmation. The Greek chorus's lofty and im-personal assertion of the general dramatic theme depends for its distinctive effect on the impact, at a point of rest in the action, of a plurality of voices and an intensified musicality: a plurality of voices, not an individualized narrator, because the function of a chorus in general, as of Conrad's in particular, is to achieve what Yeats called "emotion of multitude," which is difficult to achieve through a wholly naturalist technique for the presentation of reality; an intensified musicality because it emphasizes the requisite impersonal urgency, as in the present case Conrad's tired and yet hieratic emphasis on repetition and balance of sound and rhythm is itself the formal expression of his controlled exaltation at the prospect of the laborious but triumphant monotony offered by the endless tradition of human effort. The placing and the assertion of the passage are equally choric in nature, for Conrad seizes a moment of rest between two contrasted phases of the crew's exertion to remind us that, contrary to their longings and to what any sentimental view of existence would lead us to hope, man's greatness, such as it is, has no reward in this life or the next, and is a product only of the unending confrontation of their environment by the successive human generations, a confrontation that is unsought and yet obligatory, although "the forces of falsehood, sentimentality, and slovenliness" seek perpetually to confuse, defer, or evade its claims.

II

Mudrick's denigration of *The Nigger of the "Narcissus"* on the grounds of Conrad's rhetorical attitudinizing and of his use of point of view follows two of the major emphases of our modern criticism of fiction; and as we shall see his operative premises are typical in much else. But we must not overlook the fact that Mudrick, who has cast himself as the spectral Mr. Jones interrupting the feast celebrating Conrad's victory over the critics, is also possessed of a marked cannibalistic trait: he cannot abide the enthusiasm of his confreres for the "modish clues of myth, metaphor, symbol, etc." In his earlier essay on Conrad, Stallman's reading of "The Secret Sharer" was his main target; but he now finds *The Nigger of the "Narcissus"* subject to the same general charge: a heavy overemphasis on "catch-all" and "claptrap" symbolism which only a naïve predisposition for that sort of thing could possibly render acceptable.

That many critics have found a clue to *The Nigger of the "Narcissus"* in a unifying symbolic structure is certainly true. James E. Miller, for example, in his *"The Nigger of 'Narcissus'*: A Reexamination" (*PMLA*, December 1951), sees "James Wait and the sea as symbols of death and life; Singleton and Donkin as symbols of opposed attitudes toward death and life"; the other members of the crew hesitate whether to follow the true knowledge of Singleton or the deceptions offered by Donkin; and the conflict is only concluded when they unanimously reject Donkin's offer of a drink after being paid off—

"the crew has passed from a diversity based on ignorance through a false unity based on a lie perpetrated by Donkin, to, finally, the true 'knot' of solidarity based on genuine insight into the meaning of life and death."

Miller's analysis is, of course, presented as a confessedly simplified paradigm and I have had to simplify it further; his scheme certainly has the merit of drawing our attention to a certain number of important interrelationships which we might not have noticed: but the whole conception of a neat allegorical drama surely does violence to the patent diversity of Conrad's narrative; this may be the figure in one of the carpets but what of the many other richly furnished floors? Surely no one would have seized upon this particular pattern if he had not, in the first place, felt sure that there must be some such neat symbolic plot waiting to be discovered, and in the second, felt justified in giving decisive interpretative priority to a few selected details of character and incident which could be made to support it?

Essentially the same method—*reductio ad symbolum*—appears in Robert F. Haugh's "Death and Consequences: Joseph Conrad's Attitude Toward Fate" (*University of Kansas City Review*, Spring 1952). Briefly, from the muster, in which they each challenge the order of the ship, both Donkin and Wait are seen as "emissaries of darkness and disorder, Conrad's synonyms for evil." Donkin's level is the overt, the social, while Wait's is the religious; the book as a whole dramatizes "all of the elements in the human solidarity of Conrad's world, arrayed against those forces which would destroy them, with Wait the deeper menace since he "somehow" comes to stand for the crew's "own darker natures." This analysis seems a good deal closer to our sense of the book's chief concerns, and in the main Haugh applies it convincingly; but as soon as the stress shifts from interpretative analytic summary to the attribution of specifically symbolic meanings to characters and incidents doubts begin to arise. Wait may be "a moral catalyst . . . who brings death aboard ship in many ways," but is he himself evil? And isn't it forcing the facts to say that when, after rescuing Wait, the crew return to the deck and find that "never before had the gale seemed to us more furious," this is somehow related to Wait's influence which has "undone . . . their courage," rather than to the material fact that, being on deck again, they are more exposed to the weather?

Vernon Young's "Trial by Water: Joseph Conrad's *The Nigger of the 'Narcissus'* " (*Accent*, Spring 1952) reveals a very Galahad of the symbol. If the ship plunges "on to her *port* side," a parenthetic gloss at once nautical and symbolic reminds us that this is "the left, or sinister, side"; and if Conrad compares the *Narcissus* and her tug to a white pyramid and an aquatic beetle, "the antithesis . . . is unquestionably a sidelong glance at the Egyptian figure of the pyramid, prime symbol of direction and sun worship, and of the scarab, symbol of creative energy." It will serve us nothing to protest, for example, that this last image is patently visual, for we are in the presence of a Faith. In Young—as in many other of the more symbolically inclined critics—that faith is of the Jungian persuasion; and if I mention that I believe Jung to be a latter-day example of the same arrogant credulity which has given us astrology, the British Israelites, and the Baconian fringe, it is only because it seems to me that the kind of thinking exhibited there is exactly analogous to that in some kinds of literary symbol hunting: everything "proves x" because "proves" and "x" are defined with such accommodating tolerance—the terms of argument do not of their nature admit either of proof or of disproof.

Most of Young's essay, I must in fairness add, is concerned with elucidating a symbolic structure of a much less sectarian tendency. In its general view it is fairly similar to that of Haugh, though somewhat more schematically presented: Wait, for example, is defined as "serv[ing] a purpose comparable to that of El Negro in Melville's *Benito Cereno:* he is the spirit of blackness, archetype of unknown forces from the depths," and the mysterious adjuration of his presence "all but deprives the crew of their will to live." Allistoun and Singleton, on the other hand, stand for the superego, and they, together with Podmore, "discover, behind the mask of a dying shirker, the infrahuman visage of the Satanic."

Wait's portentous first appearance, and the way he later becomes the chief protagonist round whom the actions and the attitudes of the crew revolve, these certainly justify our impulse to look for some hidden significance in him. Some early readers no doubt thought the same, for in the 1914 note "To My Readers in America" Conrad wrote the very explicit denial: "But in the book [Wait] is nothing; he is merely the centre of the ship's collective psychology and the pivot of the action." If we set aside this disclaimer, as Young specifically (and scornfully) does, it should surely be only for the most imperative reasons; and those offered seem to be based upon the loosest kind of metaphorical extension.

Both Vernon Young and Albert Guerard make Wait's blackness their starting point, and this leads them to parallels in *Benito Cereno* and *Heart of Darkness.* Yet it is hardly necessary to adduce Conrad's antipathy to Melville to cast doubts on the former analogy: Conrad does not, in Melville's sense, believe in an absolute or transcendental "evil," and his Negro has not done any. As for the *Heart of Darkness* parallel, it is surely suspicious that Young should apply the color metaphor literally, and thus find his analogy in the "barbarous and superb woman," while Guerard, more metaphorical, plumps for Kurtz: in any case the native woman, quite unlike Wait, is conspicuous for her heroic resolution, while there seems to be little in common between

Wait and Kurtz except that they are tall, proud, have African associations, are rescued with difficulty, and die painfully. Nor is the general metaphorical implication—Guerard's statement that Wait "comes in some sense to represent our human 'blackness' "—particularly convincing. Wait, we know, was based on an actual Negro, and his color offered Conrad a whole series of valuable dramatic oppositions. These are made full use of in Wait's first appearance, where his color at once establishes his difference, his mystery, his threat: yet later in the book the color issue becomes relatively unimportant; the crew assimilates him to their group with the jocular nickname of "Snowball"; only Donkin makes a serious issue of Wait's color, calling him "a black-faced swine"; and if the narrator's own first description ends with the phrase "the tragic, the mysterious, the repulsive mask of a nigger's soul" we must remember that he is here only the spokesman of the first general and primarily visual reaction, that the color is after all "a mask," and that there is no suggestion later that the soul behind it is black.

Deferring the question of what James Wait's secret is—if any—we must surely ask why, in the absence of any convincing internal evidence or of any problem so intractable as to make recourse to extravagant hypothesis obligatory, critics capable of the perceptive felicities of Young and Guerard, to name only two, should try so hard (though not, as my present concern may inadvertently have led me to suggest, all or even most of the time) to discover some sort of occult purport in what is, on the face of it, a rich and complex but by no means equivocal narrative? More generally, why have the critics of the last decade or so put such emphasis on finding esoteric symbols? In the phrase which the hero of Kingsley Amis's *That Uncertain Feeling* uses in another connection, I can see why the critics like them, but why should they like them *so much*?

The superstition and obscurantism of our time, reflected, for example, in Young's indignation at Conrad's "fear of wholesale commitment to the irrational," will no doubt explain something, as I have already suggested; but what is perhaps more decisive is the prestige with which literary criticism is now invested. It is no longer the poet, but the critic who typically functions as the romantic seer; and a seer, of course, is someone who sees what isn't there, or at least has never been seen before. This role seems to enforce a no doubt unconscious operative strategy along the following lines: a little like the bibliophile who is too proud to deal with anything but first editions, the critic feels his status as seer jeopardized unless he can demonstrate that he saw the book first, or at least that his reading of it is the first *real* one; his version must therefore be noticeably different from any likely previous one; and since certain kinds of symbolic interpretation, unlike the emperor's clothes, are incapable of empirical proof or disproof, they are laid under contribution as offering the easiest—and safest—means toward achieving the desired novelty of insight.

This is no doubt an unfair way of putting it; and in any case such pressures would probably have insufficient force were they not complemented by the obvious fact that the novel's length makes it impossible for the critic's analysis to approach the relative completeness which that of some short poems can attain. Given the impossibility of a full account, and the somewhat pedestrian tendency of the traditional summarizing of plot and character, the discovery of some inclusive symbolic configuration appears as the readiest way to combine the imposed brevity and the solicited originality.

In the case of Conrad, it is true, such interpretations seem to find some warrant from Conrad's own statement that "All the great creations of literature have been symbolic." The question, obviously, is, Symbolic in what sense? and since the word "symbol" can be properly used in too many ways, it may clarify the discussion to suggest a set of rather ugly neologisms for the different kinds of literary symbolism that are involved in the present discussion.

The basic problem is to determine the kind of relationship between the literary symbol and its referent, between the narrative vehicle and its imputed larger tenor; most important, perhaps, are the distances between them and the basis on which the mutual rapport is ascribed. In the kind of symbolic interpretation I have been discussing, the distance between the literary object and the symbolic meaning ascribed to it is rather great: and so I would describe making Wait a symbol of evil, darkness or Satan, an example of *heterophoric* interpretation; that is, it carries us to *another* meaning, it takes us *beyond* any demonstrable connection between the literary object and the symbolic meaning given it.

Many examples of symbolic interpretation differ from this, however, in that not only is the distance between literary object and imputed meaning relatively great, but the rapport is established, not through taking a particular quality in the literary object very far, but through referring the literary object to some other system of knowledge which it would not normally be thought to invoke. Young's interpretation of the pyramid and the scarab would be of this kind, and since it depends upon an allusion to a specific body of mythical, religious or literary knowledge, it could be called a *mythophor: mythophor* would be a variety of *heterophor*, since it makes the literary object stand for something very distant from it, but the correlation would depend upon a reference to a certain story or, in the Greek sense, myth; another example of this would be Guerard's drawing the parallel between Wait and the legend of Jonah.

One particular case of *mythophor* seems to require some special term because it is common and raises peculiar problems—that case in which the body of knowledge invoked is one of the depth psychologies: this subdivision of *mythophor* could be called *cryptophor*, since it depends upon analogies which Freud and Jung agree to be hidden and unconscious; one example would be when Guerard equates the rescuing of Wait from his confinement during the storm with a "compulsive psychic descent," or when he toys briefly with the scene's "psychic geography," proposing that the Finn Wamibo figures as the "savage *super-ego*" to Wait's *id*.

Heterophor in general tends toward allegory. Guerard, for example, although he jests at the fashion for "analysis of 'cabalistic intent' " and cautions us against reading Conrad as an allegorical writer, insisting that the overt subject is also the real subject, nevertheless argues for a series of superimposed *heterophoric* significances which are essentially of an allegorical kind, as the Negro in *Benito Cereno* is conceived allegorically by Melville. I do not think that Conrad's work is symbolic in this way; even less is it *mythophoric* or *cryptophoric*. To make it so, indeed, is surely to emphasize novelty at the expense of truth; and the literary effect of such interpretation is to reduce what Conrad actually created to a mere illustration—something both secondary and—as Mudrick would argue—second-rate. For all kinds of *heterophoric* interpretation inevitably disregard the great bulk of the concrete details of character and incident in a literary work: just as T. S. Eliot's allegorical concern in *The Family Reunion*, for example, prevents us from inspecting the psychology and the dynamics of Harry's wife's death—did she fall or was she pushed?—so a *heterophoric* interpreter of Wait will be disinclined to scrutinize the manifest developing pattern of his character and actions. The details of these latter, indeed, will seem otiose compared to the few elements which, on a priori grounds, have been selected as of primary importance; and so Young can write, "Fearful of overstressing the subaqueous world of the underconsciousness, the symbol-producing level of the psyche which, in fact, was the most dependable source of his inspiration, Conrad overloaded his mundane treatment of the crew."

To demur from Guerard's statement that, on top of the various more obvious levels of narrative statement, Conrad imposed "an audacious symbolic pattern," is not to deny that *The Nigger of the "Narcissus"* is in many ways symbolic. Its symbolism, however, seems to me to be of another kind. It works, characteristically, by natural extension of the implications of the narrative content, and retains a consistent closeness to it; for this the term *homeophor* seems appropriate, suggesting as it does, "carrying *something similar*" rather than, as with *heterophor*, "carrying *something else*." When Guerard makes the parallel of the journey of the *Narcissus* and the age-old theme of the pilgrimage, his interpretation, if allowed, and at some level of generality it surely must be, would be *homeophoric* because ships and pilgrimages, to those who know anything of them, must suggest small human communities united for the purpose of a single journey.

The terms proposed are no doubt grotesque; the distinctions on which they are based would no doubt often prove difficult to apply; and considered against the complexity of the problem and the richness of its literature, the brevity of their exposition may appear unpardonable; but if they have made more manageable the problem of what kind of symbolic writer Conrad is, and, perhaps, suggested the need for further discriminations in this general area, they will have served their turn. It only remains now to show, very briefly, how Conrad's method in *The Nigger of the "Narcissus"* is symbolic in a *homeophoric* way, working through a very accessible extension of the implications of character and event. This task, however, is complicated by the need to meet the charges against Conrad's use of symbolism made by Mudrick; for, believing that, for the novelist as well as for the critic, emphasis on symbolism tends to be at the expense of character and action which, surely rightly, he takes to be the essential components of fiction, Mudrick proceeds to argue that, in *The Nigger of the "Narcissus,"* Conrad did not "aim at elaborating or examining character and incident beyond the static, repetitive point of illustration and symbol." We must therefore attempt to show, not only that Conrad's symbolism is of a very exoteric kind, but that it does not have these damaging consequences for his presentation of character and incident.

III

Mudrick gives Conrad's early presentation of Wait two eloquent and appreciative paragraphs, but he finds the later treatment of him disappointing. It is true that the first commanding air of mystery slowly evaporates as we see Wait more closely: his curious pride, it appears, is merely the defense of an alien who is aboard only because, as he tells Baker, "I must live till I die— mustn't I?"; and his climactic confrontations with Donkin, Podmore and Allistoun give increasingly clear illumination to the ordinariness of his secret, his unacknowledged terror of approaching death. These later developments undoubtedly have a deflating effect, and if we see Wait as an emissary from some spiritual chamber of horrors, they must seem mistaken; but the cumulative anticlimax can also be seen as an essential part of the book's meaning; it reveals that the influence Wait exercises on the crew is an irrational projection of their own dangerous fears and weaknesses; to put it in our terms, it asserts, eventually, that contrary to possible earlier expectation, Wait is not a *heterophor*; order and disorder on the *Narcissus* are temporary, contingent, man-made; behind the mysterious and menacing authority of a St. Kitts's Negro there is only a common human predicament; Wait is a symbol, not of death but of the fear of death, and therefore, more widely, of the universal human reluctance to face those most universal agents of anticlimax, the facts; and the facts, as always, find him out.

Mudrick, perhaps, mistook Wait for a *heterophor* and then found, as in that case I think one must, that Conrad didn't come through; but his disap-pointment has other grounds, notably that "there is no development and noth-ing mobile or unexpected" in the novel. This charge seems, specifically, to overlook or to reject the actions which focus round Wait in the fourth chapter; for when Mudrick writes that "Only Donkin—the gutter creature—'sees through' Wait" he is implicitly denying the picture of the case that is presented there. Donkin is no doubt the only person who most consistently sees Wait as an infuriatingly successful "evader of responsibility"; but everyone else has some such suspicions, and the matter is obviously not so simple. No malin-gerer is ever wholly well, even if at times he thinks so; Wait's own agonizing divisions and contradictions about his condition seem a psychologically con-vincing reaction to all the elements in his situation; and his puzzling gratifi-cation at Donkin's insults is surely an expression of the desperation of his wish to believe that Donkin really has "seen through" him.

Actually, of course, only one man—Allistoun—can be said to "see through" Wait, as we realize in the scene when, after Podmore has told Wait that he is "as good as dead already," and Wait, supported by the crew, has urged that he be allowed to return to duty, Allistoun mystifies and outrages everyone by his brusque refusal—"There's nothing the matter with you, but you chose to lie-up to please yourself—and now you shall lie-up to please me." As Allistoun explains later to the mates, it was a momentary impulse of sympathetic insight into Wait "three parts dead and so scared" which urged him to enact a form of Ibsen's beneficent lie by shielding him from the de-ception of his own wishful illusions, and letting "him go out in his own way."

That it is the most total act of sympathy for Wait which precipitates the mutiny is surely a "development" both "mobile and unexpected," and it dra-matizes one of the general themes in *The Nigger of the "Narcissus"* which is far from commonplace: pity, emotional identification with others, as an active danger to society. Nor is the treatment of the theme by any means banal; for Conrad shows that pity, though dangerous, is also a condition of human decency, by juxtaposing the Allistoun scene between two others where Wait is subjected to the cruelty of two kinds of extreme and therefore pitiless egoism: to complete the picture, we must bear in mind the qualifications implied both in the subsequent scene where Donkin brutally satisfies his malice and cupidity by tormenting Wait to his death with fiendish cruelty, and in the earlier interview where the pious Podmore, a "conceited saint unable to forget his glorious reward . . . prayerfully divests himself of his humanity" and terrifies Wait with visions of imminent hellfire.

Symbolically, Conrad seems to be saying that although pitilessness is characteristic of the selfish, yet the increasing sensitiveness to the sufferings of others which civilization brings necessarily poses grave problems of control for the individual and for society; and by making Singleton not so much unsympathetic as unaware of Wait's suffering he may be thought to have reminded us that the older and less humanitarian order was not so easily deflected from its collective purpose. Such a reading can be advanced with considerable confidence, since, as is necessarily the case with *homeophoric* extension, it is arrived at merely by extracting a more generally applicable statement from the manifest implications of particular characters and actions; and the reading could easily be supported, both by showing how the juxtaposition of certain episodes implies such a meaning, and by pointing out various explicit comments on the softening, refining and corrupting effects of pity, comments which authorize the assumption that any events which raise such issues were designed to have representative significance.

This is not to say that Allistoun, Wait, and the rest are to be regarded primarily as symbols of these attitudes and values, and I do not think that Mudrick would regard them as "elementary emblems of what they are intended to demonstrate" unless his own criteria, both of literary character in general, and of what is desirable to demonstrate, were so contrary to Conrad's.

It is undeniable that Conrad does not give us here, nor, typically, anywhere, the kind of psychological exploration focused on the individual sensibility in the manner of James or Proust: but there is surely some middle ground between this and mere "elementary emblems." If one assumes that Conrad's main objective is the ship—its voyage and its society—it is evident that, in what is little more than a long short story, not all its complement— twenty-six individuals—can possibly be particularized; nor, on the other hand, can any two or three of them be fully treated without disturbing the emphasis, which must be on the social group rather than the individual. It is inevitable that some characters of marginal importance should be portrayed with something approaching caricature—Belfast with his hypertonic Irish sensibility, Wamibo with his inarticulate frenzies of participation; and it would obviously be very unsettling to introduce characters who were flagrantly untypical of their setting. Mudrick takes exception to the stereotyped banality of the gentlemanly Creighton's daydreams—"a girl in a clear dress, smiling under a sunshade . . . stepping out of the tender sky"; and one hastens to concede that Creighton would be a more interesting character if he spent all his time at sea counting the days until he could have another stab at Kierkegaard; but what would that do to the book?

Nowadays we can swallow everything except the obvious; and one of the reasons that Mudrick singles out this particular passage for reprobation is probably that he shares our terror of whatever may seem cliché. He finds cliché, for example, when Wait talks to Donkin about his "Canton Street girl . . . cooks oysters just as I like," commenting that "Wait provided with the white man's conventional notion of the black man's secret desires" is less convincing "personally and symbolically" than "Wait with no background" at all, as at the beginning. But the girl is mentioned in a context which gives Wait just the right kind of tawdry and hopeless pathos: off the Azores, with the crew talking of the joys of London, Wait naturally thinks of the London girl he will never see; the sick man's notorious dream of food (and rations are short) explains the oysters; while the fact that the remark is addressed to Donkin makes it Wait's last—and of course unavailing—effort to achieve some sort of triumph over the one man on the ship he has been unable to soften or impress.

Mudrick, both here and elsewhere, seems to me to have imported the cliché, and for two reasons: there is the already noted demand for a degree of individualization which is impossible and undesirable in many cases, including the present; and there is exactly the same fastidious rejection of the commonplace which, under the direction of other predispositions, causes the critics he attacks to coax esoteric symbols into the text. Both Mudrick's tendencies, of course, are closely related to his earlier demand for the sharpest possible definition in prose and in point of view: all his literary criteria, in fact, have total individualization as their basic premise.

His discussion of the moral and social dimensions of *The Nigger of the "Narcissus"* is informed with the equivalent premise, expressed as ethical and political nonconformity, and it operates with the same rude vigor. Conrad's "metaphysical and moral scheme" is based on the exaltation of the "grim-jawed, nerveless, reticent men in charge"; they inhabit "a hand-me-down 'aristocratic' universe in which everybody in charge deserves to be and everybody else had better jump"; and if we examine them, "all we find beneath the gritty authoritative British exterior is a collection of soft-headed Anglophilic clichés." We have seen that Allistoun in one crucial episode, at least, is far from nerveless, and that there are some elements in the book which are neither soft-headed nor commonplace; yet to exemplify and analyze further, or to attempt to assess how severe a disablement is involved in being an Anglophile, would probably be little to the purpose. For we are in the presence of a total incompatibility: Conrad's social and political attitudes, and Mudrick's diametrically opposed convictions.

Conrad, of course, was conservative in many ways: yet surely one can be, like Donkin, Mudrick—or myself—"a votary of change" and still find that Conrad's picture of society commands respect. Even his presentation of the class issue, for example, has considerable objectivity: the hardships and the miserable economic rewards of the crew are not minimized, and we are given their cynical discussion of "the characteristics of a gentleman"; among the officers, Allistoun, with his "old red muffler" and his "nightshirt fluttering like a flag" is not a hero but a prisoner of the class to which his command has brought him, as we see when his smart wife arrives to collect him at the dockside; and our last picture of the ship shows the first mate, Baker, reflecting that, unlike Creighton with his "swell friends," he will never get a command. In any case, we can hardly make Conrad responsible for the fact that no ship was ever successfully sailed democratically; and we must also admit that, with all its rigidities and injustices, the *Narcissus* is a community with a genuine and in some ways egalitarian set of reciprocities: for the most part everyone on it knows and sees and wants the same things; while the class antipathy is qualified by the crew's recognition, in Allistoun or Baker, that individuals who in themselves are no way special or even particularly likeable can be wholly admirable and necessary in the performance of their roles. This dichotomy, of course, is an essential condition of Conrad's presentation of his characters: with the significant exceptions of Donkin and Wait, their function in one sense usurps their individuality but in another it endows them with heroic stature.

All these connections and contradictions, operating within a very restricted setting, gave Conrad his opportunity for a compressed drama which could, in part, be representative of society at large. The general values which emerge are on the whole traditional, if not authoritarian; but at least they are real values, and they are really there. If George Orwell could detect in Conrad "a sort of grown-upness and political understanding which would have been almost impossible to a native English writer at that time," it is surely because, as a foreigner, Conrad could be more objective about a social order which, for all its many faults, was in some ways admirable and rewarding; while as an exile from Poland he had cause to be presciently responsive to the existence of any viable social order at all.

Mudrick's case against Conrad, then, is largely the result of the conjunction of two value systems, neither of which happens to favor *The Nigger of the "Narcissus."* On the one hand, he takes to their logical conclusion a rather complete set of modern critical assumptions—the pieties of point of view, of prosy-prose, of authorial reticence about character and meaning, of extreme fastidiousness about permitted attitudes and endorsements; on the other, he lets loose a teeming menagerie of personal bêtes noires, ranging from symbolism, the sea and the stiff upper lip to hierarchical authorities, parvenus and Anglophiles. Mudrick had a very nice irony in "Conrad and the Terms of Modern Criticism" about how, in our too perceptive times, "nose to nose, critic confronts writer and, astonished, discovers himself"; one could find striking confirmation both of this thesis and of the *cryptophoric* significance of proper names by considering how vivid an image of Mudrick was reflected when he came nose to nose with Narcissus.

As for Conrad, we must conclude, I think, that Mudrick's impatient intransigence forces one to realize, both by its palpable hits and by what I have tried to chalk up as its misses, how *The Nigger of the "Narcissus"* is, in a number of ways, not at all the answer to our modern critical prayer. No amount of symbol-juggling will or should divert us from seeing that there is an important Romantic and Victorian element in his work; and, although Conrad was, of course, in many ways a precursor of the modern movement in fiction, his deepest originality and perhaps the chief unacknowledged cause of his popularity today, derives from an attitude to his society, both as subject and as audience, which has been shared by no other great writer of our century. Many things in himself, his life and his times, gave him as deep a sense of the modern alienation as any other of our great exiled and isolated writers; and yet Conrad's most vigorous energies were turned away from the ever-increasing separateness of the individual and towards discovering values and attitudes and ways of living and writing which he could respect and yet which were, or could be, widely shared. Mudrick has more than reminded us of the occasional cost in emphasis, repetition and cliché, but no criticism has yet adequately assessed what Conrad gave in exchange. His aim—"to make you see"—has often been quoted: but there has been less emphasis on how Conrad specified that the objects in the "presented vision" should be such as to "awaken in the hearts of the beholders that feeling of unavoidable solidarity; of the solidarity in mysterious origin, in toil, in joy, in hope, in uncertain fate, which binds men to each other and all mankind to the visible world." In the centrality of his ultimate purpose Conrad is akin to Wordsworth; and if he expresses it grandiloquently, he at least does not, in the Arnoldian phrase, give us the grand word without the grand thing.

The third chapter of *The Nigger of the "Narcissus,"* for example, is not merely a magnificent evocation of a storm at sea; it is a sequence of unequaled enactments of the theme of solidarity. It begins as we experience gratitude for the efforts of the crew to save Wait, or of Podmore, incredibly, to produce coffee; and it achieves its final resonance in the famous ending when, after long forgetting him, our eyes are turned to Singleton at the wheel, and we are told, simply, that, after thirty hours, "He steered with care." It is the climactic recognition of our utter and yet often forgotten dependence, night and day, by sea and by land, on the labors of others; and by the kind of cross-reference of attitudes which is Conrad's most characteristic way of achieving a symbolic dimension, this supreme image is linked with three other scenes: that where we later see how Singleton's endurance at the wheel brings him face to face with death; that where he has previously told Wait, "Well, get on with your dying, don't raise a blamed fuss with us over that job"; and that soon after where Donkin taunts Wait with slackness on the rope—"You don't kill yourself, old man!"—and Wait retorts "Would you?"

Singleton does, and the heroic quality of his labors reminds us, not only that what has been most enduring about human society has been the mere continuity of its struggle against nature, which is, as we have seen, the tenor of the ensuing paragraph about the sea which opens the next chapter, but also that Conrad's greatest art, in *Typhoon* and *The Shadow Line* as in *The Nigger of the "Narcissus,"* is often reserved for making us, in Auden's words, "Give / Our gratitude to the Invisible College of the Humble, / Who through the ages have accomplished everything essential." There is perhaps a moral for the critic here: for, in making us look up, briefly, to Singleton at the wheel, Conrad gives us a moment of vision in which, from the height of our modish attachment to ever-developing discriminations, we are compelled to affirm our endless, intricate and not inglorious kinship with those who cannot write and who read only Bulwer-Lytton.

EDWARD W. SAID

The Past and the Present:
Conrad's Shorter Fiction

"Men," Conrad wrote to Mrs. Sanderson on March 17, 1900, "often act first and reflect afterwards." The implications of this simple remark take us directly into the rich and confusing world of Conrad's short fiction. There, action of any sort is either performed or witnessed without accompanying reflection or interpretation, as if the overriding and immediate sensation of action done to, by, or in front of one crowds out the informing work of the reason. The exotic settings that Conrad chose underline this: the action becomes even more foreign and inscrutable to the harried mind. But there is a place for retrospection after the fact. One thinks, for example, of the beleaguered Marlow, in command of his shabby Congo steamer, who watches his helmsman inexplicably and suddenly lie down; a few minutes later he is horrified to see a spear protruding from the man's body. Only then does he understand the direct malignancy that has caused what he saw. Further on he notes in a distracted moment the stakes surrounding Kurtz's compound, standing there with ball-like ends. In time he will realize that they are dried human heads, put there as a horrifying example to others. Indeed, the whole progress of Marlow's trip until he reaches Kurtz seems incredible as it happens. As he tells his experience to his audience, Marlow wishes it understood that the experience changed his life. But during the experience he is like Rilke's Malte, realizing that "nothing in the world can one imagine before-

From *Joseph Conrad and the Fiction of Autobiography.* © 1966 by the President and Fellows of Harvard College. Harvard University Press, 1966. Originally entitled "The Past and the Present."

hand, not the least thing. Everything is made up of so many unique particulars that cannot be foreseen. . . . But the realities are slow and indescribably detailed." The details of reality, given only mute acknowledgment in action, are realized by the recollecting mind, which retraces—as Malte writes—the designs of experience. And perhaps we can sense in the style itself the partial overtaking of action by thought. In a letter to F. N. Doubleday, T. E. Lawrence once wrote of Conrad's style as a manner of writing that "hungered" for a total capture of its subject, and that constantly applied itself to actions that appeared to refuse it.

The retrospective mode of so many of Conrad's shorter works can be understood as the effort to interpret what, at the time of occurrence, would not permit reflection. And, most of the time, the action that has already occurred not only troubles the present, but also calls itself to immediate attention. Conrad's very first tale, "The Idiots," explicitly accounts for itself in this manner. The narrator is a traveler in Brittany who abruptly sees before him four idiot children. He then inquires after them, and slowly the story of their birth pieces itself together in its pathetic sadness and terror. But the content of the tale, for all its sensational operatics, still seems somewhat "obscure" to the traveler. Between the recollecting narrator and the actual tale there is a barrier that is eternally closed. For a novelist, however, a barrier is not something merely to be ignored, and this hedge of mystery, as Conrad develops it in later tales, becomes an important fact in the story.

In "The Lagoon," written a few months after "The Idiots," the visiting white man listens to Arsat's tale of betrayal as the two stand in front of the unfinished house in which Arsat's woman (for whom Arsat's brother sacrificed himself) has just died. As Arsat closes his story, he asks the white man for advice and explanation. But staring out on the quiet lagoon, the man answers with frightening passivity: "There is nothing." Arsat returns to his obscure quest for self-rectitude in an existence the white man cannot possibly understand: the placid lagoon across which the visitor travels to and from Arsat represents an eternity of uncomprehending distance between the two men. Thus there is impulsive action on the one hand and ineffectual reflection on the other.

In "Karain" and "Youth," two of the stories that follow "The Lagoon" and precede *Heart of Darkness*, the reflecting men dip into the past, as it were, to illuminate or correct what has been so uncomfortably mysterious. Karain the native chieftain is, like Arsat, haunted by the ghost of a friend whom he has betrayed for a woman. The listening English seaman, recognizing his superstitious naïveté, gives him a sixpence as a magic talisman to protect him. In "Youth," telling an odd story of his past, Marlow rhapsodizes the obscure tenacity and idealism of youth; only the evocatory magic of "romance" and "glamour" makes the incredible impulses of youth intelligible. Nevertheless, the reader (upon whose discernment Conrad relies) is made to understand that a semicomic compensation in the present cannot really change the past. Jackson, one of the men who is present whan Karain is given the sixpence, meets the narrator some years later in London. We learn that the magnificent unthinking passion of Karain's life, so cynically restructured by the white men, has captured Jackson himself. Now he does not know what is real; Jackson, like Karain, has become the perplexed victim of the consequences of impulsive action. As for Marlow's listeners, regardless of their long conversation with Marlow on the performances of youth, they are left with "weary eyes looking still, looking always, looking anxiously for something out of life, that while it is expected is already gone—has passed unseen, in a sigh, in a flash—together with the youth, with the strength, with the romance of illusions." It is significant that still another of these early tales, *The Nigger of the "Narcissus,"* draws to a close with a question whose answer is unfathomable, as conveyed by the uncertainty in the recollecting narrative voice that asks it: "Haven't we, together and upon the immortal sea, wrung out a meaning from our sinful lives?"

The price of experience is not only exacted from the individual who undergoes it in fear and mystery, but also from the person whose task it is to collect it into intelligibility. In that task there seems to be no assurance even for the most determined that a "meaning" will reveal itself. Certainly Conrad felt this crippling doubt about his own ability to communicate what *he* had so profoundly lived. He wrote, for instance, to Henry James on November 30, 1897, about the recently completed *Nigger*:

> Il a la qualité d'être court. Il a eté vécu. Il est, sans doute, mauvais. Rien de si facile comme de raconter un rêve, mais il est impossible de pénétrer l'âme de ceux qui écoutent par la force de son amertume et de sa douceur. On ne communique pas la realité poignante des illusions! Le rêve finit, les mots s'envolent, le livre est oublié. C'est la grace misèricordieuse du destin.

Marlow's hesitant voice turns the same sentiment into phrases that suit the inconclusive experience he is telling:

> Do you see the story? Do you see anything? It seems to me I am trying to tell you a dream—making a vain attempt, because no relation of a dream can convey the dream-sensation, that commingling of absurdity, surprise, and bewilderment in a tremor of

struggling revolt, that notion of being captured by the incredible
which is of the very essence of dreams.

Marlow's own captivity by the incredible is mitigated by his capacity in the
present narrative recollection: as one tells a story of incredible happenings,
one is forced to put the story in credible and familiar terms. That Marlow
speaks in terms of the credible is a compromise both comforting and frus-
trating: because he has detached himself from the incredible, he cannot now
totally command or convey the intensity of the past. All the same, he still
possesses a dark, inexpressible memory of that intensity.

As he wrote "Youth," Conrad believed he was retaining and reactivating
all of the intensity he had once experienced. He wrote H. G. Wells on
September 6, 1898, that "as to the flaws of 'Youth' their existence is indisputable. I felt what you say myself—in a way. The feeling however which
induced me to write that story was genuine (for once) and so strong that it
poked its way through the narrative (which it certainly defaces) in a good
many places. I tell you this in the way of explanation simply. Otherwise the
thing is unjustifiable." The feeling behind "Youth"—and it is interesting that,
to Conrad's sensibility here, *feeling* was almost a discrete unit—had the power
to ruin the narrative. But at least "Youth" and even *Heart of Darkness* were
written *and completed* despite the persevering intrusion of this problem. On
the other hand, his work on the unseemly "Rescuer," suffering from precisely
the same conditions, resisted all his efforts at intellectual mastery and detachment. For Conrad's conception of the story as a whole had a physical grip on
him that no amount of energy could loosen. He wrote Garnett of his miserable
captivity on March 29, 1898: "And that story I can't write weaves itself into
all I see, into all I speak, into all I think, into the lines of every book I try to
read." This was the danger he risked in each story, since no problem was
more urgent to the impressionable Conrad than that the orderly powers of his
mind, seeking expression in narrative logic, might succumb to the sentient
pressures of his overflowing heart.

Most of Conrad's short fiction, therefore, dramatizes the problematic relation between the past and the present, between then and now. It may be
Conrad's own sense of the past conflicting with his sense of the present, or
it may be a character's sense of the past disturbing his (the character's) sense
of the present—the distinction is impossible to make. Of course there are
some virtuosic variations on this simple motif, but the ground bass remains
constant. Always the tale opens upon a scene of unnatural, ominous quiet.
There is a story that needs to be told—and the inevitable analogy is the
Ancient Mariner accosting the Wedding Guest, forcing the story upon him.

In some cases the story does not involve the narrator himself: in "Falk" and *Heart of Darkness*, for example, the "I" of the story simply listens to a story told by someone else. In other instances—*The Nigger of the "Narcissus"* and "The Secret Sharer" are two—there is no specific audience and no specific occasion for the narrative, even though the tale is told in the first person. In still other works, Conrad dispenses with the first-person narrative as such, although he adheres to a "center-of-consciousness" technique similar to James's. But in each story Conrad's purpose is to consider not only the so-called plot (which has usually taken place in the past), but also the varying degrees of obscurity, difficulty, and loneliness that inevitably linger on into the present. For the past cannot, will not, be contained or circumscribed. We think we have passed out of it, but the mere thought of that reconfirms its powers over us. It is as if, to borrow an image from *The Waste Land*, each man in a prison thinks of the key that will free him and "Thinking of the key, each confirms a prison." The effect of the stories is to make solitude a universal.

According to one work on the generic characteristics of short fiction, this is exactly what should be true of stories. Frank O'Connor's *The Lonely Voice* describes short fiction as essentially the narrative of the eternal outcast, the lonely individual whose remoteness from society is made a center of intense awareness. Beyond this, O'Connor discusses short fiction as a series of individual voices (whether of Maupassant, Turgenev, or Chekhov) whose texture creates distinctive effects and delights for the reader. The conceptual scheme of Conrad's short fiction, however, is far more dramatic and subtle than a matter of delightful, if unique, effects. There is first of all the quality of attempted *intrusion*: the intrusion of the past into the present, and the intrusion of the present into the past. The real aim of the tale becomes that long, extended moment wherein past and present are brought together and allowed to interact. The past, requiring the illumination of slow reflection on former thoughtless impulses, is exposed to the present; the present, demanding that "desired unrest" without which it must remain mute and paralyzed, is exposed to the past.

Conrad's artistic solicitude for this aim made him write Galsworthy on January 16, 1898, that the writer's business is not "to invent depths,—to invent depths is no art either. Most things and most natures have nothing but a surface." He was sure that "the force of a book is in the fidelity to the surface of life, to the surface of events,—to the surface of things and ideas. Now this is not being shallow." A recollected experience of disaster disturbs the unhealthy surface calm of the present, just as a sensation of anxiety or fear bursts into consciousness and excites the atrophied mind, forcing its present situation to drop away from it. Conrad's experience as a sailor, as a man of action, had taught him the invigorating potency of danger: the threat of disaster created a "spring," as he called it, which allowed him to grapple with trouble. As a despairingly sedentary man of thought, he wrote Wells that "formerly in my sea life, a difficulty nerved me to the effort; now I perceive it is not so." At its very worst, the nightmare of his present life as a writer would permit no intrusion from the past. On September 16, 1899, he wrote Garnett: "even writing to a friend—to a person one has heard, touched, drank with, quarrelled with—does not give me a sense of reality. All is illusion—the words written, the minds at which they are aimed, the truth they are intended to express, the hands that will hold the paper, the eyes that will glance at the lines. Every image floats vaguely in a sea of doubt—and the doubt itself is lost in an unexplored universe of incertitudes." Truly, as he reminded Blackwood on April 12, 1900, it was "a dog's life! this writing out, this endlessness of effort."

It is no accident then that the *present* of almost all the stories, their "objective theatre" as E. K. Brown has called it, is inevitably one of calm, of critical delay, of time circumstantially at a standstill. The reader looks in upon an atmosphere that exudes the feeling of something wrong, which has to be examined or recollected or relived or worked out. Kayerts and Carlier in "An Outpost of Progress" have been removed from a normal European life and set down to wait for business in the depths of an eastern jungle; the *Narcissus* is voyaging across the oceans but is made to purge itself of delay, of the appropriately named Negro, Wait; Alvin Hervey in "The Return" is leading his stagnant life in London at the time that his wife is disturbing their "skimming" across the surface of life; in both "Youth" and *Heart of Darkness* there is a long pause during which the vaguely unsettled group of former sailors listens to Marlow's meditative ramblings; in "Falk" the diners have had a bad meal and must compensate for it in some way—and for their benefit an absurd episode is offered; Captain Whalley is close to the end of his tether and in order to do something attempts to start his old seafaring life all over again; the protagonist of "Tomorrow," Captain Hagberd, is existing only for the moment when his son will return, and the loitering hopefulness of his life becomes the only condition of his existence; the young captain in "The Secret Sharer" is becalmed at the moment that the runaway Leggatt boards his ship; Jasper Allen and Freya Nelson in "Freya of the Seven Isles" are awaiting to be married—the list can be extended.

Furthermore, in the technical handling of the dominant plot, Conrad attempts to achieve a causal relation between the past and the present. When he wrote once that the truth of the story consisted in its presentation, he referred, I think, to the deliberate artistic manipulation that sought to bring the past into a causal relation with the present. We are thereby invited to consider how in *Heart of Darkness* the story of Marlow's "hankering after dark places" is not merely the result of an enforced wait on the Thames, but also a cause of it. The characteristic, idiomatic twist in every Conrad story is that the attempt to see a direct relation between the past and the present, to see past and present as a continuous surface of interrelated events, is frustrated. Marlow, who wants his friends to see the outside and not the inner kernel of events (and Conrad in the famous 1897 preface to *The Nigger of the "Narcissus"* and in a letter of September 6, 1897, to Blackwood openly avowed this to be the aim of the prose writer), becomes quite invisible to his audience while, at the same time, the story he tells becomes increasingly obscure. Both story and teller seem to recede into an almost transcendent heart of darkness. This is the central and gripping paradox of Conrad's method: every attempt to establish a discipline of direct relation between events leads one further *into* the events themselves. And they yield up no single method or order by which they can be explained. Marlow quickly reminds the director of the Eldorado expedition that it is not a question of Kurtz's wrong method for getting ivory so expeditiously out of the jungle: rather, "no method at all." Nevertheless, the deep philosophical honesty of Conrad's artistic disposition preserves in each story the agonizing sense of being "a beginner in [its] own circumstances." It is almost impossible not to remark that acting first and reflecting afterwards is always the problem, with reflection hopelessly far behind, hopelessly leading one further away from an inscrutable surface of action into a confusing "beyond." There is one passage in *Lord Jim* that beautifully describes the predicament:

> After his first feeling of revolt he had come round to the view that only a meticulous precision of statement would bring out the true horror behind the appalling face of things. The facts those men were so eager to know had been visible, tangible, open to the senses, occupying their place in space and time . . . He was anxious to make this clear. This had not been a common affair, everything in it had been of the utmost importance, and fortunately he remembered everything. He wanted to go on talking for truth's sake, perhaps for his own sake also; and while his utterance was deliberate, his mind positively flew round and round the serried circle of facts that had surged up all about him to cut him off from the rest of his kind: it was like a creature that, finding itself imprisoned within an enclosure of high stakes, dashes round and

round, distracted in the night, trying to find a weak spot, a crevice, a place to scale, some opening through which it may squeeze itself and escape. This awful activity of mind made him hesitate at times in his speech.

The quandary in which, for some two hundred pages, Jim continues to find himself is singularly apposite to Conrad's own spiritual experience as a writer. Conrad's truculent and remarkably simple belief in the direct referential function of words, summed up in a letter to Hugh Clifford on October 9, 1899, corresponds to Jim's confidence in the truth of facts. "Words," Conrad wrote Clifford, "groups of words, words standing alone, are symbols of life, have the power in their sound or their aspect to present the very thing you wish to hold up before the mental vision of your readers. The things 'as they are' exist in words; therefore words should be handled with care lest the picture, the image of truth abiding in facts, should become distorted—or blurred." Conrad also knew the falsifying powers of what he once called "the crafty tracery of words." Nevertheless, like Jim, he had no choice but to employ words, risking deceit on the one hand and "awful activity" of mind on the other. He wrote Garnett on February 22, 1896, of "the cast iron impudence of [his] soul" which "can be deaf and blind but can't be mute." For "what is life worth," he continues, "if one cannot jabber to one's heart's content?" Certain things about an action or experience must be made known, in the same way that Jim feels that a meticulous precision of statement would bring out the truth. The inner knowledge Conrad had of the experience, the "cravings of [his] soul" of which he wrote Garnett on June 10, 1896, required satisfaction in a special syntax, which had to be put together with absolute fidelity and care. Sometimes, he added, he would dream for hours and hours, and then worry that he was undergoing a severe mental illness. He wrote Unwin in 1896 that the stories were "fragments of [his] innermost being," despite their wordiness and jabbering. If the words lacked what he once called "singleminded expression," it was because he had simply failed to make them represent the action—but then reflective description could never adequately grasp impulsive, and hence obscure, action. Still, he needed to talk in order to ward off a growing feeling of illusion and unreality; and surely this is the experience he so often referred to as the nightmarish silence of "the black cave." He wrote passionate and exuberant letters to his close friends, hoping that in return their voices would assure him of reality. Thus on March 26, 1897, he wrote Ted Sanderson that "one is apt to think overmuch about oneself. A barren occupation. But a friend's voice turns the current of thought into a more fruitful valley." He was always fearful of total self-absorption, and only a friend's "very life"—as he reminded Garnett on March 24, 1897—would satisfy him.

When a story was autobiographical, as most often it was, its mutually dependent temporal dimensions (past and present), receding further and further into the shadows of Conrad's own sense of self-absorption, tended to reveal too many things about himself. And those, almost invariably, filled him with a deep feeling of shame. A few lines from "The Black Mate" describe Conrad's sentiments.

> As to his remorse in regard to a certain secret action of his life, well, I understand that a man of Bunter's fine character would suffer not a little. Still, between ourselves, and without the slightest wish to be cynical, it cannot be denied that with the noblest of us the fear of being found out enters for some considerable part into the composition of remorse. I didn't say this in so many words to Bunter, but, as the poor fellow harped a bit on it, I told him that there were skeletons in a good many honest cupboards.

Although a great deal has been written on Conrad's highly developed sense of personal guilt, not enough has been said of his extraordinarily powerful sense of shame. It was shame at the responsibility he felt in common with all men for allowing personal ideals to be corrupted, shame at the will to live at all costs, at the inability to deny life in any conclusive manner, and at the difficulty of somehow remaining in life. Above all, he was ashamed of fear, and fear, as he wrote in "An Outpost of Progress," was a feeling that no amount of reflection could spirit away. His own personal history was a disgraceful paradigm of shameful things, from the desertion of the ideals of his Polish heritage to the seemingly capricious abandonment of his sea life. He had become, like Kayerts and Carlier, a creature of civilization, living in reliance upon the safety of his surroundings. Each of his stories caught him in a moment of recollection and harassed idleness. When the story progressed he found, like the two unfortunate disciples of progress, that in thinking better of himself because he was now an artist (and he wrote to Garnett that there was a special significance in the fact that Kayerts and Carlier were addicted to novels), he had laid himself open to a terrifying invasion by the unknown. What made the unknown so "irresistible, familiar and disgusting" was the fact that it tended, the more one entered it, to sound and look like something one had known and felt before but had rashly denied. The monstrous natives who emerge from the surrounding jungle to steal away the station men speak a language that sounds like one Kayerts and Carlier had heard in their dreams. When the two Europeans kill each other for a lump of sugar, their degradation is complete. The fraudulent machinery of social camouflage in which they had placed their unexamined faith has destroyed them. One need only think of Conrad's notion of the knitting machine to judge the extent to which human infection by the machine has spread.

Earlier I said that the tales attempt to create an extended moment in which past and present are exposed. By succeeding in this attempt, Conrad hoped to open the present to the therapy of the past. But now we see that the present, maddeningly quarantined from the solutions of the future, resurrects a shamefully familiar past. The more probing a study of the past, the more certain that there can be no justification in it for the present state of affairs. Because the present continues in its depressing inaction and because the past has nothing to show but an embarrassing "secret action," each tale actually intensifies its own atmosphere of horrified shame. Since Conrad in the tales keeps his authorial stance as a rescuer, the relation between past and present can be understood as an outcome of Conrad's wish to rescue meaning for the present out of the obscure past. In the earliest group of short works, which begins in 1896 with "The Idiots" and ends in 1902 with "The End of the Tether," Conrad repeatedly manipulates the tale with philosophic ingenuity in order to discover what can finally be rescued. As ever, the answer is quite simply nothing. In the second group, which includes the stories up to and including "The Secret Sharer" (1910), the conclusion is more hopeful, if contrived. Finally, with the works that end with "The Planter of Malata" (1914), there is again a falling off into despair. Yet in each of these groups the relation between past and present is treated in profoundly dramatic terms, terms that are not simply a fictional technique but an important aspect of an analytic psychology of recollection under the pressures of shame and fear.

Perhaps an analogy with one phase of Sartre's phenomenological theory of emotions will point up Conrad's admirably unerring command of *conscious* human psychology. The value of this analogy rests solely on my conviction that Conrad's choice of a narrative method depended on his habitual insight into the "mechanisms of existence" discussed . . . [elsewhere]. If his choice was sincere (and my argument is that it was sincere), the method is a direct reflection and confirmation of what he himself *knew*. But more of this later. I begin with what Sartre calls an objective reality—this is whatever one feels should be grasped as an object or entity; the equivalent is Conrad's initial scrutiny of the present. Generally speaking, says Sartre, we find it too difficult or impossible to grasp this objective reality *as it is*. So that if we see a bunch of grapes that presents itself as "having to be picked" and that is beyond our reach, we drop our hands and mumble, "they're too green." By analogy, Conrad wishes first to grasp a situation in the present in such a way as to render it in direct causal relation with the past. When this cannot be done, the urgent feeling of wanting to do something "very soon becomes unbearable because the potentiality cannot be realized. This unbearable tension becomes, in turn, a motive for foisting [on the entity] a new quality . . . which will resolve the conflict and eliminate the tension. . . . [One] magically confers upon [the entity] the quality [one] desires." But there are limits to one's "magical" alteration of a situation that is unbearably difficult: the limits are set by consciousness itself, which does not allow the object simply to disappear. If this were to happen, it would mean that consciousness must also disappear. Therefore, as Sartre says, we rely upon "magical behavior which consists of denying the dangerous object with our whole body by subverting the vectorial structure of the space we live in by abruptly creating a potential direction on the *other side*." We deny the object by turning to another. And so Conrad's return to the past—a potential direction on the other side—follows. Now if it should happen that the segment in the past to which one returns is an episode of disaster (as it usually is in Conrad's case), one is made gloomy and sad. The result is that "sadness aims at eliminating the obligation to seek new ways"—and the emotional structure is once more complete. One has only to think of the beginning and end of *Heart of Darkness*, for example, to see how a movement from the present into the past causes the gloom of the past to engulf the whole of the present. A portion of the last sentence reads: "the tranquil waterway leading to the uttermost ends of the earth flowed sombre under an overcast sky—seemed to lead into the heart of an immense darkness." But in bringing the past and present together in such a way, "it is a question," as Sartre says,

> of making the world an affective neutral reality, a system in total affective equilibrium, of discharging the strong affective charge from objects, of reducing them all to affective zero, and, by the same token, of apprehending them as perfectly equivalent and interchangeable. In other words, lacking the power and will to accomplish the acts which we had been planning, we behave in such a way that the universe no longer requires anything of us. To bring that about we can only act upon our self, only 'dim the light,' and the noematical correlative of this attitude is what we call *Gloom*; the universe is gloomy, that is, undifferentiated structure. At the same time, however, we naturally take the cowering position, we 'withdraw into ourselves.'

It can be objected, I suppose, that Conrad's narrative methods (which Sartre's theory relates to) are only some of his tools as a writer and as such should be considered either as plain technique or as manifestations of his unconscious. But narrative method, when it is intensely moving and effective, derives mainly from the fully aware author himself, not exclusively from a technical fussiness, which one would expect the merest apprentice to have outgrown, or from an unconscious over which he has no control. Conrad's letters—as we have seen—reveal him in a series of "unbearable" and "potential" situations with regard to his existential awareness. His talk of nightmares and caves shows him in need of relief, and in that need there is little of the "mythic" or the "unconscious." There would seem to be some value in the "psychographic" or philosophic method of criticism, because it can distinguish certain configurations in the author's consciousness, configurations that persist into and enliven the fictional creation. To see the manner in which the author treats these characteristic attitudes enables the critic to examine the changing course of sophistication and speculation that every major writer must go through. And this is even truer if the writer's own temperament is one that is preeminently philosophic and consciously serious.

Moreover, it does Conrad an injustice to regard him simply as a "moral" writer (and even the fine Marxist critic Georg Lukács has reduced him to this level) or as indifferent to philosophical currents. R. W. B. Lewis has said of him: "no more than other novelists writing on English soil did Conrad possess that occasional French and German talent for making the war of thought itself exciting." Yet Conrad's disposition and outlook suited him for exactly that war of thought, and his reading and heritage only sharpened his innate gifts. His close friend Galsworthy said that Conrad was deeply impressed by Schopenhauer, and one can see the relevance here of Schopenhauer's philosophy of "humanistic pessimism," with its suggestive talk of subjective correlatives, the will to live, and art as a play within the play of life. We can see, that is, how Conrad was able courageously to articulate, after the example of Schopenhauer (whom Conrad probably first knew by way of Brunetière), the artistic cosmology of narrative fiction and its dependence upon the recollecting subjective consciousness, in this way seeking salvation from the terrible will to live that enslaves every human being. Conrad was at home with these ideas and terms.

The temper of British intellectual and philosophical life (at least in its more sympathetic, less insular forms) must have also left its mark on Conrad, just as it must have influenced the thought of any serious-minded alien. Is it not possible to say that F. H. Bradley's esoteric, idealist ethics, so well known to intellectuals of the time, are movements of thought that many of Conrad's heroes take for granted? The conflict of self-realization and responsibility in "Falk" and "Typhoon," for instance, is remarkably similar to Bradley's notion of "my station and its duties." Kurtz's fall from civilized "ethics," further-more, is continually expressed in terms of fidelity to station policy—an ob-viously barbed reference to idealist ethics. Finally, there is the matter of Conrad's repeatedly affirmed affinity with Baudelaire, the poet of "stérilités nerveux," the mirror of the sea, and temperamental writing. Surely a label like "moral" or "unconscious" underestimates the sophistication of Conrad's mind. It was a mind of so natural a cultivation that not only did it endure its own fanatical self-consciousness, but it also made art of its emotional struggles; in the best *European* tradition Conrad combined fictional representation and philosophic thought into an indivisible whole. Keeping such points in mind, we can better understand the complexities of Conrad. One can then begin to see and judge his fiction in proper critical perspective.

One of the ways in which this can be done is to compare the process of structural evolution within each of the three groups of stories named earlier. Since each group has a sort of structural idiom of its own, it is feasible to show how Conrad's changing sense of himself . . . [described elsewhere] . . . influences the various advances his fiction makes. Now the one endemic char-acteristic of this idiom is the strong sense of kinship that is revealed between past and present. (I had better say first that "past and present" refer not only to the present setting and the past narrative-plot, but also to the past action—always impulsive—and the present reflection—always slower and more delib-erate. When the story is not surrounded by a frame that is distant from the main action—as in *Heart of Darkness*—and when the story takes place totally in the unfolding present, then the tale itself is a working out of what has already happened before its formal beginning. Thus, James Wait is already a dying man when the story begins, and Captain Whalley is already a man out of a job.) When the kinship is discerned, even if the discernment is only implied, the character whose situation is the central one begins himself to *make a drama* out of what he is contending with. This is equivalent, in Sartre's terms, to the magical alteration of potentially difficult objects. A dramatic role is forced upon what is past, or difficult, or ungraspable, in order to coerce it into a more amenable relation with the person who does the forcing. All of this becomes clear enough in studying the course of Conrad's short fiction before World War I.

The most painful, and in some ways the most interesting, story of Con-rad's first period is "The Return." Moser and Guerard both dismiss the work as badly written and as a failure, because Conrad could not treat sex with any skill. The real interest of the story has little to do with the plot as such. Rather, it lies in Conrad's atomistic chronicling of a man's treatment of a disaster in his immediate past (his wife's tentative unfaithfulness, her desertion of him, and her curious return to him). The ostensible subject held only a kind of manufactured interest for Conrad himself: he wrote to Garnett on October 11, 1897, that in the story he was trying to expose "the gospel of the beastly bourgeois." It is obvious that Conrad was concerned with a topical, even fashionable, subject for its tangential market value, not because of any inherently worthwhile quality. Alan Hervey, respectable, moderately well-off, incapable of real intimacy, returns to his house in a London suburb from a normal day in the city. His wife, a kind of English Nora Helmer, is like an overgrown angel, who together with him skims over the surface of life, "ignoring the hidden stream . . . of life, profound and unfrozen." He finds a letter from her at home, in which she tells him that she has left him for a fat poetaster (one of their erstwhile friends), and this is a blow that stirs up in Hervey all the feelings that God had kept hidden. For the first time, he now "looks upon the mysterious universe of moral suffering."

Everything here follows the essential pattern already pointed out. The fact of his wife's imprisonment in the past has now leaped out before Hervey in the present sterility of his heedless life, and begins its work by stirring up passions within him (and passion, Conrad says editorially, is the only thing that cannot be explained away because it is life's secret infamy). Within a few moments after receiving the news of her shameful betrayal of him, he is required by his unbearable situation to make something of it. The powerful influence of shame is what, I think, makes this story an epitome of Conrad's earliest group of short works. For within a comparatively narrow form, whose focus is an essentially simple crisis of shameful exposure, Conrad allows full scope to all his emotional responses to shame. Hervey is immediately plunged into a realm in which "inexcusable truth" and "valid pretence" are confused. In other words, he cannot distinguish at first between the fact of her betrayal and his scandalized persuasion that she should not have betrayed him. As a category, truth can have no interest for him. It is this attitude to truth that admits him into a new realm of moral suffering. In Sartre's terms, he begins his magical alteration of the objective reality; and, Conrad says of him, he now needs a fresh crop of lies (beliefs) to cultivate.

One way of finding such beliefs is to review the past in an orderly manner. By a mode of egoistic retrospection, Hervey attempts to bring his past into causal relation with the present crisis in order to determine why his wife betrayed him. He looks into the mirror; and this is a gesture that rather awkwardly communicates Hervey's own consuming sense of himself. The intensity of his feeling for himself consequently elevates his wife into an obscure symbol standing before him—for now she has returned to him (even before her actual quick return) from her unsuccessful adventure. Unshielded and alone, he sees for the first time the indestructible character of her being. "She was the incarnation of all the short moments which every man spares out of his life for dreams, for precious dreams that concrete the most cherished, the most profitable of his illusions. . . . She was mysterious, significant, full of obscure meaning. The "meaning" (so adjectival, as F. R. Leavis would say, in its description) Hervey begins to perceive sets off a train of rather self-congratulatory thoughts. It corresponds, of course, to the desire for bringing matters into simple causal connection: his wife, Hervey now explains to himself, *has been* like the dreams every man nourishes in his life. The explanation places her in an understandable category that accounts not only for what she is *now* but also for what she has done to him. There is a similarity here between Hervey's apprehension of his wife and Marlow's boyhood dream about entering the dark places of the world. Even though he had never seen Kurtz as he really is (and Hervey has never seen his wife as she is), Marlow finds that he is attracted to him because Kurtz is a *point d'appui* of Marlow's own making, a kind of secret dream, a companion of his enforced idleness. To the young and inexperienced Marlow, whose character, like Hervey's, seems formed of orderly routines until, under the influence of disaster, he is thrust into a new realm of experience, Kurtz is what Marlow would like most to find. For Kurtz is a power of ultimate efficiency that reverberates through the fantastic horrors of an unexplored universe of darkness; and, in much the same way, Hervey begins to transform his wife from a neglected doll into the central figure of a realm of crisis. Though she is his own creation, constructed out of his own distress, her "being" elusively remains hers, and Hervey feels that somehow she "tampers with him."

Conrad proceeds to develop the kind of half-blind half-lucid existential consciousness that Hervey has of himself and his wife. The wife is herself, and her being disturbs him; Hervey admits this to himself only on the level of brute sensation that admits of no intellectual sophistry. But his reflecting intellect, *feeling* what it must have to satisfy itself, continues to treat her as a symbol of what he cannot understand: he harasses her for her meaning, like a dog worrying a bone. The reason Hervey cannot accept his wife as herself is that she refuses to discuss anything more than the simple fact of her betrayal and return: her letter to him, she says, is the beginning and the end. He, on the other hand, replies that "the end—this thing has no end." Out of touch with the material universe of real sensations, he is "whirled interminably through a kind of empty universe made up of nothing but fury and anguish." The more he remains in that gray world—which in *Heart of Darkness* is identified as the realm of neutrality just between life and death, and which is Schopenhauer's world of pure will—the more his feeling demands definite, symbolic expression. All of this recalls the striking letter written about the composition of "Youth," in which Conrad's description of the feeling that had induced the story is almost a separate entity struggling to express itself through the words: here, too, Hervey's feeling for his wife as a "mute symbol" pushes its way through this empty universe of his. For all of his vaunted "symbolic" writing, the special, local *use* and relevance of the symbol for Conrad was preeminently a sense of a mute, resisting, completely inscrutable object. The object is created in spite of its own independent reality (in this case, the wife's own being) in order to restructure an unbearable situation. Hervey had formerly lived as if he were a machine, as Kayerts and Carlier had, and the orderly world has disappeared from his sight; his wife alone is before him and can therefore replace the previous medium of existence. As in the past he had wanted "to grasp [the world] solidly," to be an important man, and she, with her valuable social connections, was to have been his instrument, now she alone needs to be understood.

The psychology of this is vitally interesting. For, Conrad seems to be saying, there is a period of attrition in one's emotional attitude toward life that causes one to remain reliant upon habit. During the time of youth (and "Youth" itself is amply convincing on this point) one sees the world, and puts it into parentheses as it were, with the special tool of youth—the vision of glamour and romance. Youth itself is a grappling hook with which the world can be held. It is also interesting here to note the parallel between this belief and Bradley's system of ethics. Bradley's point, as I understand it, is that all action is self-realization; action can be understood not in a priori terms but rather as a continually reaffirmed habit of "having" the world. And society provides the individual with a place that continually forces him to have the world in the same way at all times. Hence the concept of "my station and its duties," or the ethical, active role we perforce must play. Another parallel is Schopenhauer's distinction of the intelligible, the empirical, and the acquired character. We have a sense of ourselves within us (intelligible); when put into practice (empirical) this sense is modified; and when put within the framework of the society in which we live, it becomes further modified (acquired). As a result of the interplay between the individual and the world, we endow ourselves with a sense of ethical and psychological self-location (comparable to Bradley's "station"), which in most cases stays with us all our lives. But according to Conrad, there may be a shocking unsettlement that disrupts the continuity of our hold upon life. Then we willingly fly into the new order we discern and try somehow to relocate ourselves in it. There is still one more parallel, of course, to Sartre's psychology of escape discussed earlier in this chapter. Thus Hervey is "absorbed by the tragedy of his life" and is seeking in his wife a new means of finding himself.

Nevertheless, Hervey discovers a residue of conventional emotion within himself. He berates his wife with talk of "the moral foundations of society" and the necessity of fidelity to them. Unexpectedly, she submissively assents to this without argument, and he becomes "exiled in the realm of ungovernable folly." Her submission to conventional sentiment is a radical disappointment to Hervey: as a possible "tool" with which to understand the world, his wife has offered him no assistance. She has removed herself as a symbol, has refused to provide meaning. From the world of emptiness, fury, and anguish he moves into one of total absurdity. In this new emotional universe, the "dishonouring episode seemed to disengage itself from everything actual," remaining to irritate his sensibility even more aggressively. The tension between things as they are and things as he senses them grows more painful; he consciously and fearfully clings to appeasing truths as his wife stands before him, her face ugly with the truth that comes of having abandoned all safeguards. Hervey's double awareness is described by Conrad as a look into a black hole on the one hand and into ugliness on the other. Thus the path Hervey has followed has led him from a world of conventionality to one of undifferentiated grayness, where his wife *could* have aided him by becoming a "symbolic" solidity, and finally to a world where emptiness and deeply unsatisfactory ugliness confront him. He has but one resort, which is to search for a purely simple beginning: an act that can be interpreted only as beginning their relationship afresh and keeping it totally free of implicit meaning.

The predicament in which Hervey finds himself is one that Conrad knew well from his own experience. It was that pressing need to find an unimpeachable starting point from which to continue life anew, an objective fact untainted by any of the excesses of reflective interpretation. As the Herveys begin their dinner (the act that perversely stands for a ritual communion and also is to be the vital objective act), Hervey himself is absolutely debased. Having in the first place retreated from the trouble that broke into his life (the dishonoring episode), and having sought to apprehend it in a way calculated to save him, he now believes that he can walk directly toward the placating answer and the peace he has always desired. Of course, this is finally impossible. When he had first denied the coexistence of objective truth and his own subjective awareness of it, and when he had found his provisional causal attempts totally frustrated (the failure of such thoughts as "if my wife remains a new ordering symbol, then I will see the world properly"), Hervey had lost himself in a world of violently excessive speculation. He is now caught in a net of disorderly meanings that neither he nor his wife can begin to unravel. In sheer physical terms, the weight of experience has made *of him* a new world of totally isolated "symbolic" density. Living previously as a hollow man of conventionality in a complex world, Hervey has possessed the world in a successive series of noetic acts that obliterate the distinctions between truth and illusion, time and space, himself and the darkness. To his hyper-enlarged vision, the world itself is mere representation, a sham: he himself is far richer in meaning—and he has an apprehension of the immense darkness to which he has finally penetrated. Past and present thus both become actual, and equally impossible, in his own mind. He sees the great night of the world breaking through the discreet reserve of walls, of closed doors, of curtained windows. Significantly, only the statue of a woman in the Hervey house sheds any light in the darkness. Hervey walks out of his house, never to return— though not before his wife feels that she had "confronted something more subtle than herself."

To discover a definable structure in a past that is both self-contained and disastrously unexpected is the impossible problem set by Conrad's stories of this period. Alvan Hervey, Amy Foster, Captain Hagberd, the crew of the *Narcissus*, Marlow, the young captain in "Falk," all receive into their lives the mysterious and debilitating force of detached, almost gratuitous action. Its embodiments are necessarily human—Kurtz, James Wait, Falk, Mrs. Hervey—and, to all purposes, corrupting. Each of these embodiments re-quires comprehension, at least in the minds of the characters, in a way that draws the comprehending mind into an agonizing battle with the unknown. The categorizing sensibility, insufficiently prepared and uneasy in its sterile calm, rejects and modifies what it cannot manifestly accept. Like Conrad, whose immensely distracting impressions flooded his heart in full force, each of the actors in the present makes of the past a drama that he hopes will elucidate the present. Hervey's experience remains, I think, the most sustained and well-articulated exercise in self-debasement that Conrad achieved in his written work. It is a process carried on under the influence of Conrad's under-standing of how the mind goes into shameful retreat. The gradual withering of the intellectual capacity for disinterested perception begins in outraged shame, moves to frenetic speculation, and ends in the darkness of almost inhuman solitude. And, most terrifying of all, Conrad courageously depicts the slaughter of action as in some way caused by the activity of the mind. Thus what Marlow, Hervey, and the crew of the *Narcissus* desire (an enlight-ened, orderly, and formal explanation for peculiar disaster) threatens them with darkness, disorder, and formlessness. We are left with the question: does the mind seek order *or* truth? This, we remember from Conrad's letters, is the question that runs throughout his own speculations.

In general dramatic and philosophic terms, the situation is one in which the categorizing mind, by imposing itself on the world that insolently confronts it, succeeds so well that outside itself only hollowness seems to be left. Wait's last dream, in which he sees himself as an empty husk, is an implicit commentary on the consciousness of the crew. We must then ask why it is that he troubles the crew with his presence, why Mrs. Hervey returns, why Kurtz seems to have called Marlow in, and why Falk must anger the young captain. These questions bring one to what is most profound and human in Conrad: the realization that every act of life, no matter how direct, natural, and self-sufficient, demands intellectual recognition in the consciousness of every person who is involved in it. Just as Conrad himself required the voices of his friends as evidence of their interest in him, so too, does Wait require the egoistic assurance of a common human interest in him. With terrible clarity he says, "I must live till I die."

At its most bearable, life is the egoistic assertion of one's existence so that others will feel it. If the world is a conflict of willful egoisms, as Schopenhauer saw it, then the need for recognition is the original egoism, the root from which everything else springs. In seeking the kinship of reflective understanding, however, the performer of an action inevitably is forced to reduce himself to a level below the normal limits of active human life. There is a draining of strength as the past action is sapped of all content by the reflecting present. Only the surrounding darkness remains substantially palpable. In the present, the corroding power of thought and interpretation completely absorbs the actualized situation and leads to an anarchic enlargement of the self. The mute, or nearly mute, agent who wishes himself fully understood grows more simple and direct, becomes less and less accessible to the complex, reflecting mind. And the reflecting, enervated mind, desiring relief in action, becomes even more complex, less and less able to grasp things *as they are.*

The only possible meeting between thought and action is in death, the annihilation of both. For the mind to accept death as a solution of the difficulty would be to accept the devastating irony that permits the destruction of the consciousness, the only faculty capable of enjoying the solution. Therefore Conrad's earliest tales posit a compromise in which the agent usually dies (Wait, Kurtz, Yanko) and the reflecting mind continues still uncertain, still in darkness. The breathtaking richness of *Heart of Darkness* comes from the fact that Kurtz is an arch-European ("All Europe contributed to the making of Kurtz") who undertakes the immensely egoistic, heroic, and rudimentary task of joining his action to his thought ("everything belonged to him"), succeeds ("exterminate all the brutes"), and then dies, courageously professing his success ("the horror"). Marlow, a more insular European, perceives all of this but, like Hervey, is overwhelmed by the enduring darkness. First, though, he tells a lie that simplifies the dark truth but safeguards the power of Kurtz's heroic eloquence. And that eloquence—what is it really? It is quite impossible to say. There can be no more accurate representation in fiction of the historic predicament of mind-tortured modern Europe, except perhaps Mann's *Doctor Faustus*.

If, in this group of stories, Alvan Hervey's is the most chronicled version of the interpreting quest, Marlow's the most poetic, and the *Narcissus* crew's the closest to success, then Dr. Kennedy's in "Amy Foster" is the most ironic because the past he investigates is not only the most distant from him but also the most humanly appealing. The story of Yanko Goorall, a shipwrecked young Pole who lands in England, is at first taken for a madman, and is then loved, married, and deserted (through incomprehension) by Amy Foster, is mulled over by Kennedy, who is a former adventurer. The significance of this is clear. Only Kennedy is capable of entering where others fear to tread, his detached mind allowing him the objective clarity with which to grasp the terrible unhappiness of the story. That Conrad is at once Yanko and Kennedy cannot be doubted: pathetic action and the dramatic, interpreting imagination are merged incongruously, and eternally separated by circumstance and time. Amy is the tragically ineffectual substitute for the fully understanding support that a shipwrecked man needs. A rather large degree of misfortune in the supposedly natural relation between man and woman (Hervey and his wife are excellent examples of this) depends on the fact that a woman must always be sought and is always found wanting, even debasing.

Conrad's interest in the quest I have been discussing comes to quasi-fruitful maturity in two of the last six stories he wrote before *The Mirror of the Sea*, "Typhoon" and "The End of the Tether." Both are stories of old men in periods of inordinate trial. Captain MacWhirr in "Typhoon" is an uneducated man of no distinction; even his crew holds him in some disdain. But one great virtue is his ability to face what is before him with his whole being, totally incapable of scrutinizing either tradition or the past. When a typhoon is about to descend upon the ship, his literal mind can see no alternative but to go through it. His attempted study of books on typhoons is ludicrously inept, for he cannot bring himself to understand the details. Only the fact of the low reading on the barometer and his presumption of the ship's danger trouble him. Jukes, his mate, is the interpreting man, bothered by questions of alternatives, of safety, of conflicting passions. The sustained climax of the story intensely conveys MacWhirr's steady occupancy of his position in space (always on deck) and in time (moving steadily through a stormy period). Conrad's awareness of the sacrifice MacWhirr must have made and continues to make for this choice of unreflecting fidelity to duty accounts for the seemingly irrelevant presence in the tale of MacWhirr's wife and children. Always away from them, always a silly, mindless individual to them, MacWhirr's unthinking modesty knows only that he has been through some kind of experience. His letters to them (and their reading of his incredibly prosaic storm letter ends the tale) are received with petulant patience. Yet MacWhirr has no past to live up to; everything is in the present for him. And this is what the tale advances and rejects almost at the same time. To occupy the present with a singleminded attention to immediate duty is the achievement of a man for whom thought—and broader awareness—is impossible.

Judged by itself, "Typhoon" seems to suggest that MacWhirr's way is the best after all. Set against the more interesting and credible figures in Conrad's other short fiction of this period, MacWhirr is a nonidealistically rendered individual of comparatively shallow gifts, a man temperamentally alien to Conrad himself. The dissatisfaction the reader feels at the callous treatment accorded MacWhirr by his family, especially after his unacknowledged heroism, is intensified to the point of impatient annoyance with MacWhirr and not, as might be hoped, with his family. So that while we admire MacWhirr for what he does *now*, we reject him for what he can never do *then*. To sum up: MacWhirr is in the present, on a ship in a catastrophic storm. This can be compared with Hervey's immediate awareness of his wife's betrayal. But whereas Hervey instantly leaves the immediate for the past, MacWhirr remains absolutely steady on course. There are a finite number of things to be done and he does them: to Jukes and the other sailors go the tasks of executing his orders with agony and difficulty. The importance of the story is that Conrad's conception of MacWhirr's successful coping with present disaster can be rendered only in terms of a central action that bears nothing but passivity. Offering the storm merely the resistance necessary for bare survival, MacWhirr ignores the storm's "personal" corrupting attack on him, refusing to endow it with the notion of universality that he might have created for the exigency. It is, for him, simply *a* storm, not *the* storm, not *the* darkness (as Marlow would say). The genius of the tale is that MacWhirr is both attractively human and inhuman, active and passive.

When Jukes, down in the engine room, talks with his captain over the ship's telephone, he is struck how, in a moment of titanic flooding and darkness, MacWhirr's voice and presence seem to push back the floods. But this image of defiant resistance to disaster is the only example of its kind in early

Conrad—unless one counts the taciturn Singleton, who undermines his resistance by accepting Bulwer-Lytton as a private dream. A dreamless man,
without illusions and interpretive capacities, practically a cipher: this is
MacWhirr. His opposite counterpart is Captain Whalley, the hero of "The
End of the Tether." In this touching story an old man, spiritually related to
Marlow and Falk, is almost literally crowded out of life both by circumstances
and by his own attempts to create a kind of self-consistency. With the continuity of his life broken by both poverty and responsibility for his daughter,
he becomes a co-owner with Massy, an unscrupulous and whining engineer,
of the ancient freighter *Sofala*. The central tension of the story is the connection
of Whalley's increasing blindness to his increasing sense of honor and fidelity;
the blinder he becomes, the more he clings to an outmoded code of action.
Just as Hervey cannot distinguish between truth and pretense, Whalley, the
forlorn traveler, is isolated in the present as he tries to justify and extend his
own adventurous MacWhirr-like past of glorious seafaring. His daughter,
whose name (with heavy-handed significance) is Ivy, has twined herself
around him. Like Yanko and Hervey, his whole view of existence depends on
this unhappily incompetent woman. Throughout the first part of the story
we are made aware of Whalley's noble physical bearing, which somehow does
not fit his demeaning circumstances. Carrying a burden of responsibility that
he has formulated in terms of a noble past record, Whalley continues to believe
that his life is necessary: he prolongs his agreement with Massy only because
he has to protect his investment in the ship for his daughter.

Massy and Sterne (the ship's mate) harass the old man by reminding him
not of his infirmity but of his responsibility. It is only Van Wyk, another of
those retired adventurers like Dr. Kennedy, who feels an active sympathy for
the old man. But this sympathy is viable only as a kind of helpless understanding. It is capable only of noting what it can neither fathom nor assist.

> And Mr. Van Wyk, whose feeling of outraged love had been trans-
> lated into a form of struggle with nature, understood very well
> that, for that man whose whole life had been conditioned by action,
> there could exist no other expression for all the emotions; that,
> voluntarily to cease venturing, doing, enduring, for his child's
> sake, would have been exactly like plucking his warm love for her
> out of his living heart. Something too monstrous, too impossible,
> even to conceive.

When, in his last crisis, Whalley falls into the abyss of total solitude, where
nothing is his own except his sense of duty, he has at least "carried his point."

He dies willingly then, refusing to leave the ship with whose compass Massy has tampered: now he sees the whole of life "as he had never seen [it] before."

Whalley's enlarged spiritual vision, in which everything becomes overt and manifest, pushes him out of life. He dies possessing only this; although he wants to see his daughter, he never does. From Conrad's point of view, Whalley's death closes a phase of emotional, artistic, and intellectual speculation on the supposedly liberating quest for understanding. There is a sense of decorum in Whalley's end, a decorum that shows in the difference between the ending of this tale and the ending of *Heart of Darkness* how far Conrad has come. Whereas night seems to be descending upon an already dark world at the end of *Heart of Darkness*, "The End of the Tether" closes with these sentences: "The light had finished ebbing out of the world; not a glimmer. It was a dark waste; but it was unseemly that a Whalley who had gone so far to carry a point should continue to live. He must pay the price." For the self-exploratory mission of the individual confronted with disaster, there is now only one outcome: death. Previously, men like Hervey and Marlow had the luxury of accepting the circumambient darkness even as they were overwhelmed by the difficulties of their subjective awareness. At least they can live on. Now the engulfing of the objective by the subjective—the fact of Whalley's blindness drowned in the moral severity of his private mission—leads to a pitiful death, because death is the great neutralizer in which objective and subjective do not pertain. Not only is death necessary and inevitable; it is also correct.

The further pertinence of this tale to Conrad's own life is of course that it was written in late 1902, at a time when he had broken off his relations with Blackwood and had begun the dedicated creation of a new "economical" character for himself. Like Whalley, at the end of his spiritual tether in the society that seemed to have no room for his problems, Conrad begins a new phase, having buried the Hervey-Marlow-Whalley period of his life. He undertook, within a few months of "The End of the Tether," the writing of *Nostromo* and, significantly, a series of sea sketches. He was now following the advice he had once given Galsworthy, that man lives in his eccentricities alone. The pose he would now maintain before the heedless public was that of an eccentric rather than that of a difficult novelist. And in this task, begun in *The Mirror of the Sea* and finished in the marvelous *A Personal Record*, his writing efforts play a considerable role of elucidation and support.

NORMAN N. HOLLAND

Style as Character:
The Secret Agent

"The style," so critics say, "is the man," and though we would be hard put to define either the subject or the predicate, the two do seem to have a natural affinity. We speak of works as Miltonic or Flaubertian or Kafkaesque or Kingsley Amish. From the opposite end of the sentence, the psychoanalyst, speaking of a man, will often talk of his "life-style." That usage suggests that the literary critic might find a useful model for his concept of style in the psychoanalyst's concept of character, particularly when he is puzzled about a writer's style, as when a novel like *The Secret Agent* seems sharply marked off from the rest of Conrad's work, and yet, in some half-understood way, deeply Conradian.

In "style," the literary critic seems to include three things. First, and most obviously, he means a writer's way with words: Shavian wit or Joycean puns or Shakespearean quibbles. Second, he seems to include a writer's choice of material and his characteristic form for handling it: it would be hard, for example, to think of anything but social comedy that could be said to be "in the style of Congreve," and it is hard to think of Conrad's political novels as from the same pen as his sea stories. Third, critics seem to include in the notion of style a writer's way of dealing with his audience: the snigger of a Sterne, the stage-managing of a Thackeray, the allegorizing of a Melville.

A psychoanalyst defines "character" (the classic statement is Fenichel's) as "the habitual mode of bringing into harmony the tasks presented by internal

From *Modern Fiction Studies* 12, no. 2 (Summer 1966). © 1966 by Purdue Research Foundation.

demands and by the external world." There is a certain rough correspondence between the elements the literary critic includes in style and the three terms the psychoanalyst includes in character. That is, the "internal demands" are the *Triebe*, the drives, that might lead a writer to a certain kind of material. The "habitual mode of bringing into harmony" refers to a man's defenses; they, in turn, correspond to a writer's ways of dealing with his material—form and structure on the large scale, sentence or verse manner on the small. Finally, the "external world" for a writer is his reader. Naturally, in a man, as in a work of literature, these three things interact and modify one another, but we can, I think, set up a kind of rough proportion: content is to drive as form is to defense as style is to character (defined as the habitual interactions of drive, defense, and external reality).

By these three criteria, *The Secret Agent* does not seem particularly Conradian. In terms of form, we miss the usual Conradian narrator. At the sentence level, instead of the allegorical and symbolic overtones spelled out in the language of, say, *Heart of Darkness*, we have a heavily ironic and dry verbal style. As for content, we do not have man pitting his own flawed self against nature, but rather a political story: anarchists, Verloc as *agent provocateur*, the Professor with his bombs; a story of a man and his wife, Verloc and Winnie who married him to provide for Stevie, the idiot boy. Yet some of the incidents show Conrad's preoccupations, though deviously, in the manner of parody: the fatally significant lapse, here, Verloc's using Stevie to try to blow up the Greenwich Observatory and Stevie's consequent fragmentation; the secret, both the motive and identity of the bombers and Verloc's hoard of payments from the ministry he serves; the self-sacrificing woman—Winnie and her mother. In some sense, then, the novel is "Conradian," but in what sense? Only a psychological concept of style, I think, can tell us.

Anarchic in form as well as content, *The Secret Agent* leaves us with the persistent question of the Professor, "unsuspected and deadly," just as the opening line had posed us Mr. Verloc, also unsuspected, also (in the event) deadly. Those first and last lines offer a clue to the informing principle about which the novel finds its shape and inner logic: the unsuspected—a sense throughout the book that each character has a doubleness or tripleness, a secret self. Verloc, for example—one side is the anarchist, another the bourgeois family man dealing in pornography, a third, the protector of property and servant of embassies. The late Baron Stott-Wartenheim was clever indeed to designate him Δ. The three anarchists are fat or impotent or helplessly and grossly dependent on some woman. The Professor is "frail, insignificant, shabby, miserable"—but explosive.

The police, too, share this many-sidedness, for "The terrorist and the policeman both come from the same basket." Chief Inspector Heat must mediate between the anarchists under his jurisdiction ("our lot") and the Assistant Commissioner, who in turn feels "himself dependent on too many subordinates and too many masters." He must deal on one side with Heat and on another with his wife's friend, Michaelis' patroness, and on still a third, Sir Ethelred, himself torn between the Assistant Commissioner's discoveries and the Fisheries Bill.

Stevie has the same dualistic quality: immoderate compassion matched by pitiless rage. Stevie's mother mediates between the idiot boy and his enraged father, just as Winnie herself adopts a mother's role between Stevie and Verloc: " 'Might be father and son,' she said to herself," as, unknown to her, Verloc leads Stevie to his doom. And at the moment she kills, just as she has torn Heat's pink racing form in two, "Her personality seemed to have been torn into two pieces, whose mental operations did not adjust themselves very well to each other."

The characters bisect and trisect one another, each touching only a part of the others in a chaos and maze of human relations. We begin to sense in the world of the novel the significance of Stevie's "circles, circles, circles; innumerable circles, concentric, eccentric; a coruscating whirl of circles that by their tangled multitude of repeated curves, uniformity of form, and confusion of intersecting lines suggested a rendering of cosmic chaos, the symbolism of a mad art attempting the inconceivable." Not unlike Stevie, Conrad himself seems to be drawing endless circles in his novel: coins, spectacles, wheels, clock faces, haloed street lights, bowler hats, orange peel, billiard ball, the Professor's india-rubber ball, even the great dome of the observatory. And not just circles, but T-bars (the gas lights), triangles (not only Stott-Wartenheim's, also the triangular well of streets in front of Verloc's shop)— the novel fairly bristles with geometric images, as though Conrad were trying to squeeze some sort of order out of the chaos; as though he himself were trying to act out the embassy's injunction: "What is required at present is not writing, but the bringing to light of a distinct, significant fact—I would almost say of an alarming fact."

The critical essay that tells us most about *The Secret Agent* is, of course, Conrad's own Preface, written in 1920 for a collected edition long after the novel's original publication early in 1907. Repeatedly, in the Preface, Conrad uses Wurmt's image of "bringing to light" as he speaks of "illuminating facts," their "illuminating quality," an "illuminating impression." He speaks of the idea precipitating like a geometry of bizarre and unexpected crystals in a colorless solution: "Strange forms, sharp in outline, but imperfectly apprehended, appeared and claimed attention." As against the usual setting for

Conrad's novels, the sea, "reflector of the world's light," he now saw London, as the "background" for the story, "a cruel devourer of the world's light." "Slowly the dawning conviction of Mrs. Verloc's maternal passion grew up to a flame between me and that background." "At last the story of Winnie Verloc stood out complete. . . . it had to be disengaged from its obscurity in that immense town," brought "out in front of the London background."

As one would expect from the Preface, light and dark are key images in *The Secret Agent*, notably in that dark London with its "sinister, noisy, hopeless, and rowdy night," "sullen, brooding, and sinister," broken by "soiled blood-red light." London becomes inner madness rendered as outer setting, and the city threatens throughout the novel to stifle, suffocate, submerge, overwhelm—Winnie is quite correct to fear in it hanging or drowning. London in the deepest sense is the engulfing sea or maze of irrationality—the very street numbers are as irrational as Stevie's circles. It is a "slimy dampness," a "slimy aquarium," "an immensity of greasy slime" "like a wet, muddy ditch." Miss Claire Rosenfield has very astutely pointed out that balanced against these images of water are fish: the Assistant Commissioner is busy catching a "sprat," Verloc, in order to get at the whale, dogfish, or witty fish, Vladimir. At the moment he plunges into the murky depths of London, the Assistant Commissioner himself looks like a "queer foreign fish," and, of course, Sir Ethelred is concerned throughout with his Fisheries Bill. At the end, Winnie is, as it were, thrown back into the sea.

Fishing provides the perfect symbol for the "bringing to light of a distinct, significant fact," something all the men of the novel play at. Vladimir, Verloc, Heat, even Ossipon are all investigating—but lazily, fitfully. The novel concerns Greenwich Observatory, a place dedicated to bringing facts to light, but the novel uses the observatory only in a plot to destroy it. Ossipon invokes Lombroso as an Italian peasant would his saint. Heat's wisdom is not "true wisdom"; rather, "His wisdom was of an official kind," and he is lazily willing to pin the crime on Michaelis. Two men stand out as exceptions to this general indolence. The Assistant Commissioner really tries to find the truth—and, for that, he is twice described as Don Quixote. The other truth-seeker is, of course, the mad Professor. Confronted with "this world of contradictions," "the inexplicable mysteries of conscious existence," the rest of the men in the novel want simply to relax into such facile faiths as Heat's in his favorite racing form, the easy dogmas of the revolutionaries (which Conrad describes in religious images), or Verloc's belief that he could trust any woman who had given herself to him. "Man," says Conrad, curiously echoing another melodramatic detective thriller, *Hamlet*, "Man may smile and smile, but he is not an investigating animal. He loves the obvious."

Verloc's trust in his wife suggests the key to this cheerful oblivion: "Mr. Verloc loved his wife as a wife should be loved—that is, maritally, with the regard one has for one's chief possession." "She was mysterious, with the mysteriousness of living beings. The far-famed secret agent Δ . . . was not the man to break into such mysteries." Possession substitutes for knowledge: thus Heat can rest secure on "private friendship, private information, private use of it," and Verloc, with his air of having wallowed in bed all day, can glow in his belief that he has protected "the town's opulence and luxury." Ossipon can even speak of "the even tenor of his revolutionary life." He is fat, Verloc is fat, so also Heat; Winnie's mother has triple chins and her legs are so swollen she can scarcely move. Michaelis is likewise obese. As for Yundt, "The famous terrorist had never in his life raised personally as much as his little finger against the social edifice." Appetite and eating image Verloc's grisly complacency at his murder, eating being another way in *The Secret Agent* of achieving the security of possession. For all the men in the story (save the Commissioner and the Professor), Silenus is their emblem. Lustful, lazy, fat, they rest and feed complacently on the obvious. *The Secret Agent* is, among other things, a study in sloth.

By contrast, the women are paragons of self-sacrifice. Winnie's mother commits herself (through the failure of the male trustees to investigate her) to a death-like charitable home, all for the sake of the son, Stevie. And Winnie herself gave up her butcher-boy lover for the slothful eater Verloc so as to provide for Stevie. As for investigation—"She felt profoundly that things do not stand much looking into," a note that Conrad sounds again and again as her leitmotif. The women of the story (one could take Michaelis' patron as the prototype) do not probe the mysteries of the world; instead, they offer to a world trusted and uninvestigated a bottomless compassion to the point where the only remedy for pain Stevie can even imagine is to be taken into his sister-mother's bed.

And yet, as the bed-wallowing Verloc finds out, it can be dangerous to relax into the sea of feminine compassion represented by Winnie. "The protection she had extended over her brother had been in its origin of a fierce and indignant complexion," an "ardour of protecting compassion exalted morbidly in her childhood." "Mrs. Verloc's temperament . . . when stripped of its philosophical reserve, was maternal and violent"—a curious pairing of adjectives. Ossipon sees her "twined round him like a snake, not to be shaken off. She was not deadly. She was death itself—the companion of life." Significantly, Winnie stabs Verloc as he is lolling on the sofa issuing his mating call.

In the moment of the stabbing, Mrs. Verloc literally becomes Stevie's

avenging soul, that child who seems to bring to a focus the moral world of
the novel. Miss Rosenfield notes that Stevie is the child-man who achieves
double parentage (in the manner of Moses) by being borne in a roomy "barque"
down the "lazy stream" of Mr. Verloc's life; who dies by being torn to pieces
and thus provides a grisly pun as "raw material for a cannibal feast." Conrad
is parodying the scapegoat heroes of antiquity, sacrificed and eaten that the
city may be reborn from its accumulated sins and sickness. But, alas, Inspector Heat only loses his appetite—and nearly his breakfast—at the sight
of Stevie's remains. The scapegoat provides not cleansing and rebirth but
death for Winnie and Verloc, guilt for Ossipon, failure for the forces of law
and order.

More realistically (but still not unlike the scapegoat hero), Stevie seems
always to have alternated between being seduced and being beaten. His circles
suggest the "chaos and eternity" he found in human relationships, a confusion
of intersections and hidden sides. His response to deprivation is simple, primitive, and violent: "Somebody, he felt, ought to be punished for it—punished
with great severity," and this reaction pinpoints the pattern of anarchism (at
least in Conrad's highly personal view of it): a morass of vague sentiments
from which springs a mad retaliation. "In the face of anything which affected
directly or indirectly his morbid dread of pain, Stevie ended by turning vicious. . . . The tenderness of his universal charity had two phases as indis-
solubly joined and connected as the reverse and obverse sides of a medal. The
anguish of immoderate compassion was succeeded by the pain of an innocent
but pitiless rage." He alternates between lazy, mindless compassion and sudden, violent action; Vladimir, Verloc, his sister-mother, and all the anarchists
do the same.

Balanced against this moral and emotional anarchy are the police and the
other forces of government, "the House which is *the* House, *par excellence*,"
but very distinctly not a compassionate home. Government tries to impose
on this violence-in-violence some sort of control and order, a constant watch,
"rules of the game." And it is the aim of Vladimir, Verloc, and the rest to
provoke the very forces of control into anarchy. As the Professor puts it: "To
break up the superstition and worship of legality should be our aim. Nothing
would please me more than to see Inspector Heat and his likes take to shooting
us down in broad daylight with the approval of the public. Half our battle
would be won then; the disintegration of the old morality would have set in
its very temple." This theme of control brings us to Conrad himself. The
idea that informs the novel is anarchy masked over by control or indolence.
The "secret agent" in human affairs, the "unsuspected," is the potential for

violence in each of us—and, presumably, in Conrad himself (who once sprang at Ford Madox Ford's throat when Ford interrupted his proofreading).

The Secret Agent seems to stand apart from the main line of Conrad's writing. It is set in the city, not the sea; government, not navigation, is his subject. Yet this novel is perhaps more deeply Conradian than any of the others. Albert Guerard has shown that Conrad's basic theme is the conflict between the mariner and the outlaw; between the man who seeks to establish control by finding his place among the hard, infallible objects of external reality and that other, darker figure who immerses himself in the destructive, chaotic jungle within and without. Although it is clearest, perhaps, in "The Secret Sharer," between the anonymous captain and his outlaw double, we see the contrast all through Conrad's works: the twinned figures of Marlow and Kurtz, one returning from, one sinking into the *Heart of Darkness*; MacWhirr battling the "Typhoon" without and the passengers' riot within his ship; the skillful young captain threatened by the anarchic spirit of the dead one in *The Shadow-Line*; Haldin and Razumov, the outlaw rejected and his betrayer, in *Under Western Eyes*; the captain and crew of *The Nigger of the "Narcissus"* striving to exorcise by seamanship the deadly thing within their ship; Lingard and Almayer in *Almayer's Folly*; Heyst and Jones in *Victory*; and we sometimes see the same dualism of control and anarchy, fidelity and betrayal in single figures, Lord Jim (notably) or Karain. Given such a preoccupation with the dualism of controller and controlled, how, in a sense, could Conrad have failed to write a novel about anarchy? And he wrote two, *The Secret Agent* and *Under Western Eyes*.

In *The Secret Agent*, the earlier of the two, we find Conrad's usual dualism doubled. There is controller and controlled but then a doubleness to what is controlled: the police try to keep under surveillance and rule a violent, masculine rage which itself punctuates a feminine, complacent compassion. Thus, the atmosphere of the novel consists of indolence, obesity, dependence on woman, bureaucracy, compassion, Stevie's circles, and all this in the foggy, dark, damp, grimy maze of London. In the night journey of Winnie's self-sacrificing mother, Conrad brings all these elements together and at the same moment sinks his novel to its deepest, most obscure point in the maze. The action of the novel (as contrasted to its atmosphere) is best described in the diplomat's phrase, "the bringing to light of a distinct, significant fact . . . an alarming fact": the explosion itself, the sacrifice of the scapegoat Stevie, the emergence of his nametape, the Professor's detonator, the Commissioner's quest for Vladimir, or even Verloc's bank account (the prosaic equivalent of the buried treasure in *Nostromo* and other Conrad tales). But nothing is brought to light. Instead, at key points in the novel, the lights are turned off. All this fishing in the slimy dampness of London produces no catch: Winnie sinks into the ocean, the buried treasure slips into Ossipon's pocket, and we are left with the Professor, "unsuspected and deadly." "An impenetrable mystery seems destined to hang forever over this act of madness or despair."

Psychologically, it would be difficult and unnecessary to say what that swamp or sea might have stood for in Conrad's mind—it undoubtedly stood for many things. Death; passivity; sexuality; human relations and communication; woman or the feminine side of Conrad's own nature; betrayal or loss of fidelity, particularly the expatriate's failure to carry on his forefathers' fight for Polish independence: the writer landlocked at his farmhouse desk as against the onetime heroic seaman; perhaps the irrational in the largest sense, particularly irrational or self-destructive aggression (there is evidence that Conrad himself once attempted suicide)—all these and many others may be represented in that "immensity of greasy slime" the novelist fought to keep his head above. One thing, however, is clear: Conrad was deeply tempted to let go his hold, lose control, and sink into it (as so many of his heroes do). Not only *The Secret Agent*, but all his novels deal with the control or punishment of such an impulse.

This problem of control creates not only the events and characters of the Conradian novel, but also its form, for, psychologically, form is to content as defense is to impulse. It is surely no accident that a novelist so preoccupied with action as a defense should choose a style which Henry James saw was "the way to do a thing that shall make it undergo most doing." As though Conrad felt the very writing of his stories as a tempting but threatening anarchy, he interposed in most of them a dispassionate narrator, ironically commenting on and distancing us (and Conrad) from the fictive world. He thus defended against communicating not only with his material but also with his readers. A number of his stories (but most notably "Amy Foster") deal with problems of communication; we hear from Ford Madox Ford about his Flaubertian search for *le mot juste* and his composing his richest sentences in French (for English was his third, not his second, language). Critics galore have noted (and some complained of) the fog of adjectives Conrad puts between his material and his reader.

In *The Secret Agent*, Conrad put aside the margin of safety the narrator represented (and his wife has written how depressed he became during the writing of this particular novel). He relied instead entirely on the adjectives. He created a comic, ironic style that swings between an involved periphrasis, almost neoclassic in manner, and sudden, grimy, realistic details. The result can be such delicious ironies as our last view of Ossipon: "Already he bowed his broad shoulders, his head of ambrosial locks, as if ready to receive the leather yoke of the sandwich board." In sentence after sentence and scene after scene, a "distinct, significant fact" comes to light against the prevailing murk: the fly on the window of Vladimir's office, for example, or the little cracked bell in the Verlocs' shop that marks each passing from the outer world to the inner. His artistic aim, Conrad said, was "before all, to make you see."

In structure no less than sentence style, we see him try either to flee the "immensity of greasy slime" or to bring out from it some distinct fact that can then be seen and controlled. In *The Secret Agent*, Conrad (who was the first great writer to tackle the screenplay) constantly uses flashback, as though he were retreating from the immediate material into some safer matter elsewhere. *The Secret Agent* is a detective thriller—indeed, Alfred Hitchcock has made a film of it—but it does not grow as the usual thriller does from an initial problem to a mass of revelations at the end. Instead, Conrad gives us little secrets which are soon revealed and replaced by other secrets, as though he could not stand a sustained buildup of uncertainty and mystery; rather, there must be a constant "bringing to light."

Further, the novel, in its ending, pirouettes away from the complexities of politics and policing developed in its first three-quarters; at the end we are left with two characters so peripheral they become symbolic of the two poles of the novel: the morally complacent Ossipon and the madly violent Professor. Throughout the book, Conrad seems almost to be running away from his characters as his focus shifts successively from Verloc to Vladimir to the other anarchists to Heat to the Assistant Commissioner to Winnie Verloc's mother to Winnie to Ossipon and finally and ultimately to the Professor. We sense in the structure—or lack of it—another version of Stevie's circles, Conrad's flight from and return to his material: "I had to fight to keep at arm's length the memories of my solitary and nocturnal walks all over London in my early days, lest they should rush in and overwhelm each page of the story."

By the structure of individual sentences and of the whole, Conrad enlists us in his defensive action of "bringing to light a distinct, significant fact," but does he make us feel the need for the defense? In most of Conrad's works in which the characters sink into the moral swamp, he represents the morass as tempting or alluring, justified by compassion or sheer self-defense. *The Secret Agent* provides no such temptation toward the fat, slimy, repellent world of the anarchists—except for one thing. Conrad plays on our curiosity; on just the first page, for example, we hear "nominally," "ostensible," "discreetly but suspiciously," "hinting at impropriety." He tempts us to probe the secrets of the controllers and the controlled—but warns us they are both rather dreary. At only one point does he draw us into the novel unequivocally: the chapter of the murder where both the danger of being overwhelmed and the vengeful justification for overwhelming reach a peak. We come in on the side of Winnie and feel, as she does, the power of the terrible absurd urge to destroy and be destroyed into utter, total blackness. It is no wonder that all the many critics of this novel, though they differ as to its merits, find the murder its high point.

The critics, I think, are saying Conrad's special style (or character) succeeds in that chapter, much less so in the rest of the novel. But the novel as a whole is no less Conradian for that. In content, the novel lets us over the side, as it were, into the London sea of anarchy. Psychologically, such a content is a drive: Conrad describes as "a fascinating temptation" the Assistant Commissioner's "descent into the street . . . like the descent into a slimy aquarium." The defense is to get back out of that anarchy or indolence—as form, the defense becomes all Conrad's devices for extricating and distancing us from that tempting sea: the dry, ironic style, the shifting of focus from one character to another, flashback. Then, drive and defense, content and form come together as the style and theme of the whole, pervading and informing its individual sentences: "the bringing to light of a distinct, significant fact . . . an alarming fact." The style is indeed Conradian, for, as he defined his own aim in the "Preface to *The Nigger of the 'Narcissus'* ": "The artist descends within himself, and in that lonely region of stress and strife," if he succeeds, he can "hold up unquestioningly, without choice and without fear the rescued fragment before all eyes . . ." "And when it is accomplished—behold!—all the truth of life is there: a moment of vision, a sigh, a smile—and the return to an eternal rest." The aim is a noble one, truly and stoically Conradian, and because we can understand his style psychologically, we can feel what he felt as something of the moral function of literature: to bring back to light, almost in the manner of a detective, a character and style of life buried in our own dark, anarchic past.

R. W. B. LEWIS

The Current of Conrad's Victory

The opening sentences of *Victory* introduce us half-playfully to a number of "close relations," the surprising similarities between seeming contrasts—coal and diamonds, the practical and the mystical, the diffused and the concentrated, an island and a mountain. All of them have their literal and thematic importance in the story, which describes a profound conflict rooted in opposition and likeness, and which has to do with coal, diamonds and an island; but the first effect of such dialectical teasing is the imparted sense of enlargement and creativity, of some idea or insight being made to grow. The last sentences of *Victory*, and especially its last word, are something else again:

> "And then, your Excellency [says good Captain Davidson], I
> went away. There was nothing to be done there."
> "Clearly," assented the Excellency.
> Davidson, thoughtful, seemed to weigh the matter in his mind,
> and then murmured with placid sadness:
> "Nothing!"

Between that initial sense of conceptual growth, with its cautious jocularity, and the thoughtful sadness of the closing negation there lies the truth of *Victory*, and its reality.

Victory is, in fact, a novel intimately concerned with questions of truth and reality, as it is with lies and illusion. Those big considerations force

---

From *Twelve Original Essays on Great English Novels.* © 1966 by Wayne State University Press, © 1977 by Charles Shapiro.

themselves on the imagination of the characters, and hence upon that of the reader; for it is that kind of novel, the kind Conrad normally attempted to write. In his preface to *The Nigger of the "Narcissus,"* Conrad defined art as the effort to render the highest justice "to the visible universe, by bringing to light the truth, manifold and one, underlying its every aspect." That creative ambition found an exact analog in the experience narrated in *The Nigger of the "Narcissus"* itself, in the story's movement from the emphasized darkness of the ship's nighttime departure to the sunlit morning that greets its arrival in the English channel—after a voyage featured by the crew's effort to bring to light the truth and reality incarnate in the dying dark man, James Wait. And measured by Conrad's own standard, *Victory* achieves the conditions of art; for the manifold *and* unitary truth of things is just what Conrad succeeds in making real and visible, and what the persons of his island drama are most vitally concerned with. How the process is managed in this particular instance is the subject of present examination. But we have first to take a hard pull on our intellectual reins.

Revisiting *Victory* today, one cannot help being struck by its "existentialist" qualities—by how much it shares the intellectual preoccupations and postures notable in continental literature during recent decades. Here, for instance, is an elaborated image of human isolation: the isolation not only of man from man but even more of man from his metaphysical environment— Axel Heyst, the rootless drifter, who has settled alone upon a singularly remote little island, near an abandoned coal mine, there to meditate in silence his late father's reflections upon "the universal nothingness" and "the unknown force of negation." Here, too, is the familiar counterattack upon metaphysical isolation, the unsteady impulse towards human fellowship—those compassionate gestures towards Morrison and the girl called Lena which belie Heyst's habitual detachment and are the source of his misfortunes and maybe of his redemption. Here is the articulated obsession with the feeling of existence and of nonexistence, as clues both to character and action. "If you were to stop thinking of me, I shouldn't be in the world at all," Lena says to Heyst; and, "I am he who is—" announces plain Mr. Jones, in a breathtaking moment which, in context, has an overpowering propriety. Here are modes of nihilism yielding to modes of self-annihilation, in the oddly similar catastrophes of both hero and villain. Here, in short, is a tale of violence that oscillates richly between the fundamental mysteries of being and nothing. Conrad, we are inclined to say, is the still insufficiently acknowledged grandfather of the most recent literary generation.

To say so is not necessarily to praise Conrad; and it is more likely, indeed, to impose upon him a false identity. *Victory* is not—and it cannot be discussed as—a novel of ideas, for example, in the manner of Malraux's *Les Noyers de L'Altenburg*. Nor is it a calculated work of metaphysical revolt, like Camus's *The Plague*. Conrad did of course display attitudes, and he had a stiff little set of convictions. But E. M. Forster has rightly, if unsympathetically, made the point that Conrad had no "creed"—no coherent order of intellectual principles; and no more than other novelists writing on English soil did Conrad possess that occasional French and German talent for making the war of thought itself exciting. He wanted to exploit the power of words, as he said, in order "to make you hear, to make you feel—before all to make you *see*"; and the end of each of his best novels was simply its own composition. He did not believe with Malraux that art is "a rectification of the universe, a way of escaping from the human condition"; and he would scarcely have understood Camus's parallel and derivative contention that "the novel is born simultaneously with the spirit of rebellion and expresses, on the aesthetic plane, the same ambition." *Victory* dramatizes basic aspects of truth and being; but as regards the human condition, its main aim is only to observe it in the way of art—with that idle but no less intense and sustained attention for which Conrad accurately thought he had a natural ability, and with which he recalled observing the living model for *Victory*'s heroine.

The novel's final word—"Nothing!"—is, accordingly, less a cry of appalled metaphysical recognition than the quiet acknowledgment that the adventure is over and the art that described it has peacefully exhausted itself. It is in the mood less of Camus's Caligula than of Shakespeare's Hamlet: "The rest is silence." The drama is done, and everybody who had a significant part in it is dead. Lena is dead, accidentally shot by Mr. Jones. Heyst has died by fire; Jones has died by water; and both deliberately, as it seems. Ricardo has been killed by Jones's second try at him; and Pedro has been dispatched by Wang, the houseboy. "There are more dead in this affair," Davidson remarks to the Excellency, "than have been killed in many of the battles of the last Achin war." The bungalow and the other two houses are burned to ashes; the boat has drifted out to sea; a corpse lies rotting on the scorched earth. To close the account, only the word "nothing" needs to be uttered.

And yet. If there is no metaphysical vision or purpose at work in the novel, there can nevertheless be felt running through it something like a metaphysical tide. Or better, perhaps, one senses the active presence, the dangerous undertow, of a metaphysical current giving the story its energy and its direction. In the same way, if the tale is not plainly intended as an allegory, one feels in it nevertheless something like an allegorical swelling, as though everything were about to become bigger than itself. That very impression affects the nerves of the persons in the book. "I have a peculiar feeling about this," says Mr. Jones. "It's a different thing. It's a sort of test." In the long list of Conrad's writings, *Victory* also comes to us as a different thing and a sort of test. It is Conrad's test of the nature of fiction: in general, of the ability of drama to move towards allegory while retaining intact its dramatic form and essence; and in particular, the ability of fiction to move towards drama while retaining its identity as fictional narrative. It is a test of the way truth and reality can become the subject matter of a novel which hangs on to its novelistic nature. And the result, in my judgment, is indicated by the last word Conrad actually did write to this book, as he tells us: the single word of the title.

Victory (1915) is itself the last of those works both Conrad and his critics have agreed to call major; and it ranked with *Nostromo* (1904) as Conrad's personal favorite. Conrad's appraisal of his writings was, I think, both sound and suggestive. He always had a special fondness for *The Nigger of the "Narcissus"* (1897), recognizing it for what it was, his first genuine artistic accomplishment; and his satisfaction with *The Secret Agent* (1907) was grounded correctly in his belief that he had succeeded, in that novel, in treating "a melodramatic subject ironically," as he wrote in the copy he gave his friend Richard Curle. But he disagreed with readers and critics who thought that *Lord Jim* (1900) was his best book; he felt the tale did not justify the great length of the novel, and suspected that he should have stuck to his original idea, which was to restrict the narrative to the pilgrim ship episode. The most he could say for *Under Western Eyes* (1910) was "rather good." We should probably speak more warmly, but the pain of composition clings to the pages of *Under Western Eyes*; and the congealing of the action (for example, in Part III) is for long stretches greater than all the interpolated reflections on the art of fiction can overcome. About *Chance* (1913), in a manner not uncommon with authors, he began to talk deprecatingly the moment it became so huge a success. But he remained steadfast in his conviction that his two supreme efforts were the vast tale of the South American seaboard and the tight little story of Axel Heyst.

Surely he was right. *Nostromo* was, as Conrad knew, his largest canvas and his "most anxiously meditated work." It is also one of the greatest novels in English, with a greatness so complex and extensive that only belatedly and partially has it become appreciated. *Victory* is a triumph of a different kind, of a nearly opposite kind. Here Conrad has presented almost all the themes that interested him, but he has refracted those themes through the closely observed conduct of a tiny group of people in a tiny and absolutely isolated setting. *Nostromo* and *Victory* thus stand in a relation similar to the relation between *King Lear* and *Othello* (or perhaps like that between *The Possessed* and

Crime and Punishment). Both *Nostromo* and *King Lear* comprehend more of the world and of human experience than the mind can comfortably contemplate; both are made up of a variety of parallel plots and involve several different groups of persons; in each we discover what Francis Fergusson calls "action by analogy," and the action so richly exposed in its multiplicity of modes reveals something not only about the individuals concerned but about the hidden drift of history, the secret and tragic movement of the universe. Both works engage the artist's most disturbing power—the prophetic power, which is of course not the ability to read the particular and immediate future, but the ability to read the future implicit in every grave and serious time, the future man is perennially prone to. In *Victory*, on the other hand, as in *Othello*, the action emerges directly from the peculiar temperaments of a few eccentric individuals. What happens, both artistically and psychologically, happens as a result of the impact of one unique personality upon another. This is not to deny any largeness to *Victory*; it is only to identify the source of the special largeness it does reveal. It is to say that the novel shows an allegorical swelling rather than an allegory, and that the creative force is less a preexistent design the characters are reenacting (for example, the myth of Eden, of the man and the woman in the garden and the invasion by the serpent) than the jarring effect of the human encounters.

The germ of *Nostromo* was an anecdote, the theft of a lighter-full of silver. But the germ of *Victory* seems to have been the remembered look of several unrelated persons glimpsed at sundry times and in sundry places. *Nostromo* houses characters enough for half a dozen novels; but it says something about Conrad's attitude towards them that he took most of their names from an old book of memoirs (G. F. Masterman's *Seven Eventful Years in Paraguay*, published in 1869) which gossiped about people called Carlos Gould, Monygham, Decoud, Fidanza, Barrios and Mitchell [*sic*]. Conrad's inventive power in *Nostromo*, I am suggesting, was mainly or at least primarily directed to the exposure of action through plot. In *Victory*, however, we remark a thinness, almost a casualness, of plot invention; for Conrad's attention here was directed initially towards people—towards the exposure of action through character. The distinction is exaggerated, and with luck we can make it collapse; but for the moment it can be helpful. It is intended, in any case, as a slight revision of the wonderfully fertile distinction offered by Jacques Maritain, in *Creative Intuition in Art and Poetry*—the distinction between "the poetry of the novel" and "the poetry of the theater." The latter, Maritain argues, is essentially the poetry of the action; action comes first in the dramatic composition, and other elements—character, especially—are subordinated to and controlled by the shape of the action, which it is their chief function to illuminate. The poetry of the novel, Maritain continues, is the poetry of the agent, for the aim of fiction is not so much to present an action as to shed light upon the human heart. The incidents in a novel are accordingly selected in order to illuminate the peculiar and representative nature of individual human beings. M. Maritain's remarks and my respectful revision of them help explain the sense in which *Victory* is a test of the nature of fiction. For the "agents" of the book did come first in Conrad's planning and in his writing. But by his manipulation of his characters, Conrad brought into being an action virtually invulnerable in its design.

"Conrad was fond of discussing characters in *Victory*," Curle reports; and in his author's note, Conrad discusses little else. He shares with us the memories that went into the making of the novel: a professional cardsharper he had seen once in the West Indies in 1875; the silent wide-eyed girl in a café orchestra in the South of France; the wandering Swedish gentleman who became "the physical and moral foundation of my Heyst." "It seems to me but natural," Conrad says, "that those three buried in the corner of my memory should suddenly get out into the light of the world." The reference was actually to the three bad men, Mr. Jones and Martin Ricardo and Pedro; but it applies equally to the three key figures in the story. They gathered together irresistibly in Conrad's imagination, just as they gather together for the culminating experience of each of their lives on Heyst's island. They are made known to us exactly through the process of gathering. And indeed the first and most obvious way to chart the unfolding scheme of the book is to point to the important moments in that process.

We meet Axel Heyst on the first page. We hear of Lena thirty-six pages later in Mrs. Schomberg's reluctant mutter to Davidson: "There was even one English girl." Mr. Jones makes his appearance fifty-five pages later yet: "a guest who arrived one fine morning by mail-boat . . . a wanderer, clearly, even as Heyst was." Conrad then devotes nearly seventy pages to acquainting us with the three desperadoes, and with the critical differences between them. But even before he begins that section, the gathering process has been at work in the meeting and the drawing together of Heyst and Lena, and their flight to the island refuge. The entire group of major characters (the Schombergs, of course, excluded) is not assembled in a single place until a little more than halfway through the book: when Wang interrupts the moment of deepest intimacy between Heyst and Lena to announce that a boat (containing, as we learn, Mr. Jones and his henchmen) is approaching the jetty. From that instant, the whole of the novel is caught up in the collision of personalities—in what Henry James (speaking about one of Ibsen's plays) called the lunging of ego against ego, the passionate rocking of soul against soul; every ego against every ego, in Conrad's masterful treatment of it, and every soul against every soul. From the instant the boat is sighted—or more accurately, from the instant Heyst goes down to the jetty to stare in amazement at the spectacle of the three white men drifting in from nowhere, seemingly more dead than alive— Conrad's complex artistic purpose becomes clear and begins to fulfull itself. The individual characters, explored individually or in small combinations, now meet and join in an adventure which becomes an action larger and more significant than any of them. The novel, that is, begins to assume the defining quality of drama.

Throughout the course of it, however, Conrad continues to exploit the peculiar resources of the novel, for the traditional aims of the novelist; but he does so, at the same time, as a way of heightening and solidifying the dramatic design. In elaborating the distinction I have mentioned, Jacques Maritain observes that since the shape of the action is determining in a drama, contingencies and coincidences and simple accidents have no place there; but that these devices are proper to fiction, since they can be exactly the occasion for some special insight into character. During the latter half of *Victory*, the plot is heavily dependent upon a series of "evitable" incidents, of which two may be cited as typical: the theft of Heyst's gun by Wang, and the shooting of Lena by Mr. Jones. The latter is pure accident: Jones had intended to kill Martin Ricardo. The former is a contingency—Wang might have had a gun of his own, or Heyst another revolver hidden away somewhere. Each incident is important to the plot as plotted. But alternatives can easily be imagined, and neither incident seems indispensable to the larger purpose. Yet both incidents serve to shed light on the characters involved and are insofar novelistically justified; and in the light they shed, a truth and a reality begin to appear, as elements towards which an action is steadily in motion.

These incidents, in short, are literally accidental, but they are symbolically inevitable and dramatically appropriate. The theft of the gun tells us a good deal about the curiously hidden nature of the houseboy, his swift and agile selfishness with its portion of quiet cruelty; and it reinforces the sense pervading the world of the book, that in it the distance between men is nearly absolute. At the same time, by rendering Heyst physically defenseless, it provides an "objective correlative" for his more fundamental defenselessness, that of a man of thought like himself in the hour of necessary action. The time spent in puzzling and worrying over the absence of the gun is time artistically well spent. The death of Lena has a still higher degree of propriety. Mr. Jones's bullet, though aimed at Ricardo, only grazed Ricardo's temple before burying itself in Lena's heart, just "under the swelling breast of dazzling and sacred whiteness"—the accident is compounded by the terrible chance that the bullet should strike her exactly there. Yet we need little instruction from the Freudians to perceive that the accident probably masked an act of deepest deliberation. Towards Ricardo, Mr. Jones felt only fury mixed with a lively sense of danger; but towards Lena, towards any woman, he felt the much more destructive emotion of radical disgust. The shooting of Lena is one of the last and most meaningful of the gestures by which we take the full measure of plain Mr. Jones—the evil ascetic, the satanic figure whose satanism springs from a loathing of women and a horror of sex. (Graham Greene, who has written a short essay called "Plain Mr. Jones," and who is indebted to Conrad on many counts, has provided a comparable image in Pinkie Brown, the inflamed ascetic of *Brighton Rock*.) And in the mode of her death, we have the final revelation and indeed the vindication of Lena's character. Hers is the touching figure of the young woman of smudged virtue who prays she may lose everything for the sake of the man she loves (again, a figure we encounter in Graham Greene). She has drawn upon herself the death that threatened Axel Heyst. To do so is not only a part of her character. It is a part of her plan.

Each of the main figures in *Victory* has his or her private plan; and in this respect, *Victory* too, like *Nostromo*, has a number of plots—as many as the number of central characters; the plot in each case being what happens at last to the individual plan. As each plan is lit up for us, so much more of the action comes into view. In human terms, the separate plans are catastrophically irreconcilable, and in their difference they provide the "manifold" truth—to use Conrad's word—that the novel brings to light. But artistically, they form a living pattern of parallels and contrasts, and so provide the unitary truth Conrad equally envisaged.

Each of these secret programs of conduct is rooted in the mystery of one or two absolute characteristics. Schomberg's malice, for example, is an absolute trait of character, as unmotivated as the malice of Iago. Like Iago's hatred of Othello, Schomberg's hatred of Axel Heyst can pretend to a specific reason: Heyst's snatching away of the girl, which led to the funny Faulknerian madhouse involving Schomberg and the orchestra leader Zangiacomo, over which Conrad used to laugh reminiscently. But the hatred existed already, existed even before the episode, which Schomberg so evilly misrepresented, of Heyst and poor Morrison. Schomberg's private plot, rooted in his malice, is the business of his so-called revenge upon Heyst, along with the business of diverting the outlaws from his own hotel to the safe distance of Heyst's island. In its vicious way, it is successful, but not because it has anything to do with the facts about Heyst and Lena. Schomberg's plot is strictly his own creation; it is not nourished to any real extent by external circumstances. The same is true of his malignancy. It is a key factor in releasing the terrible events of the book; but it is not developed by outside pressures, it is *revealed* by them. Thus it is with the determining features of the other people in *Victory*. For here, as is customary in Conrad's work, the characters do not grow, they only grow more visible. That is the precise effect of their mutual impact.

Mr. Jones is perhaps the most fascinating instance in the novel of the motion towards visibility, if only because it is the most paradoxical. What becomes fully and finally visible about him is a kind of absence, a nothingness. His plan is the least reconcilable of all the plans, and hence the most irreducible symptom of the "manifold" aspect of *Victory*: because Mr. Jones's plan opposes not only the substance of all the others but the very terms of their existence. Ricardo, we remember, has his own particular reasons—reasons he cannot disclose to Mr. Jones—for urging the invasion of Heyst's island; and no doubt some dumb dream of conquest occupies the primitive skull of Pedro. But the mission of Mr. Jones undercuts all that. It has to do with the condition of his being, which is as it were a mockery of being itself. Heyst reports to Lena on his conversation with Jones:

> "'I suppose you would like to know who I am?' he asked me.
> "I told him I would leave it to him, in a tone which, between gentlemen, could have left no doubt in his mind. He raised himself on his elbow—he was lying down on the campbed—and said:
> "'I am he who is—.'"

"No use asking me what he meant, Lena," Heyst adds. "I don't know." What Jones meant was probably a theatrical blasphemy. In very similar words, according to the Old Testament, God announced his name and his nature to his chosen people: "I am," or "I am that I am." Jones, of course, is not godlike, and especially not godlike in the sense of representing the source of being itself. He is devil-like—his character bulges in the direction of the devil (he is not *the* devil, any more than *Victory* is an allegory); and exactly because he represents the source of nonbeing.

The association with Satan gratifies Mr. Jones immensely. He describes, in an echo from the Book of Job, his habit of "coming and going up and down the earth"; and Heyst replies that he has "heard that sort of story about someone else before." Jones at once gives Heyst a ghastly grin, claiming that "I have neither more nor less determination" than "the gentleman you are thinking of." But the nature and end of his determination emerge from a later allusion to the devil. Jones speculates for Heyst's benefit that a man living alone, as Heyst had been living, would "take care to conceal [his] property so well that the devil himself—." Heyst interrupts with a murmured "Certainly."

Again, with his left hand, Mr. Jones mopped his frontal bone, his stalk-like neck, his razor jaws, his fleshless chin. Again, his voice faltered and his aspect became still more gruesomely malevolent, as of a wicked and pitiless corpse.

Those last four words summarize the character of Mr. Jones and point to his unswerving purpose: he is not only deathly, he is the cause that death is in others. To Schomberg, too, Jones had seemed "to imply some sort of menace from beyond the grave"; and in Heyst's first view of him, Jones is "sitting up [in the boat], silent, rigid and very much like a corpse." At the outset of their duel, Jones seems to exert a greater force of sheer existence than Heyst; for Heyst, as he confesses mournfully in language highly reminiscent of one of Hawthorne's isolated men, has lived too long among shadows. But Heyst's determining quality has only been lying dormant; he is like the indolent volcano, to which he is lightly compared on the second page of the book; he is moving—though moving too late and too slowly—towards existence and reality. Jones's characteristic movement is all in the other direction.

The force in Jones is all negative, though not the less emphatic for being so. That is why he hates and fears women, for they are fertility incarnate and the literal source of life. Jones's particular and personal plot is not really to seize Heyst's alleged treasures but to inflict his deathiness upon others. He comes as an envoy of death, disguised as an envoy of the living: of death not in the sense of murder but in the sense of a fundamental hostility to existence. He is the champion of the antireal, and he arrives at just the moment when Heyst, because of the presence and love of Lena, is feeling "a greater sense of reality than he had ever known in his life." Jones's plan, too, is superficially successful: everyone he has brushed against on the island is dead. Jones is dead also; but he has not been killed, he has simply shrunk, collapsed, disintegrated. He has reached the limit of his true condition. And what is visible of him at the end is exactly the outward signs of that condition. "The water's very clear there," Davidson tells the Excellency; "and I could see him huddled up on the bottom between two piles, like a heap of bones in a blue silk bag, with only the head and feet sticking out."

Mr. Jones's most astute enemy in the book is not Heyst but the girl Lena, though Jones and Lena never in fact confront one another. But Lena is the one person able to understand not only the threat represented by the invaders but the very threat of the threat; and she understands it so well that, as things develop, she can formulate her own plot and purpose to herself with exactness—to "capture death—savage, sudden, irresponsible death, prowling round the man who possessed her." Lena stands for a possibility of life. Yet curiously enough, her role as the actual source of Heyst's sense of being is rendered less visible—rendered, that is, with less apparent success—than are the deadly negations of Mr. Jones. Lena is the one member of the cast who remains in partial darkness. Many critics have remarked upon this, and some have gone on to say that Conrad rarely had much luck with his women. But his achievement elsewhere is not always unimpressive: Winnie Verloc, in *The Secret Agent*, seems to me one of the most compelling females in modern literature; and one has little difficulty making out the attractive features of Emily Gould and Flora de Barral, in *Nostromo* and *Chance* respectively. It may even be that a kind of haziness, a fragility of substance was intended in the portrayal of Lena. She *is* like that, and the frailty of her being determines the nature of her plot. For her aim is precisely to win for herself a greater measure of reality, by forcing upon the man she loves a greater recognition of her. She lives in his acknowledgment of her: "If you were to stop thinking about me I shouldn't be in the world at all. . . . I can only be what you think I am." This is a trifle unfortunate, since Heyst, the only human being who could have seen Lena, can never manage to see quite enough. Richard Curle observes nicely about Lena that she is "the supreme example of a 'one-man' woman, so supreme that even the reader is kept out of the secret." Heyst peers at her in the half-light, and we peer over his shoulder, dimly discerning a creature of considerable but only guessed-at bodily appeal and intense but only partially communicated spiritual desire.

Her desire is stated plainly enough for us, as it takes form after Ricardo's attempt to rape her. From that moment onward, "all her energy was concentrated on the struggle she wanted to take upon herself, in a great exaltation of love and self-sacrifice." And we know enough about her history to find that exaltation plausible. We have heard of her mother's desertion of her father, of her father's career as a small-time musician and of his removal to a home for incurables; we have heard of her bleak childhood and adolescence, her blurred unhappy life with a traveling orchestra; we can easily imagine what Heyst's compassion must have meant to her. "I am not what they call a good girl," she has said; and through Heyst's impression of her, we are struck by her mixture of misery and audacity. She alone fully understands that it is Schomberg who has put the outlaws on Heyst's trail, and she can comprehend the hotelkeeper's motiveless motive. Lena's plot, accordingly, is the most coherent of all the plots, and the most important. It is also the most private, since it requires of her that she lie both to the man she hates and the man she loves. She is altogether successful, at least as successful as Schomberg or Mr. Jones. She does disarm Ricardo, literally and psychologically; the dagger she takes from him is indeed "the spoil of vanquished death" and "the symbol of her victory." By dividing Ricardo from Jones, she creates a situation in which, as the demonically brilliant Jones instantly realizes, Ricardo must be killed; and through a chain reaction, she is responsible also for the death of Pedro and Jones himself. All this we know, understand and can rehearse. But Conrad has nonetheless not finally managed to fulfill his ambition with respect to Lena. He has not made us see Lena completely. Between her and ourselves, there falls a shadow. It is, of course, the shadow of Axel Heyst.

If the victory is Lena's—if her end, as Conrad insisted, is triumphant— the major defeat recorded in the novel is that of Heyst. His is the ultimate failure, and for the reason he gives in almost the last words we hear him speak: "Ah, Davidson, woe to the man whose heart has not learned while young to hope, to love—and to put its trust in life." But that very statement demonstrates that Heyst, by acknowledging his failure and perceiving its cause, has in the literary manner of speaking been saved. He is, at the last, completely in touch with truth. And similarly, if Heyst's personal plan—which is not only to rid the island of its invaders and to protect Lena but also to join with Lena in an experience of full reality—if that plan is the least successful plan in the book, Heyst is nonetheless the true and steady center of the novel from its beginning to its end. So central is Heyst within the rich composition of *Victory*, that neither his character nor his conduct may be clearly seen apart from that composition. They are identified only through a series of analogies and contrasts, and as the vital center of the book's design.

As analysis moves to the figure of Axel Heyst, it moves of necessity from the Many to the One—from the many separated individuals with their irreconcilable differences of purpose to the pattern in which they seem to echo and reflect and repeat one another. It is the felt flow of the Many into the One that accounts for the feeling one has of a strong metaphysical current running deep through the novel, of very real human beings and events gathering together in a way that suggests an allegory of universal proportions. Let it be emphasized again that we have to do with a process, not with an imposition. And as it develops, we begin to detect parallels between contrasting and inimical elements, continuities between divisions—and by the power of the book's current, more radical contrasts between newly observed parallels. At the center is Axel Heyst, whose entire being—*artistically*, within the actual pages of the book—is created by the play of likeness and difference.

We must, accordingly, approach Heyst by way of those relationships— which is to reconsider some of the persons already inspected, but to consider them now not in their enormous differences, but in their unexpected similarities: an undertaking the first page of *Victory* (with its references to the similarities between coal and diamonds, an island and a mountain) has warned us would be the key to the novel's meaning. Between Lena and Ricardo, for example, between the mystically devoted young woman and the thick-headed roughneck who plunges headlong through the blue serge curtain to assault her, an unexpected likeness is uncovered. It is a fatality in Ricardo's crude imagination that he should exaggerate it. "You and I are made to understand each other," he mumbles, after a stupor of surprise and admiration at the vigor of Lena's resistance. "Born alike, bred alike, I guess. You are not tame. Same here! You have been chucked out into this rotten world of 'ypocrits. Same here!" Because of his conviction of their likeness, Ricardo trusts Lena more simply and unquestioningly than Heyst trusts her; Ricardo trusts what there is in Lena of his own animal and prehensile nature, and he dies of that trust, as Heyst dies of mistrust. But within disastrous limits, Ricardo is right—he and Lena do have a good deal in common. "Perhaps because of the similarity of their miserable origin in the dregs of mankind," Lena realizes, "she had understood Ricardo perfectly." Even her physical strength and tenacity match his: "You have fingers like steel! Jiminy! You have muscles like a giant." That is scarcely the pathetic child seen through Heyst's impression of her, the child suffering helplessly the venomous pinchings of Mrs. Zangiacomo; and the ferocity of her response to Ricardo's attempted rape correctly suggests a ready perception, based on experience, of that kind of jungle behavior. It also suggests the strength in Lena which has been brought to the surface since the Zangiacomo days: brought to the surface and focused as a powerful instrument, through the effect upon her of Heyst.

An important ingredient in her strength is a talent for lying, exercised for the sake of truth. Ricardo is quite justified in attributing to Lena a duplicity equal to his own; he knows that both of them have had to become skilled in duplicity as the one indispensable resource in the world's hypocritical "game of grab." "Give the chuck to all this blamed 'ypocrisy," urges Ricardo. Lena seems to agree, and she embarks deceptively upon a plot to deceive Heyst— "her gentleman," as Ricardo calls him—which notably parallels Ricardo's systematic deception of *his* gentleman, Mr. Jones. It seems to Ricardo natural that Lena should lie to the man who has befriended her; such is the norm of behavior in the world he inhabits: that is, the world of *Victory*. It is what people do to each other in that world: witness Mrs. Schomberg's trickery of her own gentleman, her fat braggart of a husband. The cluster of duplicities has, up to a point, a common element, for each aims initially at the salvation of the man deceived. Mrs. Schomberg, when she helps frustrate her husband's plan (his "insane and odious passion") by helping Lena to escape, imagines she is keeping Schomberg out of serious trouble and preserving their wretched marriage. Ricardo's organization of the invasion of Heyst's island is a contrivance to rescue his chief from the habitual state of sloth into which Jones had fallen. To do so, Ricardo must cunningly keep silent about the presence on the island of a young woman; since, were Jones to hear about it, he would instantly abandon the adventure. Only later does Ricardo's helpful deceit deepen into betrayal. And as to Lena, "she was not ashamed of her duplicity," because "nothing stood between the enchanted dream of her existence and a cruel catastrophe but her duplicity." She will deceive everyone, and she will especially deceive Heyst; she will wear the mask of infidelity to save the life of the man towards whom her fidelity is the very assurance of her existence.

The relationship between Lena and Ricardo thus illuminates one of the major themes of the novel—the theme of truth-telling, and the significance of truth-telling, as a value, in the scheme of human behavior. By the same token, Lena and Ricardo illuminate the character of Axel Heyst; for it is almost a weakness in Heyst that—at the opposite extreme from Mr. Jones and his self-association with the Father of Lies—he has an absolute regard for truth. He is so obsessed with truth that he becomes literally disempowered when confronted with lies; and he is so inflexible towards truth that only lies can save him. Even more than the theft of his gun, as it seems, it is the lies Schomberg has spread about Heyst's treatment of Morrison that, when they belatedly reach Heyst's ears, succeed finally in rendering him defenseless by provoking in him the emotion of paralyzing disgust. His only defense thereafter is the multiple duplicity of Lena.

It is not inappropriate that such should be the case, for between Morrison and Lena, too, there is a revealing similarity. Lena shares with Ricardo a certain seamy background and a certain practical toughness; but with Morrison, the unfortunate master of the trading brig *Capricorn*, she has shared the magnanimity of Axel Heyst. The story of Morrison is a sort of rehearsal for the story of Lena; for like Lena, Morrison is not only the object; he is in a sense the victim of Heyst's compassion. Morrison is miraculously rescued by Heyst in a way that, as events work out, both leads to and makes plausible the rescue, not long after, of Lena; and the consequence in both cases is a fresh involvement, a chance for life, that results in fact in their death. Both look upon Heyst as a kind of god, especially because to both Heyst's conduct appears purely gratuitous, like the undeserved and disinterested mercy of God. It is not purely pity; Heyst's father had advised him to "cultivate that form of contempt which is called pity," but the salvaging of Morrison and the benevolent theft of Lena are due to no such calculated attitude. They reflect rather a temperament which, as we are told, was incapable of scorning any decent emotion—a temperament so fine and rare as to seem literally godlike to the bedevilled of the book's world. When Heyst offers Morrison the money to save the latter's boat, Morrison gazes at him as though "he expected Heyst's usual white suit of the tropics to change into a shining garment down to his toes . . . and didn't want to miss a single detail of the transformation." In the procedure typical of *Victory*, a reaction which will later become serious, complex and tragic is presented in the early pages in simple and partly comic tonalities. Lena's reaction to Heyst's rescue of her is less extravagant and open-mouthed; but it partakes of a still deeper awe and of a genuinely self-sacrificial reverence.

In the same way, it is Morrison who first strikes the note, in his droll and touching way, which will develop into a theme close to the tragic heart of the book. Morrison wonders in panic if Heyst is joking about the money. Heyst asks austerely what he means, and Morrison is abashed.

> "Forgive me, Heyst. You must have been sent by God in answer to my prayer. But I have been nearly off my chump for three days with worry; and it suddenly struck me: 'What if it's the Devil who has sent him?' "
>
> "I have no connection with the supernatural," said Heyst graciously, moving on. "Nobody sent me. I just happened along."
>
> "I know better," contradicted Morrison.

That moment has its louder and more serious echo a couple of hundred pages later, when Heyst catches sight of Jones and his henchmen approaching the jetty. He stares at them in disbelief: "[He] had never been so much astonished in his life."

> The civilisation of the tropics could have nothing to do with it. It was more like those myths, current in Polynesia, of amazing strangers, who arrive at an island, gods or demons, bringing good or evil to the innocence of the inhabitants—gifts of unknown things, words never heard before.

"Gods or demons, bringing good or evil. . . ." Those ambiguous phrases greet the first glimpse Heyst and Jones have of each other; and they frame and give shape to the most telling of the patterns of similarity and contrast that *Victory* has to offer—the one that says most about Heyst himself, and the one that best reveals the drama of which he is the protagonist. Between Heyst and Jones, the differences are of radical dimensions. Heyst is a bringer of good (though the recipients of his gifts suffer evil by consequence). Jones is a bringer of evil (though his gift is the occasion of greatest good for Lena, and her victory). Heyst has some godlike element in his nature; but the insinuation makes him highly uncomfortable. Jones has a kind of private understanding with the Devil, and that insinuation never fails to excite him. But between Axel Heyst and plain Mr. Jones, there is a vibrant flow of analogies, a movement back and forth like electrical currents.

A likeness is registered at the instant Jones first turns up in the novel; a guest at Schomberg's hotel arriving from Celebes, "but generally, Schomberg understood, from up China Sea way; a wanderer clearly, even as Heyst was." Both men are drifters by profession—"I'll drift," Heyst had decided as a young man; both have occupied themselves for many years by "coming and going up and down the earth." Both men are gentlemen, in the conventional meaning of the word and within the book's definition as pronounced by Martin Ricardo: "That's another thing you can tell a gentlemen by, his freakishness. A gentle-man ain't accountable to nobody, any more than a tramp on the roads." Heyst invokes a comparable notion: "I, Axel Heyst, the most detached of creatures in this earthly captivity, the veriest tramp on this earth. . . ." As gentlemen and as tramps, both Jones and Heyst are products of highly civilized society who have chosen the career of the rootless outsider. Both are well-born, per-haps aristocratic; they are elegant, sophisticated, mannerly; both have an ex-cessive vein of fastidiousness, a too easily outraged austerity. And both are outcasts who in different ways are outside the law: Heyst by being in some manner beyond and above it, Jones by being several degrees beneath it. With one of his ghastly grins, during their first interview, Mr. Jones confesses to Heyst that the latter was not the man he had expected to meet. For he sees or thinks he sees, startlingly, *son semblable, son frère.*

Jones misjudges Heyst just as Ricardo misjudges Lena, and with the same limited warrant. "We pursue the same ends," Jones remarks; and he argues that his presence on the island is neither more nor less "morally rep-rehensible" than Heyst's. Jones assumes that, like himself, Heyst is simply a gentlemanly scoundrel, sharing with him the impulse common to gifted men—the criminal impulse. About this mistake there is something as ridic-ulous as it is fatal; but Jones has intuited a fragment of the truth. Heyst does share with Jones a basic indifference to the habitual practices of society and to its moral verdicts. He appraises the world in terms nearly identical to those of Jones: "The world's a mad dog," Heyst tells Davidson. "It will bite you if you give it a chance." These two lean and handsome gentlemen, these radical drifters, have an extraordinary amount in common, and Jones's contention is justified—"Ah, Mr. Heyst . . . you and I have much more in common than you think." Jones and Heyst reflect each other with a sort of perfection, the way an object is reflected in a mirror. Each is the other seen wrong way round.

That is why they are dramatically indispensable one to the other—the visibility of each is dependent upon the presence of the other. They come from opposite ends of the universe, and they meet where opposites are made to meet: in a work of art. The strength of each often appears as an extension of the other's weakness and vice versa; which is one reason why the conflict between them, as it assumes its form, seems to extend endlessly, to enlarge almost beyond the reach of human reckoning. It brushes the edge of allegory, and touches briefly on the outskirts of myth—one of "those myths, current in Polynesia, of amazing strangers . . . gods or demons." But the drama hangs on to its human vitality and its immediacy and continues to draw its force from the peculiar nature of the two men involved—the man of intellectual sensibility with an inadequate but incipient trust in life; and the man of occasional action with a strenuous but insufficiently examined faith in the power of death. Mr. Jones's tendency to sloth, which leaves him spread motionless over three chairs for hours at a time, is reflected in Heyst's long periods of meditation on the hostility of thought to action, while he lounges on the verandah and smokes his cheroot. But Jones's condition has the terrible and explosive power of an ancient sin; and Heyst's skepticism is marred by a vein of tenderness. If Heyst had mistrusted life more completely, he would perhaps have been a better match for Jones from the outset. As it is, the novel catches him at the moment when mistrust is giving way to an urge toward reality and communion.

He had long since, so he tells Jones during their last conversation, divorced himself from the love of life; but then he adds, with painful accuracy, "not sufficiently perhaps." So he acts and reacts without "distinctness." His conception of the world, taken from his father, had for too many years been of something "not worth touching, and perhaps not substantial enough to grasp." The experience of Lena was beginning to put substance into the world; but Heyst can neither participate fully in that experience nor resist it, for he has absorbed either too much or too little of his father's doctrine that "the consolation of love" is the cruelest of all the stratagems of life. He can still insist that "he who forms a tie is lost," but his actual feeling is that he is about to find himself, that Lena is giving him "a greater sense of his own reality than he had ever known in his life."

Greater: but still inadequate to fit him for the challenge that arises. For that challenge is exactly the embodiment of the challenge his father had honorably faced. "With what strange serenity, mingled with terrors," Heyst thinks about his father, "had that man considered the universal nothingness! He had plunged into it headlong, perhaps to render death, the answer that faced one at every inquiry, more supportable." It is only four pages later that Wang arrives to announce the approach of a strange boat. And Mr. Jones, the corpselike figure at the tiller of the boat, is himself the harbinger and representative of that "universal nothingness." He is the body of that death "that faced one at every inquiry." Trapped between a waning skepticism and an undernourished sense of reality, Heyst cannot emulate his father; cannot make the plunge or launch the assault. All he can do, at the end, is to take death upon himself, purgatorially, by fire.

But, if Heyst is unable to plunge, Jones (like Ricardo on his lower level) plunges too incautiously. The sinister mission he engages on is unsupported by the necessary amount of cold intelligence—of just that kind of intelligence that Heyst possesses supremely. Heyst begins finally to exercise it at Jones's expense during their climactic interview, after Heyst has learned the reason for the invasion of the island—Schomberg's preposterous falsehood about treasures hidden on it. At this instant, a reversal is effected, and Heyst takes command of their relationship; it is his strength now which becomes visible because of the revelation of Jones's weakness. "You seem a morbid, senseless sort of bandit," Heyst says with weary contempt. "There were never in the world two more deluded bandits—never! . . . Fooled by a silly rascally innkeeper," he goes on remorselessly. "Talked over like a pair of children with a promise of sweets." It is the logical weakness of Jones's asserted belief in universal fraudulence that it must contain in itself an element of the fraudulent. If he had been wholly convinced of the depravity of all the inhabitants of a wholly vicious world, Jones would have trusted less in the strength of his authority—his graveyard power—over Martin Ricardo; and he would not have overlooked the possibility of mere vulgar vindictiveness in Schomberg. He leapt too swiftly from sloth into action, in a way that, in retrospect, invests one of Heyst's casual pronouncements, made early in the book, with prophetic implications: "Action is the devil."

Heyst and Jones need each other for artistic visibility; but both of them need Lena, as she needs them, to make clear the full shape of the drama they have begotten between them, when the current of the novel carries them (this is one's impression) into a dimension beyond the dimension occupied by all the other persons in the book. The action disclosed by the effect of those three upon each other is the gradual location of that dimension, of the very domain of reality and truth. The domain lies somewhere between the dialectical stirrings of the book's first page and the observation of nothingness on its last—somewhere, as it turns out, between the intellectualism of Heyst and the deathiness of Jones. Between the two kinds of failure, Lena's victory is squeezed out in a way that is a victory both for her and for the novel in which she has her being. As against Jones, Lena has dedicated herself to the actual cause of living; and as against Heyst, she has seized with fingers of steel upon the immediate and necessary facts of behavior. Her practicality (again the book's first page is recalled) derives from a mystical exaltation that transcends the particular situation and attains to universal value while remaining sharply and intently focused upon the single figure of Axel Heyst. Lena's accomplishment reflects the accomplishment of the novel. *Victory* is, in a sense, a reproach to the fascination with death of so much modern fiction. But even more, perhaps, it is an admonition about the tendency of both fiction and criticism to intellectualize the art—to lose the drama in the allegory; or to deform the art—to lose the novel in the drama. The form of *Victory* grows dramatic, and it gives forth intimations of allegory. But it remains faithful to its own nature, for it never makes the mistake of Mr. Jones—it never fails to take account of the variable and highly unpredictable character of individual human beings.

IAN WATT

Impressionism and Symbolism
in Heart of Darkness

The fiftieth anniversary of Joseph Conrad's death brought few signs of converging agreement about the essential nature of his creative achievement or his place in literary history. There remains, for instance, the unresolved paradox that although Conrad is often categorized as an Impressionist novelist he is also often considered a major precursor of the modern literary tradition; and, at least since Edmund Wilson's *Axel's Castle* in 1931, this tradition has often been viewed as mainly a continuation of the French Symbolist movement.

The contradiction remains largely unexamined; critics who treat Conrad as an Impressionist do not mention Symbolism, and vice versa. Thus Ford Madox Ford wrote in 1924 that Conrad "avowed himself impressionist," and implies that they together worked out a new fictional technique which was more lifelike than others because, through such devices as the time-shift, it more closely imitated the way our knowledge of others is actually built up in a casual, confusing, and often unchronological way. That Conrad employed such a technique—among others—is undoubted; but his own use of the term is far from suggesting any doctrinal endorsement. Thus when Conrad writes of a sailor asking "in impressionistic phrase: 'How does the cable grow?' " his usage implicitly defines impressionism as a concern with noting external appearances as opposed to stating what is "really happening"; and there is an explicit note of derogation when, speaking of Stephen Crane's story "The

From *The Southern Review* 13, no. 1 (January 1977). © 1977 by Ian P. Watt.

Open Boat," Conrad makes the judgment: "He is *the only* impressionist and *only* an impressionist." This was in 1897, and Conrad's sense of the limitations of Impressionism apparently hardened later; thus in 1900 he praised the "focus" of some Cunninghame Graham sketches, and added: "They are much more of course than mere Crane-like impressionism."

The preface to *The Nigger of the "Narcissus"* is often read as an Impressionist document; but much of Conrad's critical position there is also consonant with that of the Symbolists—it is, for instance, very close to Paul Verlaine's "De la musique avant toute chose" (*Art poétique*) in making it the supreme aim of literary style to achieve "the magic suggestiveness of music." Conrad also wrote in a letter dated January 27, 1897, that in *The Nigger of the "Narcissus"* he had tried "to get through the veil of details at the essence of life"; and this avowal of a transcendental perspective, which is equally reminiscent of Plato, Schopenhauer, and the French Symbolists, later recurs even more explicitly: "How fine it could be . . . ," Conrad wrote to Ford, "if the idea had a substance and words a magic power, if the invisible could be snared into a shape."

Conrad expressed this wish to make the idea visible a month before he began *Heart of Darkness*, a work which, among other things, is generally reckoned the supreme example of Conrad's importance in the modern literary tradition. Marvin Mudrick, for example, declares with almost pardonable hyperbole that "After *Heart of Darkness*, the recorded moment—the word—was irrecoverably symbol." Mudrick's analysis is based on the way Conrad developed "the moral resources inherent in every recorded sensation"; and he thus surely implies that in *Heart of Darkness* Conrad gave a larger symbolic meaning to an Impressionist recording of particular experience. *Heart of Darkness* is the key work for examining the relation of Symbolist and Impressionist elements in Conrad for another reason: the fact that the nature of its symbolism continues to provoke much critical controversy.

I

At the beginning of *Heart of Darkness* the primary narrator explains that the meanings of Marlow's tales are characteristically difficult to encompass:

> The yarns of seamen have a direct simplicity, the whole meaning of which lies within the shell of a cracked nut. But Marlow was not typical (if his propensity to spin yarns be excepted), and to him the meaning of an episode was not inside like a kernel but outside, enveloping the tale which brought it out only as a glow

brings out a haze, in the likeness of one of these misty halos that
sometimes are made visible by the spectral illumination of moonshine.

The distinction between the ordinary story and Marlow's uses a metaphor based on contrasted arrangements of two concentric spheres. In the first
arrangement, that of the typical seaman's yarn, the direction given our minds
is, to use a term from Newtonian physics, "centripetal"; the narrative vehicle
is the shell, the larger outside sphere which encloses a smaller sphere, the
inner kernel of truth; and as readers we are invited to seek this central core
of meaning. Marlow's tales, on the other hand, are typical "centrifugal"; the
relation of the spheres is reversed; now the narrative vehicle is the smaller
inside sphere, and its function is merely to reveal a circumambient universe
of meanings which are not normally visible and cannot be seen except in
association with the story, just as the haze appears only when there is a glow.

Conrad's metaphor clearly implies the complementary, even the sym-
biotic, relationship of the Impressionist and the Symbolist aspects of the narrative as a whole. The Symbolist aspect mainly depends on the geometric
nature of the haze, the outer sphere of larger meaning. It is intangible and
theoretically infinite, since, like St. Augustine's God and unlike the husk of
a nut, it lacks any ascertainable circumference; and yet it depends on the finite
glow. Thus the combination of Marlow's two spheres constitutes a symbol
precisely in Thomas Carlyle's sense of it—"the Infinite is made to blend itself
with the Finite, to stand visible, and as it were, attainable there."

The Impressionist component of the passage is mainly evident in the
sensory qualities of Conrad's two spheres. The narrative depicts a meaning
which is only as fitfully and tenuously visible as a hitherto unnoticed presence
of dust particles and water vapor in what normally looks like a dark void. In
this there is a clear parallel with one of the new features of Impressionist
painting. Claude Monet, for instance, said of the critics who mocked his
obscurity: "Poor blind idiots. They want us to see everything clearly, even
through the fog." The difficulty of seeing is not a gratuitous defiance of the
public; haze in Monet—and even more explicitly in Conrad's image—is not
an accidental atmospheric interference which stands between us and the "real"
object; the difficulty and the obscurity are essential parts of what the artist is
trying to convey.

Much the same idea, and expressed in a similar metaphor, occurs in a
classic later statement on the novel in "Modern Fiction," Virginia Woolf's
1919 essay. There she exempts Conrad, together with Thomas Hardy, from
her charge against the "ill-fitting vestments" of the traditional novel, and of

the Edwardians, H. G. Wells, Arnold Bennett, and John Galsworthy. Her basic objection is that if we "look within" ourselves we see "a myriad impressions" quite unrelated to anything that goes on in the traditional novel; and if we could express "this unknown and uncircumscribed spirit" of life freely, "there would be no plot, no comedy, no tragedy, no love interest or catastrophe in the accepted style, and perhaps not a single button sewn on as the Bond Street tailors would have it." For, Virginia Woolf finally affirms, "Life is not a series of gig-lamps symmetrically arranged; life is a luminous halo, a semi-transparent envelope surrounding us from the beginning of conciousness to the end."

Virginia Woolf 's basic metaphor, the luminous halo, is Impressionist in nature; but it is used to describe an aim for the novel very like the characteristic Symbolist attempt to reach outward, to penetrate the semitransparent, and therefore semiopaque, envelope of the world outside. With the Impressionist painters, the first object of creation is light; and with the Symbolists it is most characteristically an inner light of the spirit which illuminates a part of the surrounding darkness.

II

Before applying the description of Marlow's mode of storytelling to a passage from *Heart of Darkness*, a brief historical perspective seems necessary; for, both in their origins and in their later course through modern literature, Impressionism and Symbolism are essentially manifestations of various general tendencies which first came to prominence in the Romantic period; both are antitraditional assertions of the private individual vision; and they both took their full shape during the epistemological crisis of the late nineteenth century, a crisis most familiar to literary history under the twin rubrics of the death of God and the disappearance of the omniscient author.

"Impressionism" as a specifically aesthetic term was apparently coined in 1874 by a journalist, Louis Leroy, to ridicule the affronting formlessness of the pictures exhibited at the Salon des Indépendants, and particularly of Monet's painting entitled "Impression: Sunrise." In one way or another all the main Impressionists, from Monet to Renoir, made it their aim to render the appearance of objects as they saw them under particular atmospheric conditions, an aim which, as E. H. Gombrich has shown, allots the Impressionists a decisive role in the process of art's long transition from portraying what all men know to portraying what the individual actually sees.

This transition is recorded in the history of the word "impression" and its cognates, a history which embodies in more general terms the growing disjunction between public systems of knowledge—what all men know—and the ephemeral indefiniteness of private experience—what the individual actually sees. The *Oxford Dictionary* documents a semantic flow beginning with the root meaning, from *premere*, to "press" in a primarily physical sense, as in the "impression" of a printed book, to more psychological and mental senses, meaning "the effect produced by external force or influence on the sense or the mind" (1632); and it later adds: "especially in modern use a vague or indistinct survival from a more distinct knowledge." This last usage surely reflects one aspect of the process whereby the concentration of philosophical thought upon epistemological problems from Descartes and Hume onward has made the relation between individual sensation and ascertainable truth increasingly problematic. The disjunction found more radical expression at the end of the eighteenth century, when the increasingly pervasive authority of a mechanistic and sensational psychology in effect drove the religious, imaginative, emotional, and esthetic orders of being into the private and internal world of the individual. After the Romantics this process took a more deeply skeptical direction, which was most memorably expressed in the famous "Conclusion" to *The Renaissance* (1868–1873), where Pater speaks of how "each mind keeping as a solitary prisoner its own dream of a world" can actually experience directly only "the passage and dissolution of impressions, images, sensations. . . ."

The critical thought of Pater, and of the nineties, are embodiments of a fusion between various Impressionist and Symbolist tendencies which had reached their fullest expression in France. The French Impressionists and Symbolists were exactly contemporary; Verlaine, Rimbaud, and Mallarmé wrote during the heyday of the Impressionist painters in the seventies, although Symbolism as a conscious movement came a little later—in poetry when Jean Moréas wrote his manifesto in 1886, and in painting at the Café Volpini exhibition in 1889. Compared to the views of earlier painters and writers, there were many parallels between the attitudes of the adherents of Symbolism and Impressionism in both painting and poetry; they fully agreed in rejecting intellectual conceptualization and established artistic traditions in the name of expressing a directly apprehended personal and subjective vision.

In one important respect, it is true, the Impressionists and Symbolists took logically opposite directions. The Impressionist painters began with the outside world as it appeared to their own subjective perception, whereas the Symbolist painters wished, as Gustave Moreau put it, to "clothe the idea in perceptible form"; in effect the two schools differed in approaching their task from different ends of the same newly intensified polarity between individual consciousness and external reality. In literature the Symbolists, especially

Mallarmé and later Paul Valéry, while just as opposed to logical conceptual-ization as any Impressionist, nevertheless wanted to get larger ideas into lit-erature somehow, although they were ideas of a very special kind; ideas which belonged only to the inner world of the consciousness, which could only be summoned through the portals of the imagination, and which were only man-ifested to the senses of the artist or his audience in the shape of symbols.

Here Symbolism must be seen as part of the same historical process which produced the individualist and subjective direction of Impressionism, since the imagination and the symbol are distinctively Romantic and post-romantic preoccupations. The process by which the individual mind attrib-uted a larger intellectual or emotional meaning to particular objects and events was hardly a problem in earlier periods, because the whole universe was generally assumed to constitute a fixed order in which every item had its communally agreed meaning—most obviously in mythology—which gave a spiritual role to everything in the external world. Men could hardly be con-sciously concerned with symbolism when the larger meaning of objects was already established, as with the cross, for instance, or the apple. But the Romantic writers felt impelled to assign their own personal symbolic meanings to natural objects, to mountains, birds, and flowers; and they did so by creat-ing new orders of meaning which were not those of the established orthodoxies but of the individual imagination. After Blake and Wordsworth, it was com-monly assumed that the poet had access to previously unknown immanent connections between the external world and spiritual reality. This general epistemological assumption is reflected in one of the characteristic expressive idioms of modern literature. The postromantic symbol is likely to be private rather than public; but it is not intended to stand for a single and definable concept. Even the poets who were most attached to esoteric or transcendental beliefs tended in their writing to rely primarily on the many natural conno-tations of their images; Shelley's skylark, Keats's nightingale, or the swans of Mallarmé and Yeats—none of these are univocal or allegorical symbols; their meanings arise from the varied inherent suggestions of the poetic object, and only to the extent that these are mobilized in the poem so that the reader concretely experiences all the implications of seeing and not seeing, singing and not singing, soaring and not soaring. Thus the essential meaning of the symbolic image is established in a way quite unlike that of allegory, and one which is consistent with Yeats's contrast between a symbol, which was "the only possible expression of some individual essence, a transparent lamp about a spiritual flame," and allegory, which was "one of many possible represen-tations of an embodied thing or familiar principle, and belong[ed] to fancy and not imagination. . . ."

Yeats's metaphor of the lamp and the flame for the inherent, natural and personal way that object and meaning are associated in modern symbolism is fairly close to Conrad's metaphor of the two spheres; and both of them implicitly require a special kind of symbolic interpretation from the critic.

The significance of any particular symbolic object or its verbal sign is usually established either by arbitrary convention, as in algebra, or, more commonly, by an extension of its normal properties. Thus we understand that "the apple of my eye" means a beloved object merely by an extension of our knowledge that an apple has the properties of looking beautiful and being good. As with many other objects, however, the apple has also been assigned various conventional or allegorical meanings which can only be understood by reference to specific bodies of knowledge. The story of Discordia at the wedding of Peleus and Thetis, for instance, is the item of special knowledge required to interpret the conventional phrase an "apple of discord." This distinction between two kinds of symbol can be summarily expressed by the neologisms *homeophor* and *heterophor*: "the apple of my eye" is a *homeophor* because we can arrive at its symbolic meaning by an imaginative extension of the *same* or *similar* properties as are normally possessed by the object; the "apple of discord" is a *heterophor* because its symbolic meaning is carried by *something else*—in this case by another body of knowledge.

There are obviously many historical reasons why allegory should have gone out of general favor in a period characterized by less and less community of belief in any body of knowledge, and thus why modern literature should predominantly rely on *homeophoric* symbolism. It also follows that, in fiction as well as in poetry, modern writers should have developed an expressive idiom which activates this kind of symbolic response.

To begin with, the symbolic images described by Yeats can only carry multiple suggestions to the extent that they evoke all the potencies of particular individual experience; and the Symbolist method therefore makes much the same primary demand as Impressionism or Imagism in requiring the writer to render the object with an idiosyncratic immediacy of vision which is freed from any intellectual prejudgment or explanatory gloss. The reader must also feel that he is in the presence of an unfamiliar hierarchy of attention—it is, for instance, the emphasis on some details and the absence of others which makes it clear that the birds in the poems of Mallarmé or Yeats are presented not for their ornithological or autobiographical interest, but for some other purpose, some larger complex of connecting values and meanings. These values and meanings are not stated, but only the hypothesis of their hidden presence, it seems, could explain the special emphases with which the writer's perceptions are conveyed; the obtrusive disparity between a particular image and the significance apparently attributed to it creates a semantic gap which we feel called on to fill with our own symbolic interpretation.

One logical result of this semantic gap, and more generally of the characteristic idiom and objectives of Impressionism and Symbolism, has been to give a much more important, but also a much more difficult, role to the literary critic. He is faced with the task of explaining to the public in discursive expository prose a literature whose authors deliberately kept their works as free as possible from rational or conceptual definition. He confronts an incompleteness of utterance, an indeterminacy of meaning, a seemingly unconscious or random association of images, which simultaneously demand and defy logical exegesis. In the fiction which belongs primarily to the Impressionist school, such as that of Stephen Crane, or to its Imagist and later heritages, such as that of Ernest Hemingway, the idiosyncratic sequence of vivid particularities asks to be construed and translated into the realm of public discourse; but once translated into that expository language not much is left and its residue of general meaning is likely, in the critic's rendition of it, to seem both meager and ambiguous. The difficulty is even greater for writing with a strong Symbolist element, where there is, in addition, a semantic gap to be bridged and an intangible unifying essence to be discovered. In either case the critic is asked to provide a commentary which will transcend the very epistemological problems which dominate the expressive idiom of the literature he is analyzing; no wonder, then, that the modern critic is prone to an excessive metaphysical abstraction in aims and language, and to a notorious compulsion for extravagant symbol hunting.

This last tendency, which was particularly powerful during the apogee of the prestige of literary criticism in the fifties, seems to have been partly based on the idea that the essence of Symbolism lay, not in its attempt to suggest the larger possibilities of meaning behind individual experience but in its use of an essentially esoteric purpose and method. In the case of *Heart of Darkness*, this *heterophoric* approach often concentrated its attention on the episode where Marlow receives his appointment from the Trading Company, to which, at long last, we can turn.

III

A narrow and deserted street in deep shadow, high houses, innumerable windows with venetian blinds, a dead silence, grass sprouting between the stones, imposing carriage archways right and left, immense double doors standing ponderously ajar. I slipped through one of these cracks, went up a swept and ungarnished staircase, as arid as a desert, and opened the first door I came to. Two women, one fat and the other slim, sat on straw-bottomed chairs, knitting black wool. The slim one got up and walked straight at me—still knitting with down-cast eyes—and only just as I began to think of getting out of her way, as you would for a somnambulist, stood still, and looked up. Her dress was as plain as an umbrella-cover, and she turned round without a word and preceded me into a waiting-room. I gave my name, and looked about.

Marlow is ushered into the presence of the Director, and then

In about forty-five seconds I found myself again in the waiting-room with the compassionate secretary, who, full of desolation and sympathy, made me sign some document. I believe I undertook amongst other things not to disclose any trade secrets. Well, I am not going to.

I began to feel slightly uneasy. You know I am not used to such ceremonies, and there was something ominous in the atmosphere. It was just as though I had been let into some conspiracy—I don't know—something not quite right; and I was glad to get out. In the outer room the two women knitted black wool feverishly. People were arriving, and the younger one was walking back and forth introducing them. The old one sat on her chair. Her flat cloth slippers were propped up on a foot-warmer, and a cat reposed on her lap. She wore a starched white affair on her head, had a wart on one cheek, and silver-rimmed spectacles hung on the tip of her nose. She glanced at me above the glasses. The swift and indifferent placidity of that look troubled me. Two youths with foolish and cheery countenances were being piloted over, and she threw at them the same quick glance of unconcerned wisdom. She seemed to know all about them and about me too. An eerie feeling came over me. She seemed uncanny and fateful. Often far away there I thought of these two, guarding the door of Darkness, knitting black wool as for a warm pall, one introducing, introducing continuously to the unknown, the other scrutinising the cheery and foolish faces with unconcerned old eyes. *Ave!* Old knitter of black wool. *Morituri te salutant.* Not many of those she looked at ever saw her again—not half, by a long way.

Several critics have made the two knitters a primary basis for a large-

scale *heterophoric* interpretation of *Heart of Darkness* in which Marlow's whole
journey becomes a symbolic version of the traditional descent into Hell, such
as that in the sixth book of Virgil's *Aeneid*, or in Dante's *Inferno*. Marlow
certainly presents his experience in the general perspective of the pagan and
Christian traditions of a journey to the underworld; this is sufficiently explicit
when he talks of the knitters "guarding the door of Darkness," and of the two
youths "being piloted over." But it is surely only a primary assumption that
there was a single kernel of truth to be extracted, that a thoroughgoing *heterophoric* interpretation was a good idea, which could have impelled one critic
to assert that there is "a close structural parallel between *Heart of Darkness* and
the *Inferno*," and proceed to make the Company Station Limbo, the Central
Station the abode of the fraudulent, and Kurtz both a "traitor to kindred"
and a Lucifer.

Marlow goes on to make some further *heterophoric* references; but they
are also surely intended merely to place the two knitters in the ageless perspective of the heartless unconcern of spectators at an ordeal which may be
fatal to the protagonists. This unconcern is also evoked by the *tricoteuses* cal-
lously knitting at the guillotine, and by the Roman crowds to whom the
gladiators address their scornful farewell in Marlow's rather pretentious in-
terjection: "*Ave!* old knitters of black wool, *Morituri te salutant*." These parallels, however, are surely as local in function as the earlier historical allusions
to Drake and Franklin; once made, they are dropped, if only because keeping
the parallel going would detract both from the immediacy of the narrative and
from its freedom to evoke other associations and suggestions.

Certainly, if we are seeking an interpretation which makes *Heart of Darkness* as a whole an essentially *heterophoric* work, we are likely to alert our
attention too exclusively to clues of a specific kind. Why does Conrad give us
only two fates? Which one is Clotho the spinner? and which is Lachesis the
weaver? Did the Greeks know about knitting anyway? Where are the shears?
What symbolic meaning can there be in the fact that the thin one lets people
in to the room and then *out* again—a birth and death ritual, perhaps? Thus
preoccupied, however fruitfully or unfruitfully, our attention will hardly be
able to respond fully in the immediate *homeophoric* suggestion of how the thin
knitter: "got up and walked straight at me—still knitting with downcast
eyes—and only just as I began to think of getting out of her way, as you
would for a somnambulist, stood still, and looked up. Her dress was as plain
as an umbrella-cover. . . ."

If we submit ourselves to the vivid impressionistic particularity of these
details, their connotations take us far beyond our primary sense of the fateful,
uncanny, and impassive atmosphere of the scene to a larger awareness of a

rigid, mechanical, blind, and automatized world: the thin knitter does not speak or see or even move in relation to others; her shape recalls an umbrella and its tight black cover; there has been no effort to soften its hard and narrow ugliness with rhythmic movements, rounded forms, or living colors. It is not her reminding us of the classical Fates that really matters, but that she is herself a fate—a dehumanized death in life to herself and to others, and thus a prefiguring symbol of what the Trading Company does to its creatures.

A full analysis of the scene would no doubt reveal an inexhaustible network of expanding symbolic suggestions; one incidental reason for the vogue of *heterophoric* criticism may be that it bypasses the endless and necessarily tentative explication which is theoretically entailed by Symbolist writing. Here, however, there is room only for a very summary illustration of how the typical features of the Impressionist and Symbolist expressive idiom combine to illuminate one of the general themes of *Heart of Darkness*.

The Impressionist elements in the rendering of the scene are present in the way we see it entirely and manifestly through Marlow's remembering mind, and without any canonical gloss by an omniscient author. This limited and subjective nature of the report is made most explicit when Marlow says of the tycoon, "He shook hands I fancy." Marlow's comment enforces our awareness that we are inside a consciousness that does not notice or understand much of what is happening in the world outside his mind. This has the effect of legitimizing and emphasizing whatever external details do emerge. The older knitter, for example, with her wart and her flat cloth slippers, becomes a stark visual image of physical and spiritual deformity combined with imperturbable self-complacence, an image which recalls the grotesque crones of Dégas or Toulouse-Lautrec.

If we scrutinize the whole episode to see what is and is not recorded by Marlow, the pattern in his hierarchy of attention becomes apparent. He omits much that would be mentioned in an autobiography, or a Naturalist novel; we are not given, for instance, the name of the city, the title of the company, or the details of Marlow's contract. Here, as often, Conrad's method follows the Symbolist injunction, as expressed in Mallarmé's "Nommer un objet, c'est supprimer les trois quarts de la jouissance de poème . . . le suggérer, voilà le rêve." [To name the object is to destroy three-quarters of the enjoyment of the poem . . . to suggest it, there is the dream.] Marlow reports much else in the briefest and most general terms; for instance, the tycoon is merely a "pale plumpness" because big bureaucrats typically eat too much, don't exercise outdoors, are featureless and somehow abstract. But on the other hand, the very incompleteness and apparent randomness of what details are given forces the reader to extract whatever unifying symbolic intimations he can.

There must, we feel, be a reason why Marlow's attention to particulars is so intermittent; if he often despecifies the external and the factual, it may be because he is trying to specify the internal and the moral; and so we come to see that what Marlow essentially registers with increasingly agonized incredulity is his inward reaction to an initiation into what is perhaps the most fateful of modern mysteries—how the individual confronts a vast bureaucracy, and in particular how he gets a job from it.

Marlow begins his rites of passage with a representative ecological sequence: approach through unfamiliar streets and arid staircases; passive marshalling from waiting room to grand managerial sanctum; and forty-five seconds later, a more rapid return thence through the same stages, with a delayed and demoralizing detour for medical examination. The sequence of routinized human contacts is equally typical: the impassive receptionists; the expert compassion of the confidential secretary; the hollow benevolence of the plump tycoon; the shifty joviality of the clerk; and the self-congratulation of the medical examiner.

When the scene ends Marlow is left with a sense of doubly fraudulent initiation: the Company has not told him what he wants to know; but since Marlow has been unable to formulate the causes of his moral discomfort, much less voice any protest or ask any authentic question, his own tranced submission has been a double betrayal—indirectly of the Company and directly of himself.

This prefigures one of the larger and more abstract themes of the story—the lack of any genuinely reciprocal communication anywhere. For instance, Marlow's most extended dialogue at the Company's offices is with the doctor. In part it merely typifies this particular aspect of bureaucratic initiation: the formulaic insult ("Ever any madness in your family?"); the posture of disinterested devotion to scientific knowledge (measuring Marlow's cranium); and the pretendedly benevolent but actually both impractical and deeply disquieting counsel ("Avoid irritation more than exposure to the sun"). Such details might be said to operate partly in a centripetal way, since they point to specific later issues in the narrative, to Kurtz's skull and those on his fenceposts and to Marlow's physical and mental collapse at the end; but the details also have larger and more expansive centrifugal overtones. The horrors of the modern secular Hell are not merely the affronting mumbo-jumbo of the medical priesthood; Marlow has illuminated the haze which hangs like a pall over the society of which the doctor, the clerk, the knitters, and the pale plumpness are representatives; and we are led outward to see the complete impossibility of genuine communion with anyone else's intellectual or moral center.

Beyond that we are again left with an overpowering sense of Marlow's

fateful induction into the vast overarching network of the silent lies of civilization. No one will explain them—not in the Company offices, certainly—if
only because the jobs of the personnel depend on their discretion, and because
the division of labor restricts each individual to knowledge of a very small
part of the system—none of the people there seem to have been to Africa, for
instance. The great corporate enterprise has made itself, and it has no voice;
yet men cannot help attributing moral meanings and intentions to all its appearances because they are the only available manifestations of a power which
controls their lives.

The semantic gap exists at higher thematic levels. Marlow doesn't fully
understand the meaning of what is happening; there is no Virgil in sight,
much less a Beatrice; and no one will help him, or even admit that the problem
exists. Later the narrative reveals that this gap extends throughout Marlow's
world, and we see that the silent, lethal madness of the civilization for which
the Trading Company stands enacts the intellectual and moral impasse whose
narrative climax is to be the forced lie to the Intended. This gap, in turn,
can be seen in a much wider perspective as a reflection of the same impasse,
the same breakdown of the shared categories of understanding and judgment,
as had originally imposed on Conrad and his peers among the artists of the
period, the indirect, subjective, and guarded strategies that typify the expressive idiom of Impressionism and Symbolism.

Conrad wrote in the preface to *The Nigger of the "Narcissus"* that his aim
was "before all, to make you *see*." One could argue that the distinctive aim,
not only of Impressionist painting but of much modern literature is, to put it
a little more explicitly, "to make us see what we see." For this, the essential
requirement in our reading and our criticism is surely a primary commitment
to the literal imagination. In this case it involves a receptiveness to the whole
scene which can discern in the knitters symbolic meanings which are essentially *homeophoric* extensions of their own inherent qualities, and which combine to extend these symbolic meanings in a centrifugal way which extends
far beyond the literal vehicle of the narrative.

The opposite kind of critical reading gives priority to an esoteric interpretation of particular objects—knitters are *heterophors* for the fates—and combines them into a centripetal interpretation of the work as a whole—*Heart of
Darkness* is essentially about a descent into Hell, or into the unconscious. One
suspects, incidentally, that this kind of criticism has also had unfortunate side
effects for literature. Some recent novelists write fiction as if it were supposed
to fit a *heterophoric* prescription in mythological acrostics, or engineer gratuitous semantic gaps so that they can be bridged by symbol-finding critics—
Last Year in Marienbad is a likely candidate.

As regards *Heart of Darkness*, such criticism is surely contrary to the implications of the primary narrator's image, which asks us to reach out, not in, to expand, not to narrow the range of meaning. *Heterophoric* criticism, on the other hand, inevitably bypasses much of the narrative because it burrows beneath it in quest of a single edible kernel of truth presumed to be hidden deep below the surface. It is surely curious, and saddening, to reflect that there have appeared a dozen or more studies which take a *heterophoric* view of the knitters, and none which see them and the scene in which they figure as *homeophoric* symbols of the great corporation and the civilization for which it stands.

IV

It would certainly be lengthy, and it would probably be inconclusive, if one attempted to assess how close the affinities of *Heart of Darkness* are to the general spirit and methods of the French Symbolists. Many difficulties arise from the extreme diffuseness and variety of the Symbolist tradition, and from the inherent differences between literary genres—a symbolic image obviously cannot have the same autonomous and controlling importance in a long prose narrative as in a short poem. Another major difficulty is that Conrad's most explicit theoretical comments are, as usual, puzzling and unhelpful.

In 1918 Conrad wrote to a critic that "All the great creations of literature have been symbolic." This might mean no more than that Oedipus or Don Quixote portray universal human characteristics and situations: one of the commonest uses of the term "symbolic" means little more than "representative." Here, however, Conrad seems to imply something rather more specific, for he goes on: "A work of art is seldom limited to one exclusive meaning and not necessarily tending to a definite conclusion. And for the reason that the nearer it approaches art, the more it acquires a symbolic character. This statement may surprise you who may imagine that I am alluding to the Symbolist School of poets or prose writers. Theirs, however, is only a literary proceeding against which I have nothing to say. I am concerned here with something much larger. . . ."

The fact that Conrad implies a polar opposition between a work of art, which is symbolic, and other modes of discourse, which have exclusive meanings and definite conclusions, certainly starts from a view of literature similar to that of the French Symbolists. But, while disclaiming the Symbolist doctrine, Conrad characteristically abstains from any further explanation of his own views.

In 1902, when the publication of *Heart of Darkness* in book form had provoked further discussion, Elsie Ford made various objections to what Conrad called "my pet Heart of Darkness." He allowed only one of them: "What I distinctly admit is the fault of having made Kurtz too symbolic or rather symbolic at all." Conrad probably meant only that he would have liked Kurtz to be more convincing as a character; perhaps Conrad came to regret the experiment he had made, and felt that he had failed in trying to combine some general Symbolist aims with more traditional fictional values and methods, although one notes that characterization is hardly the strong point either in the novels of Villiers de L'Isle-Adam and Huysmans, or in the plays of Maeterlinck and Jarry.

Another clue to the essential nature of Conrad's achievement is supplied by the fact that Henry James did not much like *Heart of Darkness*. In her unpublished diary, Olive Garnett reports Elsie Ford as saying that James "objected to the narrator mixing himself up with the narrative in 'The Heart of Darkness' and its want of proportion" (January 5, 1903). James's phrase about Marlow's "mixing himself up with the narrative" surely discloses a myopic resistance to the technique of *Heart of Darkness* which only James's invariable veneration for his own methods can explain. Marlow is certainly very different from the Jamesian central intelligence; in effect, he flouts what James thought the essential objection to the first-person method—the fact that the narrating "I" has "the double privilege of subject and object." But if James believed that there was an "object" to be clearly seen, Conrad did not; it is precisely because Marlow is both subject and object that *Heart of Darkness* prefigures how the modern novel was to reject, much more fully than did James, the assumption of full authorial understanding and, in its formal posture at least, restrict itself to showing an individual consciousness in the process of trying to elicit some personal order or meaning from its impressions of past and present experience. If we see Conrad as decisively closer to us than James, it is surely because he gave much more radical expression to the skeptical and subjective attitudes which also characterized the Impressionist and Symbolist movements; and in the context of these traditions we can recognize *Heart of Darkness* as a landmark in the literature of modern solipsism.

Conrad shrank from all literary schools and doctrines, and he was certainly not a Symbolist with a capital "S." The available evidence at most strengthens the view that he is closer to the Symbolist tradition than any previous English novelist, and especially close in *Heart of Darkness*, although two later short stories, "Tomorrow" and "The Secret Sharer," are near contenders. Conrad's earlier work had already shared some of the general features of French Symbolism—the simple plots, the musical, suggestive and poetic nature of the prose, the intensity of attention to physical objects. *Heart of*

Darkness added some further elements of similarity: the spiritual voyage of discovery, especially through an exotic jungle landscape, which was a common Symbolist theme, in Baudelaire's "Le Voyage" and Rimbaud's "Bâteau ivre," for instance; the pervasive atmosphere of dream, nightmare, and hallucination, again typical of Rimbaud, and especially of "Une Saison en enfer"; the very subject of Kurtz recalls, not only Rimbaud's own spectacular career, but the general Symbolist fondness for the lawless, the depraved, and the extreme modes of experience; and in *Heart of Darkness* Conrad is making his supreme effort, in Baudelaire's phrase about Delacroix, to reveal "the infinite to the finite."

This intention is suggested in the title. What is most characteristic about the Symbolist tradition is certainly not the use of particular objects and acts as *homeophoric* symbols, a use which is almost equally common among the Impressionists and Imagists. Thus in his Imagist manifesto Ezra Pound defines an image as "that which presents an intellectual and emotional complex in an instant of time," and makes the ringing polemic affirmation "the natural object is always the *adequate* symbol" ("A Stray Document," 1913). Insofar as any specific feature of Symbolist literature can be identified, it is more probably the centrifugal way in which the meaning of the work as a whole is conceived. Thus the Symbolist poets often made their titles suggest a much larger and more mysterious range of implication than their works' overt subject apparently justified—one thinks of the expanding effect of T. S. Eliot's *The Waste Land* for example, or of *The Sacred Wood*—and this centrifugal direction in the title was sometimes produced by an obtrusive semantic gap, a coupling of incongruous words or images that forced us to look beyond our habitual expectations.

Such is the final effect of Conrad's title. Compared with the particularity of Conrad's earlier and more traditional titles such as *Almayer's Folly* and *The Nigger of the "Narcissus," Heart of Darkness* strikes a very special note; we are somehow impelled to see the title as much more than a combination of two stock metaphors for referring to "the centre of the Dark Continent" and "a diabolically evil person." Both the nouns are too densely charged with physical and moral suggestion; and together they generate a puzzle which compels us to expect something beyond our usual moral and literary experience; the words do not name what we know, but ask us to know what has, as yet, no name. The more concrete of the two terms, "heart," is attributed a strategic centrality within a formless and infinite abstraction, "darkness"; the combination defies both visualization and logic: How can something inorganic like darkness have an organic center of life and feeling? How can a shapeless absence of light compact itself into a formed and pulsing presence? And what are we to make of a "good" entity like a heart becoming, of all things, a controlling part of a "bad" one like darkness? *Heart of Darkness* was a fateful event in the history of fiction; and to announce it Conrad had hit upon as haunting, though not as obtrusive, an oxymoron as Baudelaire had for poetry with *Les Fleurs du Mal*.

JOAN E. STEINER

"The Secret Sharer":
Complexities of the Doubling Relationship

Because "The Secret Sharer" is among those works given the most attention by Conradian critics, one is tempted to conclude that little or nothing significant remains to be said about it. Endlessly debated, for example, is Leggatt's role as doppelgänger—since the captain-narrator specifically refers to him no less than eighteen times as "my double" and employs variant terms, "my other self," "my second self," "my secret self," and "my secret sharer," as many or more times, it is impossible to ignore. While the doubling here is, in some respects, less complicated than that in some of Conrad's other works, such as *Heart of Darkness* and *Victory*, it confirms his thorough mastery of a convention that had already undergone considerable development in the hands of his nineteenth-century predecessors. By using the double as the central image in a tale exploring a number of ostensibly clear-cut dualities and, simultaneously and paradoxically, as the focus of persistent ambiguities that blur those dualities, Conrad transforms the device into one peculiarly his own. Thus more does remain to be said about Conrad's handling of the doubling relationship in "The Secret Sharer."

In his study, *Doubles in Literary Psychology*, Ralph Tymms traces the evolution of the doppelgänger from its origins in primitive belief, where it was frequently associated with dreams and hallucinations and with such visual phenomena as mirror images, shadows, and supernatural manifestations,

From *Conradiana: A Journal of Joseph Conrad Studies* 12, no. 3 (1980). © 1980 by the Institute for Textual Studies, Department of English, Texas Tech University. Originally entitled "Conrad's 'The Secret Sharer': Complexities of the Doubling Relationship."

through its major appearances in literature up to the end of the nineteenth century. In so doing, he points to the development of two conceptions, doubling by duplication, in which the counterpart appears as a twin or, in its essential aspects, a physical duplicate, and doubling by division, in which the counterpart represents one major facet of character, customarily spiritual or psychological in nature. In addition, he describes the alternation between allegorical or ethical doubles, which express dualism in human nature in terms of good and evil, and realistic or psychological doubles, which depict dualism in terms of reason and emotion of the conscious and unconscious.

Of particular importance in the development of the doppelgänger was E. T. A. Hoffmann. Intrigued by the discoveries of the Mesmerist psychologists, who clinically developed theories of dual consciousness and postulated the existence of a "night side" of the mind, Hoffmann incorporated their ideas in his fiction. Reviewing a number of representative tales, Tymms finds Hoffmann's greatest contribution to be his identification of the unconscious self with another individual and in some cases subjective transference of this part of the personality to that physical double, either real or imaginary. By associating inward dualism with outward physical likeness, Hoffmann thus combined the previously separate concepts of doubling by division and doubling by duplication. Moreover, influenced by the observation of the Mesmerist psychologist, G. H. Schubert, that "emotions (which act most directly on the unconscious mind) are ambiguous in character," Hoffmann placed greater emphasis on psychological than on allegorical aspects of the doppelgänger relationship.

Examining the portrayal of Leggatt in light of this information, I find it significant that Conrad alludes directly to Hoffmann's tales in *Under Western Eyes*, the work he interrupted to write "The Secret Sharer," for the correspondences are too great to ignore. Thus, like Hoffmann, Conrad combines doubling by duplication and doubling by division in his representation of Leggatt and also places greater emphasis on the psychological than on the allegorical aspects of Leggatt's relationship with the captain.

With respect to Leggatt's role as double by duplication, the captain, in addition to making numerous references to their identical attire and observing that the "sleeping-suit was just right for his size," initially notes other physical similarities between Leggatt and himself, including age and appearance, and concludes with an image associated with the double from the beginning: "It was, in the night, as though I had been faced by my own reflection in the depths of a sombre and immense mirror." Throughout the story, moreover, the captain frequently reminds us of this physical similarity.

By noting experiential parallels as well, Conrad extends his portrayal of the double by duplication beyond that of most of his predecessors. Thus both the captain and Leggatt, we learn, served on the Conway maritime training ship. Moreover, accounts of Leggatt's experiences on the *Sephora* indicate that he, like the narrator, was "the only stranger on board," making his first voyage as an officer among men who had been together for some time and who distrusted him." Because Leggatt appeals to him "as if our experiences had been as identical as our clothes," the captain is able to understand the circumstances of the murder "as though I were myself inside that other sleeping-suit."

Because critics have concentrated on Leggatt's role as double by division, many have taken an extreme position on his significance. Some, following the lead of Albert J. Guerard, who has variously interpreted Leggatt as "some darker, more interior, outlaw self" and as a "more instinctive, more primitive, less rational self" revealing man's "potential criminality," regard him as a predominantly negative figure. Others, by contrast, view Leggatt as the embodiment of that "ideal conception of one's own personality" that the captain has secretly set up as a standard by which to measure his behavior. While each position has some validity, both fail to consider sufficiently all aspects of Leggatt and hence the ambiguities inherent in his character, as well as in his relationship with the captain.

Heretofore ignored by critics, Conrad's remarks in *The Mirror of the Sea* concerning his own first command aboard the *Otago* provide some insight into his view of Leggatt. Specifically, he asserts that the two qualifications necessary for a trustworthy seaman are, paradoxically, a healthy sense of insecurity and "an absolute confidence in himself," both of which Leggatt reveals by the time he meets the narrator, but neither of which the narrator initially possesses. The latter's serenity at the outset, reflected in the opening descriptive paragraph, is disrupted when, just before the "tide of darkness" obliterates the scene before him, he notices the presence of another ship, which destroys for him the "solemnity of perfect solitude," as the "multitude" of stars and "disturbing sounds" from the crew destroy "the comfort of quiet communion" with his ship. Thus his preparation for Leggatt has begun.

Subsequently, the captain reveals facets of his character that further suggest his readiness for Leggatt's arrival and for their ensuing relationship. Acknowledging that he is "somewhat of a stranger" to himself and aware that he is "doing something unusual," he impulsively takes the anchor watch himself. Motivated partly by compassion for his men, he suggests this "unconventional arrangement" chiefly because he wishes to be alone in order to "get on terms" with his strange ship. Under the illusion that "the sea was not likely to keep any special surprises expressly for my discomfiture," he proceeds to commit a further breach of discipline by leaving his watch to go below for a cigar and, presumably, to put on his sleeping suit, then returns to rejoice naïvely "in the great security of the sea as compared with the unrest of the land, in my choice of that untempted life presenting no disquieting problems." Just as his initial description of the indistinguishable welding of land and sea reflects a naïve sense of integration, so this simplistic dichotomy between land and sea reflects his growing sense of duality.

Immediately thereafter, he is confronted with a disquieting problem that results directly from his impulsive behavior and destroys his sense of security. Annoyed at finding that a rope ladder has not been hauled in, he asks himself "whether it was wise ever to interfere with the established routine of duties even from the kindest motives." After discovering Leggatt, however, he impulsively commits another breach of discipline by letting him come aboard. Upon noting the establishment of a "mysterious communication" with him and providing him with a "sleeping-suit of the same grey-stripe pattern" as his own, the captain makes the first reference to him as "my double."

That the self-confident Leggatt is presented, in part, as a positive figure of light, i.e., of life and strength, is, I think, indisputable. Three times while he is in the water he is described as "phosphorescent," and as he sits naked on deck before putting on the sleeping suit, he appears "glimmering white in the darkness." Moreover, we learn later that it is the riding light, burning "with a clear, untroubled, as if symbolic flame, confident and bright in the mysterious shades of the night," that directs him to the ship and saves him from having to swim "'round and round like a crazed bullock.'" And at the end, of course, he leaves the hat, "white on the black water," that serves as the "saving mark" for the captain.

Through most of the story, the captain, despite his feeling of identity with Leggatt, contrasts his own deficiencies with Leggatt's strengths. After Leggatt's account of the murder and his subsequent confinement, for example, the narrator notes, "There was nothing sickly in his eyes or in his expression. He was not a bit like me, really," and imagines the manner of his thinking over the incident as "a stubborn if not a steadfast operation; something of which I should have been perfectly incapable." Later, when the captain feels that he is "appearing an irresolute commander," he envies Leggatt's looking "always perfectly self-controlled, more than calm—almost invulnerable." And after the incident of near-discovery, he marvels at "that something unyielding in his character which was carrying him through so finely. . . . Whoever was being distracted, it was not he. He was sane."

Leggatt's strength of character was also evident during the storm aboard the *Sephora*. "'It wasn't a heavy sea,'" Leggatt says, "'it was a sea gone mad!

. . . a man may have the heart to see it coming once and be done with it—but to have to face it day after day . . .'" When the sea produced a corresponding madness in the crew, everyone on the *Sephora* failed. Most culpable of all was the captain, Archbold, whose "'nerve went to pieces altogether.'" After watching the main topsail blow away, he was unable to give the order for the reefed foresail, but "'whimpered about our last hope.'" This experience, according to Legatt, "'was enough to drive any fellow out of his mind. It worked me up into a sort of desperation,'" yet he maintained enough presence of mind to give orders and set the foresail.

As commander of the *Sephora*, Archbold theoretically should be a strong figure, one whose "seven-and-thirty virtuous years at sea, of which over twenty of immaculate command," ought to make him an ideal example to the narrator. Instead, he serves as kind of pathetic double whose moment of failure forcefully emphasizes the ever-present dangers facing the narrator and the precariousness of his position, both personally and professionally. Unlike Leggatt, Archbold appears "completely muddled" about what has happened, unable to face the implications of his behavior or to comprehend his share in Leggatt's guilt. In addition to serving as a reminder of the possibility of failure, he both figuratively mirrors the narrator's inability to master his command, his growing sense of madness, and his fear of the crew, and literally intensifies the suspicion and distrust of that crew.

Despite Leggatt's positive aspects as a figure of light, his act of killing identifies him also with darkness. Leggatt, like many of Hoffmann's doppelgängers, serves as the embodiment or projection of the unconscious and that the captain's relationship with him, as Guerard observes, takes the form of the archetypal night journey or "provisional descent into the primitive and unconscious sources of being," resulting in spiritual change and rebirth. Thus, Leggatt arrives at night, appearing to the captain initially as a "naked body" flickering "in the sleeping water"—at once actual environment and metaphor of the unconscious—and then as a being "complete but for a head. A headless corpse," i.e., one without intellect. Moreover, as we have seen, the captain's discovery of him comes as the direct result of his own impulsive behavior, just as Leggatt, by his account, has impulsively jumped off the *Sephora* and, on arriving here, impulsively asked for the captain.

Once Leggatt is on board and dressed in a sleeping suit, which he wears throughout his stay, the captain, as if to check his bearings, examines his double's face under a lamp before the "warm, heavy, tropical night closed upon his head again." Thereafter, Leggatt is identified predominantly with night, for it is then that he and the narrator communicate in whispers, it not being "prudent to talk in the daytime." Finally, Leggatt plans his escape for night, noting "'as I came at night, so I shall go.'" Here, night and darkness have traditional connotations of the mysterious and irrational.

In addition to this identification of his "second self" with night, the narrator's frequent allusions to the sleeping suit, "the garb of the unconscious life," are in keeping with the traditional psychological representation of the doppelgänger as a manifestation of the unconscious or "night side" of the mind. Traditional, too, are the narrator's metaphorical allusions to his double as a ghost, suggesting his "possession" by Leggatt. Shortly after Leggatt's arrival, for example, the captain surmises that if his chief mate were to come on deck, "he would think he was seeing double or imagine himself come upon a scene of weird witchcraft; the strange captain having a quiet confabulation by the wheel with his own grey ghost." To prevent such an occurrence, the captain takes Leggatt below to his cabin, where Leggatt must be "as noiseless as a ghost" in the attempt to keep "my second self invisible." And when that attempt is subsequently threatened by the incident of near-discovery, the captain observes, "An irresistible doubt of his bodily existence flitted through my mind. Can it be, I asked myself, that he is not visible to other eyes than mine? It was like being haunted. . . . I think I had come creeping quietly as near insanity as any man who has not actually gone over the border."

Indeed, under the stress of the emotional crisis brought on by Leggatt's sudden appearance and his own self-doubt, the captain, like many of the protagonists in Hoffmann's tales, experiences an increasingly acute dissociation or disintegration of personality, leading to incipient madness. After his double has gone to bed, for example, he tries to clear his mind of "the confused sensation of being in two places at once." The next morning, he forces himself to leave the cabin to go on deck and to breakfast with the crew, noting that "all the time the dual working of my mind distracted me almost to the point of insanity." Then, after Archbold's visit, he fears that he is making a bad impression on his first mate because "with my double *down there*, it was most trying to me to be on deck. And it was almost as trying to be *below*. . . . But on the whole I felt less torn in two when I was with him." (my emphasis)

While Conrad's portrayal of Leggatt reveals his thorough familiarity with and dependence on the traditional doppelgänger, his depiction of the ambiguity of Leggatt's character and behavior also reflects his originality and independence. That such ambiguity was intentional is evident in his reworking of materials of the *Cutty Sark* incident to soften the character of the first mate and introduce extenuating circumstances. Thus, unlike Sidney Smith, Leggatt had to contend not only with the exhausting strain of the storm and serious threat to the ship but also with a captain who had gone to pieces. Moreover, his ability to give orders and take action in such a crisis clearly enabled him to save the *Sephora* and the lives of her crew. Finally, the victim, presumably a repeated offender " 'simmering all the time with a silly sort of wickedness,' " disobeyed Leggatt not once but twice, and at the moment of their second encounter they were struck by a wave whose ferocity lasted for over ten minutes, causing Leggatt instinctively to keep hold of his assailant's throat.

The captain, knowing "the pestiferous danger of such a character where there are no means of legal repression," pronounces his double "no homicidal ruffian," yet he also recognizes Leggatt's "guilt." And Leggatt does not absolve himself of responsibility. Considering the killing " 'very wrong indeed,' " he confesses, " 'It's clear that I meant business, because I was holding him by the throat still when they picked us up.' " Moreover, while he later indicates that he wants to prevent more killing, he twice admits the possibility of his committing further acts of violence.

To interpret Leggatt as an essentially "outlaw" or "criminal" self and as a predominantly negative influence on the captain is to distort his significance, however, for he demonstrates that the irrational or instinctive elements in human nature can be a source of strength as well as weakness, good as well as evil. Recognizing this ambiguity, the captain understands how "the same strung-up force which had given twenty-four men a chance, at least, for their lives, had, in a sort of recoil, crushed an unworthy mutinous existence." Leggatt's effect on the captain is similarly ambiguous but ultimately, I think, more positive than negative.

After a few words of conversation with the "calm and resolute" Leggatt upon his arrival, for example, the captain indicates that "the self-possession of that man had somehow induced a corresponding state in myself." And the following morning, despite his fear of Leggatt's discovery, he reflects, " 'I must show myself on deck.' " Facing his suspicious officers, who have heard about his strange behavior, he deftly handles them by giving his "first particular order" and remaining to see it executed. Moreover, feeling "the need of asserting myself without loss of time," he reprimands the second mate for insolence and seizes the opportunity to have "a good look at the face of every foremast man." Though all these actions are deliberate and self-conscious rather than instinctive, they reveal a positive effort to assert control.

Simultaneously, however, the captain's constant awareness of Leggatt, "as dependent on my actions as my own personality," intensifies his sense of duality and incipient madness. Emphasizing the division between his rational and irrational selves, he notes that during the day, Leggatt sits in "the recessed part of the cabin" where he is "half-smothered" by coats. The dangers of the split are evident when enough wind arises to get the ship underway. Although pleased to feel "for the first time a ship move under his feet to his own independent word," he is disturbed by the realization that "I was not wholly alone with my command; for there was that stranger in my cabin. Or rather, I was not completely and wholly with her. Part of me was absent," i.e., his instinctive self:

> There are to a seaman certain words, gestures, that should in given conditions come as naturally, as instinctively as the winking of a menaced eye. A certain order should spring on to his lips without thinking; a certain sign should get itself made, so to speak, without reflection. But all unconscious alertness had abandoned me. I had to make an effort of will to recall myself back (from the cabin) to the conditions of the moment.

Beyond the influence directly attributable to his function as doppelgänger, Leggatt affects the captain's behavior in other ways that are equally ambiguous. Newly appointed to command, he begins the voyage, as we have seen, as a stranger. At the outset, his isolation is "imposed" by circumstances and by youth. Although Leggatt's situation on the *Sephora* was similar initially, his severe physical and moral isolation began only after the killing, when he was confined to his cabin for nine weeks. Thus, on his arrival at the ship he indicates that he has had " 'a confounded lonely time' " and is grateful that the captain saw and spoke to him, for " 'I wanted to be seen, to talk with somebody.' " Through his relationship with the captain, he temporarily becomes less isolated psychologically, while the latter becomes less a stranger to himself.

Yet their relationship has moral and physical, as well as psychological, consequences for the captain. On the one hand, by harboring a fugitive from justice, he places personal or individual loyalty above the traditions of the community. In effect, then, he betrays his function as captain, for his failure to perform any but the most perfunctory duties prevents his getting to know his ship and crew, while his increasing anxiety promotes hostility and distrust that intensify his moral and physical isolation. On the other hand, his loyalty to Leggatt not only demonstrates admirable compassion, but leads to the self-knowledge and self-mastery he must have if he is to succeed both personally and professionally and avoid the weaknesses demonstrated by Archbold and Leggatt.

While he discovers the advantages and dangers of unconscious or instinctive forces in human nature, however, the captain also comes to realize that awareness of one's "second self" does not necessarily lead to desirable or predictable results, for his own nature and/or "accidents which count for so much in the book of success" may cause him to be unfaithful to his ideal conception. Temporarily immobilized by this knowledge, he must summon the courage and self-confidence to act in spite of it. Once again, it is his "calm and resolute" double who forces the issue by his "sane" insistence that he be marooned as soon as possible, making the captain realize that his hesitation is "a mere sham sentiment, a sort of cowardice."

The maneuver to facilitate Leggatt's escape initially involves little risk, for the narrator plans only to take the ship in to "half a mile" from shore, "as far as I may be able to judge in the dark," yet Leggatt's warning to " 'be careful' " makes him realize that "all my future, the only future for which I was fit, would perhaps go irretrievably to pieces in any mishap to my first command." As if to avert this possibility, the captain spends most of his time on deck giving firm and calm commands to his dubious crew and only sufficient time with his "double captain" to work out plans for the escape.

What alters the original plan is Leggatt's unexpected behavior. Going below to see him just before supper, the captain notes that "for the first time there seemed to be a faltering, something strained in his whisper." Moreover, later in the sail locker, when he impulsively rams his hat on his "other self," Leggatt at first "dodged and fended off silently." Immediately after returning to the deck, the narrator decides "it was now a matter of conscience to shave the land as close as possible—for now he must go overboard. . . . Must! There could be no going back for him." As a result, he finds himself facing a test similar to that in which Leggatt succeeded/failed. There is a significant difference, however, for not only does he once again impulsively create a morally ambiguous situation out of loyalty to Leggatt, unnecessarily risking the lives of his crew and the safety of his ship, but his external challenge is provided by the land rather than the sea.

That the captain has "absorbed" the unyielding character of his double and achieved insight into his own potential weaknesses is clear from his description of his behavior during the risky maneuver. Immediately after deciding to "shave the land," he tells us that "my heart flew into my mouth at the nearness of the land on the bow. Under any other circumstances I would not have held on a minute longer." Gaining command of his voice, he issues orders quietly in an attempt to calm his understandably nervous crew. Even when "the black southern hill of Kohring seemed to hang right over the ship like a towering fragment of the ever-lasting night," and later, when the ship is "in the very blackness of" the land, "already swallowed up as it were, gone too close to be recalled, gone from me altogether," he maintains self-control and continues to give orders confidently. Then in an incident parallel to that confronting Leggatt on the *Sephora*, the chief mate, resembling both Archbold and the mutinous sailor, goes to pieces and starts talking back to the captain. Unlike Leggatt, however, the captain maintains control of himself, subduing the mate by clinging to and shaking his arm, not his throat, while firmly issuing orders. Finally, as the ship's "very fate hung in the balance," he suddenly remembers that he is "a total stranger" to her and does not know how she is to be handled. Only the appearance of the white hat, which indicates the backward movement of the ship, enables him to give the saving command. Having demonstrated confidence and self-control, he hardly gives a thought to his "other self" and regards him now, not as a spiritual double, but as "mere flesh."

The hat not only suggests a transference and ultimate reintegration of personality, but also, as it were, a transference of destiny. The narrator must subdue his unrestful, self-conscious, and overly introspective "land" self which has proved potentially harmful to his success as captain. Yet he must retain some measure of that insecurity prompted by his newly acquired recognition of ever-present danger from within and without. His description of his confrontation with the land, juxtaposing events on board ship with frequent references to darkness and night and images of death and Hades, graphically conveys his awareness of the significance of this test. By consciously facing danger and challenging his vulnerability, the captain overcomes his crippling sense of duality and demonstrates his ability to command, thereby belatedly earning the respect of his crew.

Yet ability alone does not save the ship, for without the assistance provided by the hat, the captain might have had many more deaths to account for than Leggatt. Aided by circumstance in avoiding actual betrayal, he is free to establish a bond of fellowship with his crew and pursue his chosen profession at sea. Deprived of similarly fortunate circumstance, Leggatt commits an act of betrayal, a breach of human solidarity, that condemns him to moral and physical isolation. However, just as he helps the captain to prepare for a "new destiny," so the latter serves a similar function for him. In presenting this mutual aspect of the doubling relationship, Conrad further demonstrates his originality. Specifically, in addition to saving Leggatt's life and relieving his loneliness, the captain is able to give him what he most needs—compassionate understanding—and with it an increasing capacity to reflect, as well as a renewed determination, with which to face his exile on land.

Thus, while the narrator notes that Leggatt, on his arrival, seems "to struggle with himself," expressing "something like the low, bitter murmur of doubt. 'What's the good?'" Leggatt, subsequently confirming this impression, emphasizes that "'you speaking to me so quietly—as if you had expected me—made me hold on a little longer.'" Thereafter, the narrator's references to necessary lengthy silence, combined with his descriptions of Leggatt's posture during the day, which as Thomas R. Dilworth observes, is that of a thinker or mediator, suggest that Leggatt becomes increasingly introspective. Further suggesting this process is the narrator's growing number of references to Leggatt's head and to Leggatt and himself with their heads together. Thus, having initially seen Leggatt as "complete but for a head," the narrator ultimately envisions him with his "homeless head."

The results of Leggatt's introspection and the narrator's understanding are apparent in his comments on his predicament. As we have seen, he acknowledges the murder from the outset. Considered in the context of his allusions to being " 'a Conway boy' " and the son of a parson, his question, " 'Do you see me before a judge and jury on that charge?' " seems to be prompted not by a desire to avoid punishment but rather by shame at having failed to live up to the traditional values of his family and his profession. A similar motive is suggested when, in describing Archbold's refusal to let him escape, he says he wanted " 'nothing more' " and then bitterly compares himself to Cain.

This scene with Archbold is symbolically reenacted when Leggatt, asking the captain to maroon him, once again indicates that he wants " 'no more' " and refers to Cain's fate. There is a crucial difference here, however. He now wants to avoid a trial not because of shame but because, never having faced a crisis in which rapid, instinctive action is imperative, the men trying him would not be able to understand his behavior: " 'What can they know whether I am guilty or not—or of *what* I am guilty, either?' " he asks. He is willing to accept Cain's punishment, he tells the captain, " 'as long as I know that you understand. . . . It's a great satisfaction to have got somebody to understand. You seem to have been there on purpose.' "

Earlier, the narrator has remarked of Leggatt, "The very trust in Providence was, I suppose, denied to his guilt." Now, however, Leggatt says that he is " 'not naked like a soul on the Day of Judgment. I shall freeze on to this sleeping-suit. The Last Day is not yet.' " In short, acting somewhat in the role of Providence, as Leggatt acts for him in leaving the hat, the captain gives Leggatt compassion and protection not unlike that which God demonstrated toward Cain in allowing him to expiate his guilt by wandering the earth. Just as he has had to subdue some of his "land" self in preparing for life at sea, so Leggatt must subdue some of his "sea" self in preparing for life on land, a process symbolized by the captain's view of him looking at the navigation chart, "following with his eyes his own figure wandering on the blank land of Cochin-China, and then passing off that piece of paper clean out of sight into uncharted regions." As noted earlier, the transference not only of personality but also of destiny is suggested when, visualizing himself "wandering barefooted, bareheaded, the sun beating on my dark poll," the captain gives Leggatt his hat. Subsequently marking the spot where he "lowered himself into the water to take his punishment" and where the captain gains control of his ship, the hat contributes to Leggatt's redemption, making him "a free man, a proud swimmer striking out for a new destiny."

Metaphorically, the lowering of Leggatt into the water and passing "out of sight into uncharted regions" suggest the resubmergence of the captain's unconscious and the reintegration of his personality. Thus, during his night journey, the narrator has moved, with the assistance of his double, from immature and naïve integration through a period of severe disorientation and disintegration to a more mature reintegration resulting from self-knowledge and self-mastery.

DANIEL MELNICK

The Morality of Conrad's Imagination:
Heart of Darkness *and* Nostromo

In a letter written as he was beginning *Lord Jim*, Conrad describes the problem of discerning and firmly holding the values by which life may be lived, and his remarks identify an issue central to the reading and criticism of his works: the difficulty of defining Conrad's values. In his letter, the same English novelist of decent commitments who would write that Jim is "one of us," speaks with the voice of the profound pessimist of obscure European origin.

> There is no morality, no knowledge and no hope: there is only the consciousness of ourselves which drives us about a world that is always but a vain and floating appearance.

What exactly was the novelist's view of the social and moral condition of human life? The difficulty of answering the question grows out of the conflict between Conrad's basic yet sometimes only suggested pessimism and his explicit affirmations. His finest novels lead the reader into a world of "vain and floating appearance," into a symbolic heart of darkness where he is made to doubt the reality and effective value of all social and personal order. Yet, in the face of the evoked moral disintegration, Conrad's narrators often affirm a morality of decency and fidelity, of "human solidarity." This contradiction between pessimism and affirmation is a complex and integral part of our experience of reading the novels.

I want here to examine the elements of the contradiction—this ambiguous

From *Missouri Review* 5, no. 2 (Winter 1981–82). ©1982 by the Curators of the University of Missouri. Originally entitled "The Morality of Conrad's Imagination."

tension—in Conrad's finest work. Central to his pessimism is a subversive perception of the vacant, indeed malevolent nature of reality, a perception which grew steadily in the mind of Conrad, most of whose childhood was spent with a sick and pessimistic father in political exile from his native Poland and who spent half of his manhood without roots in any homeland, sailing the world's oceans as a merchant seaman. In his view, reality provides man with a shattering test to the endurance of his human identity, to the value of his every thought and act. And in each of Conrad's best novels, the heart of the vision of reality toward which everything leads and from which all falls away is hollow, both literally and symbolically an inhuman and thus malevolent core. In *Heart of Darkness*, the center and climax of vision is Kurtz's "hollow voice," compelling, horror-struck, and perverted. The center of the reality richly envisioned in *Nostromo* is Mount Azuera with the silver which is its issue, both inevitably and destructively indifferent to human life.

Yet, Conrad's pessimism is ambiguous. The "heart of darkness" into which his finest fiction leads the reader is itself at the center of a vision rendered by a vital imaginative richness of language, scene, and character. There are, for example, those expansive and detailed impressionistic visions of human life in the disintegrating Costaguana of *Nostromo*, in anarchic and oppressive London of *The Secret Agent*, or Europe's imperialistic venture in the Africa evoked by *Heart of Darkness* itself. These visualizations are brilliant, rich, and surely constructed; yet as each is imagined, the envisioned life is, of course, profoundly precarious—threatened or, indeed, destroyed by forces within characters, societies, and nature.

The reader is made to penetrate and to question the reality and value of a world which has been given the illusion of depth and substance. This paradox in Conrad's best novels is central to their power, and to their modernity. For the modern consciousness is concerned with the relativity and potential destructiveness of all ordering, and the modern imagination in Conrad—as in the works of later twentieth century novelists—exists amid the disordered ruin of disintegrating social and moral reality. Given such a desperately paradoxical situation, what values can modern fiction embody? Must it, indeed, project a nihilistic acquiescence to meaninglessness? This is the question posed implicitly when, in the face of evoked moral disintegration, Conrad's narrators often affirm a basic code of decency and commitment. The novelist's allegiances seem here to be divided between two supposed world views: that human experience is inevitably destructive, and that man must strive to confront life with all possible integrity and honesty. Such ambiguous paradox poses the major difficulty in every discussion of Conrad, and the judgments required to explore and resolve the problem of defining Conrad's values constitute an unusually challenging and important task for his reader.

I

The sense of Conrad's values which I want to explore is that the basis of his deepest moral commitment is located in neither affirmation nor pessimism, but in Conrad's reliance on the reader's ability to use his own imagination, a reliance which Conrad often voiced. In the novels, the idealist, the steeled cynic, and the human stoic are each maimed or destroyed by the anarchy, the mystery, and the extremities of fate which constitute the malevolent nature of the reality Conrad envisions. Only the observing eyes of the reader and in a sense those of narrators survive the ruin of human experience; human vision alone endures. Conrad's finest novels subtly project this crucial reliance on and respect for the reader who is able imaginatively to face and judge disintegrating experience.

Conrad describes this most central imaginative capacity for a rich and enduring awareness in an essay on Henry James.

> When the last aqueduct shall have crumbled to pieces, the last airship fallen to the ground, the last blade of grass have dried upon a dying earth, man, indomitable by his training in resistance to misery and pain, shall set this undiminished light of his eyes against the feeble glow of the sun.

Surviving the projected destruction of life and human culture is, then, the ability to see, to illuminate with the "light" of the imagination. This passage is quoted by Robert Penn Warren in his brilliant effort to define Conrad's affirmation, in an essay which became the preface to the Modern Library edition of *Nostromo*. When he tries there to locate precisely what values Conrad affirms, Warren—in an ambiguous and sympathetic manner characteristic indeed of Conrad himself—tends to narrow and obscure his profoundly sensitive insight into the fictive vision, into man's precarious balance there between the inward and outward abysses of the self and of malevolent nature. The narrowing of focus occurs particularly when he uses the notion of "the undiminished light" in human eyes to support his view that Conrad would honor a purged idealism which sustains the precarious human balance. Conrad does not finally let us take comfort from such values which, like poignant dreams, are offered at moments by his characters—the values of the 'revolutionary' yet classic liberalism in Natalie Haldin's remarks about love in *Under Western Eyes*, or Mrs. Gould's purged and sympathetic idealism in *Nostromo*, or even the knowledge of evil offered by "the gaunt Buddha-like" Marlow. These are in different ways too illusory or insecure to help us face the destructive indifference which in the novels takes on the symbolic forms of sea or jungle and the social guises of tyranny, revolution, materialism, or "progress." Only the deeply seeing eyes of our human imagination are able fully to face destructive reality, to observe the momentary triumphs, and to secure the lasting triumph of human awareness.

When we look to Conrad for a vindication of ideals which are regenerative and progressive, and when we emphasize the rage against disintegration in statements like that from the essay on James, we must not overlook the darkening shadow which Conrad's sense of last things "upon a dying earth" as well as the novels themselves cast over the affirmation. Conrad's idea of imaginative perception is, in actuality, quite desperate and pessimistic. The value of perception is illusive and in part self-defeating. To observe with understanding—deeply to see—is a final imaginative act and the only human affirmation left to the man who witnesses the disintegration of the social and moral order of his world. The reader of Conrad must look with an undiminished gaze on that profoundly difficult and dark vision of the world, using his capacity purely and deeply to see, a naked and most enduring form of imagination. It is in this sense that we can speak of Conrad's morality not of fidelity or of idealism, but a morality of the imagination.

Later in his essay on James, Conrad develops and deepens his vision of the writer's and his reader's imaginative engagement. He suggests that the value of fiction, in an apocalyptic time, depends on the difficult-to-achieve "heroism of the hearers"; his image of the need for moral heroism in a final human encounter with fiction reveals the extremity not of James's as much as of Conrad's own perspective. His vision expresses both a tortuously achieved perception of the ethos of his time, and his awareness that the modern novel severely challenges the reader. In his concluding remarks on James, Conrad defines a central aspect of that challenge to the reader, as the "rejection" of the "finality," which readers may seek in the novelist's vision; the writer must refuse to acknowledge an ending to the temporal flux in the novel's closing pages, or to violate "the sense of . . . life still going on" there. The reader is, in this way, challenged finally to take up the role of interpreter discerning an on-going human meaning even in the face of apocalypse; and it is this role which requires at least a form of the moral heroism Conrad describes—from the reader engaging an intentionally open-ended and ambiguous fiction which is like life in assaulting his sensibility and expectations.

To Conrad, the modern novel is a vital product of the imagination only when it is engaged and enlivened by the reader's response, and the novelist's descriptions of his own encounters with particular readers are crucial and meaningful illuminations of his notion of fiction's value; the encounters enact the elemental drama and morality of Conrad's vision. In *A Personal Record*, he presents the story of his first reader, a dying consumptive who reads the incomplete manuscript of *Almayer's Folly* while on board a ship Conrad helped to command. His response to Conrad is to acknowledge, with a severe nod of the head, that he has been deeply stirred by the work. That first reader meets the imagined life of Conrad's first novel and, almost immediately, his own death with expressive and stoic reticence; indeed, the author's oblique and suggestive "interpretation" of life is there met by the, if possible, more oblique and suggestive response of a heroically enduring sensibility. This first reader, Conrad writes, helped him to believe in the worth of his work by affirming his "conviction" in the existence of another human being's imagination: "What is a novel if not that conviction . . . strong enough to take upon itself a form of imagined life?" Here and in many other places, Conrad affirms what is finally his respectful and reliant trust to the reader's creative participation in achieving the meaning of his work. The novelist, in looking for a recipient of his vision, for a reader, searches finally for the hero of his vision who can carry on the struggle for human awareness in an ever-darkening world.

II

At the center of vision, then, Conrad locates a profound and desperate opposition between disintegration and the creative engagement stirred to life in his reader. The narrative voice is one of Conrad's primary means of challenging the reader to understand and affirm the value of such an engagement, of imaginative perception. The confrontation between imagination and disintegrating reality is, in part, expressed by the tension in the voice of the Conradian narrator who views the collapsing world yet affirms his survival as an observer. A suggestive image of the narrator's role is that of Marlow in *Heart of Darkness*, seated "in the pose of a meditating Buddha," who—in telling his tale—grapples with the impressions and significances of his journey into the Congo to meet Kurtz, the dark extension of his own psyche. The narrating voice of Marlow on board ship is pitted against the darkness which engulfs it. Occupying that darkness are his own voice, the framing shipboard narrator's, Kurtz's, and many other subsidiary voices in the night, over the water of the Thames, and from each benighted human settlement. And in Conrad's work, the malevolent and neutralizing expanse of darkness is also made to include the reader's world. The structure of suggestive and insinuating voices confronts the perceiver, forcing him to absorb its assault on his consciousness.

I want later to discuss *Heart of Darkness* in more detail, but here let me briefly explore the significance of Marlow's narration as he penetrated deep into the Congo. He seeks of course to hear the reassuring voice of the gifted and 'liberal' imperialist Kurtz who seems to possess

> "the gift of expression, the bewildering, the illuminating, the most exalted and the most contemptible, the pulsating stream of light, or the deceitful flow from the heart of an impenetrable darkness."

Marlow's grasping bitterness here increases in the face of the failure of Kurtz's voice and spirit, grown mad and corrupt in his inner-most settlement; and Marlow's own voice becomes increasingly more strident, at times fragmenting under its weight of desperation.

> "And I heard—him—it—this voice—other voices—all of them were so little more than voices—and the memory of that time itself lingers around me, impalpable, like a dying vibration of one immense jabber, silly, atrocious, sordid, savage, or simply mean, without any kind of sense. Voices, voices—even the girl herself—now. . . ."
>
> He was silent for a long time.

The voices Marlow perceives and that he projects form here, and throughout the work, an assaulting structure; indeed, his voice is driven repeatedly towards silence by the pain of uttering and sustaining its disharmonies. As he describes the failure of Kurtz's voice, the despair and anxiety distorting his narration are ambiguous. The suggestive disintegration of the prose here points to Marlow's own self-doubt. Its outreaching ambiguity poses the question whether communication is possible or valuable in the face of Marlow's disastrous insights, and that question implicates the reader with his threatened reliance on Marlow's self-doubting perception and judgment. So the pattern of ambiguity reaches out to involve and implicate the reader.

Conrad places narrators like Marlow between the reader and the agonized inhabitants of each novel's vision, and at their best these narrators begin to have the qualities of maturity, truthfulness, and controlled irony that would make them the bearers of Conrad's ethic of the imagination. Yet, as with Marlow, his narrators' observing role becomes a severe test of their capacity to sustain both perception itself, and their own identities. As the disintegration they observe menaces their role and identity, their responses are strategically less than Conrad's aesthetic demands. We find his narrators sometimes desperately half-rejecting their vision in favor of simple pieties or simpler truths as Marlow at times does, or they cynically condescend to their vision as do the narrators of *The Secret Agent* and, at times, *Under Western Eyes*. The narrative voice in Conrad is meant only provisionally to take up the role and imaginative responsibility which he finally gives to the reader. The disintegrating ambiguity in their voices challenges the reader to engage the author's test of the power of man's imagination to endure the assaults of experience.

Conrad allows his fictions to fall short of the poised and ironic balances achieved by his partly Flaubertian contemporaries, Henry James and later Joyce. That Conrad desperately risks a sort of failure in fiction is suggested by the strained evasiveness of his narrations; and the remarkable, intended effect of the desperation in Conrad's narrative art is to give the reader a profound responsibility, the obligation to bring to the narrative the imaginative insight and judgment approached but strategically not achieved by the narration. This strategy is, in fact, the key to the great richness and redemptive power of his novels. The moral and emotional center of his art is, finally, located neither in a single character's disastrous fate nor in the disintegration which besets him. And that center is not in the author's or a narrator's untrembling voice. Meaning in Conrad is dependent on the survival and, as important, the courage and depth of the reader's creative response; it is a function of the perception and judgment Conrad's best novels require and form in the reader. The reader strategically becomes the meaning of Conrad's finest novels; it is Conrad's desperate and powerful use of this strategy which links him to other writers of radically out-reaching narrative, Emily Brontë for example and D. H. Lawrence.

III

In the Preface to *The Nigger of the "Narcissus,"* Conrad directly addresses the question of how he would confront the reader with the intellectual, emotional, and moral challenge of his fiction. He would attempt to achieve a magic, symbolist "suggestiveness" in fiction, and that ambiguous suggestiveness in narration, symbolic image, and time scheme challenges his reader to discover self-implicating possibilities for meaning in his own responses to the flux of impressions, the husk of suggestive ambiguities in Conrad's best fiction. The novelist's aim here is "above all to make you see," to offer "that glimpse of truth for which you have forgotten to ask" and which one suffers in the shock of self-recognition. His task is exactingly to evoke the "movement" of a moment of experience, "its form, its colour, and so to reveal the substance of its truth—to disclose its inspiring secret." The ideas of the French symbolists, of Schopenhauer and Nietzsche, and of English writers like Walter Pater are shaping influences on Conrad's conception here, and his Preface stands at the climax of a tradition which saw art as the revelation of the "secret history" of man's driven experience. The moment of experience which Conrad's art would penetrate and reveal is, indeed, treacherous: time is "remorseless," fate "uncertain," and origins "mysterious." Yet the aim of Conrad's fiction is not to present merely a pessimistic vision of life which the reader then passively comprehends; his aim is actively to awaken the reader to the discovery of the meaning menacingly obscured by human experience yet vitally rooted in it. The novelist would "attain to such clearness of sincerity that at last the presented vision . . . shall awaken in [the reader] that feeling of unavoidable solidarity . . . which binds men to each other and all mankind to the external world."

Conrad's fiction calls upon the reader to take up the responsibility for moral exploration and judgment that arises from the experience of reading such work; the narratives are by design lifelike, both in assaulting the reader's temperament and expectations, and in offering him an opportunity to explore and affirm his own capacity for human awareness. The sort of moral heroism Conrad hopes fiction can draw from the reader is summoned up in him by the novel which stirs to life his capacity to face and judge a world where traditional human order seems to fall apart. Conrad's art compels the reader to place his own capacity for self-examination at the center of his imaginative experience. In *Nostromo*, for example, the narrative's complexity projects the shattering tension between human aspiration and reality with its subverting impact on Decoud, Mrs. Gould, and each provisional narrative center of perception; the value and meaning of the novel depend finally on the insight, the independent judgment, and the heightened imaginative and moral rigor of the response which the assaulting flux of such form draws from the reader. In the following pages, I explore the ways in which *Nostromo* and *Heart of Darkness*, two of Conrad's finest novels, challenge the reader to find meaning and transcendence in his own investment of creative energy. In the visions these two novels offer, the survival of the human spirit depends on the awakened imagination of the reader, on his acceptance of a crucial and difficult place at the center of the form of the novels. Conrad's strategy is that the fiction's meaning becomes the engagement and revelation of the reader's own sense of human possibility, and that strategy underlies the aim and value of his finest works.

IV

Nostromo is Conrad's attempt to present the morality of his vision on the largest scale. Particularly the first three hundred pages of the novel involve

the reader in the difficult and challenging task of penetrating and comprehending an entire society, not only the symbolic fate of one character. In the
first half of the novel, the impressionistic dislocation in the presentation of
scene, character, and time makes the reading experience the fictional equivalent
of how the mind actually works in achieving a growing yet fragmentary awareness of reality and the self. The reader's experience is, finally, a test and
affirmation of his imaginative capacity to survive and richly to confront the
nature of reality. As we move back and forth between our encounters with
the Goulds, Nostromo, Viola, Decoud, Antonia, Dr. Monygham, and so on,
the pattern of fictional illumination is uneven and complex. The profound
reason why the form of the rendered history of Sulaco is not consecutive and
'logical' is that the reality of man's history for Conrad is a destructive darkness
difficult to penetrate.

The reader's penetration, as it is shaped by the first half of the narration,
lays bare exactly the failure of Sulacans to perceive and endure what we learn
history to be: that is, the conflict—destructive to man—between human illusion (embodied by Gould's idealization of his silver) and the reality of human
experience, its shattering indifference to human aspiration. This conflict results in the destroyed or disintegrated lives of Gould himself, his wife, Nostromo, Decoud, and the others. Gould, obsessed and mistaken, idealizes a
physical presence, his mountain of silver, as a constructive force giving Sulaco
progressive order and power. And the silver reveals itself to have an opposite
power; it embodies the destructive indifference of external reality, finally of
materialism and Gould's imperialistic venture, to the human community. In
the end, the destructive domination of the silver, a central and most powerful
image in the novel, extends over all passion, politics, history, and morality.
In the face of the early images of complex malevolence, the freely shifting
narration here implicitly relies on the reader to discern and affirm the necessity
of his own, independent judgment of the silver's triumph.

In the second half of the novel, we see a momentary and ironic triumph
of silver-based, progressive politics in bringing a new, "orderly" regime to the
secessionist Occidental Republic. The reality of this triumph is hollow and
destructive. To present the victory, Conrad relies on the limited and rigid
narrative consciousness of active characters; this creates an ironic and simplified atmosphere that diminishes the challenging imaginative intensity and
complexity of the narrative. Also, it emphasizes the hollowness of the apparent
triumph of the politics of silver. In this latter half, not only have the material
interests of the silver fed and then disintegrated the idealism particularly of
the Goulds, the cynical commitment of Decoud, and the vanity of Nostromo
(so vital to the progress of the "interests" that corrupt him). Not only have

they uprooted and alienated the human sympathies of Mrs. Gould, who perceives how the ideal of material interests possesses and destroys her husband and her community. The triumph of the silver is hollow and destructive in the end because—though it underlies all human order in Sulaco—it exists only for itself. As an image, the silver joins the menacing and inhuman abstractions of the Golfo Placido and Mount Azuera.

The responsibility for the imaginative center of consciousness falls to several narrators in *Nostromo*. Except implicitly with the impressionistic and assaulting narration in the first several hundred pages, no narrator fully understands and accepts that responsibility. Indeed, the reader's task is to see how each character is differently unaware of the full meaning and potential power of the imagination. The narration of this anarchic and often ironic history enables the reader alone to develop a full awareness of both the failure of human order and the capacity for imaginative choice. Such is the work's crucial strategy, and it enables the reader to achieve the imaginative response which the work's fragmented form itself stirs in him.

Decoud is a central character here, who narrates some of the events of the Monterist revolution in a letter to his sister in Paris. Though Decoud is more realistic than, for instance, Kurtz or Lord Jim, he, too, fails fully to take up the deeper obligations of the imagination. A sometimes frivolous skeptic, he perceives the fragility and corruption of all political order in Costaguana and the fanatic idealism of Charles Gould's commitment to his San Tomé Silver Mine. In spite of his skepticism, however, he acts; he acts from passion for Antonia Avellanos, the politically committed daughter of a dying progressive leader. First, he formulates a "progressive" plan for the secession of Sulaco with its mine from the Monterist dictatorship, and then he steals away with a silver shipment in order to secure bargaining power for the "liberal" Gould.

In his study of Conrad, Albert Guerard sees two Decouds here, one cynical and the other committed. The two, however, become one if we consider the nature of his view of life. Decoud is skeptical of all ideals and motives; although at times frivolous, he has an acute insight into how constructive aims can become destructive. At key points, however, he immaturely exempts himself, for he believes that he acts without illusions; such is his illusion. His cynical pose blinds him to his own idealism in serving his love; that pose dangerously obscures the fact that such a commitment is finally a consciously chosen fiction of redeeming power. When all human order disappears into the impenetrable and indifferent mists of the Golfo Placido, the defiance of illusion which was fueled by his passionate ideal is weakened, and Decoud commits suicide. To drown himself, he uses the silver which he is keeping from Montero's hands, and which symbolizes the indifference of material reality to life. In the face of Decoud's partly tragic failure of perception, the reader more than ever becomes the only enduring bearer here of the full responsibility for imaginative perception.

Mrs. Gould's consciousness also dominates the narrative at important points, and she, too, is unable to take imaginative hold of her reality. For her, the world fostered by her husband's idealism becomes an unconquerable nightmare. In spite of her sensitive involvement with the lives around her, her vision reduces her to passivity, a woman half asleep, having a nightmare:

> She saw the San Tomé mountain hanging over the Campo, over the whole land, feared, hated, wealthy, more soulless than any tyrant, more pitiless and autocratic than the worst government ready to crush innumerable lives in the expansion of greatness. He [Gould] did not see it. It was not his fault. He was perfect, perfect; but she would never have him to herself. . . . An immense desolation, the dread of her own continued life, descended upon the first lady of Sulaco. With a prophetic vision she saw herself surviving alone the degradation of her young ideal life, of love, of work—all alone in the Treasure House of the World. The profound blind, suffering expression of a painful dream settled on her face with its closed eyes. In the indistinct voice of an unlucky sleeper, lying passive in the toils of a merciless nightmare, she stammered out aimlessly the words:
> "Material interests."

In contrast to Mrs. Gould, Dr. Monygham's vision and his perception of the dark symbol of the silver form an integral part of his consciousness. He can state Mrs. Gould's paralyzing insight in impersonal terms:

> "The time approaches when all that the Gould concession stands for shall weigh as heavily upon the people as the barbarism, cruelty, and misrule of a few years back."

Conrad places the Doctor's consciousness at the narrative center of much of the less complex and imaginatively dense last part of the novel. Dr. Monygham's deepest commitment is not fully to the effort to form an imaginative, self-revealing meaning from the fragments of his world. He does have a deeper awareness of himself than, say, Decoud; unlike the latter, he extends his pessimism to himself. This self-awareness is the result of an experience with the barbarous tyrant Guzman Bento, an experience that destroyed his expectations of his own character and identity. In this way, he is like a deeper Jim, whose experience did not kill him and who thus has gained knowledge of himself and reality. Yet his commitment to such knowledge is secondary in him to his love for Mrs. Gould. Skeptical but without—in Conrad's strategic sense—an active and ennobling imagination, at the least he is ennobled, in part unwittingly, by that love. For example, he involves himself in a revolutionary intrigue for the sake of his love, though he perceives that Sotillo, and through him the force of the silver, will very likely kill him. The part of the book which Monygham dominates, therefore, has a quality of melodrama and of ironic lack of perception which heightens its overt suspense but lessens its imaginative intensity; the same effect is felt through most of the novel's second half, for instance in the sections involving Nostromo alone. An example of this effect is the final incident of the novel which takes place before Monygham's imperceptive eyes. He is unaware of the silver's corruption of Nostromo as well; from his imperfect grasp of events issues an irony which undercuts his response to Linda's dramatic cry and his belief in Nostromo's apparent triumph there. Only the silver is actually triumphant as her cry "seemed to ring aloud from Punta Mala to Azuera and away to the bright line of the horizon, overhung by a big white cloud shining like a mass of solid silver."

In the second half of the novel, Conrad also uses the—for us—ironic commentary of Capt. Mitchell to narrate the "historical" events of the counterrevolution and of the prosperity of the Occidental Republic. Though the Captain is an enjoyably ironic and informative character, this use of him is shallow; for he unconsciously capitulates to the symbolic force of the silver, to the politics of material interests. Our difficultly achieved awareness of the darkness shadowing history clashes particularly with Mitchell's pompous and jolly piety. The ironic use of the Captain and, more subtly, of Dr. Monygham expresses the growing and sometimes insurmountable difficulty of the author's imaginative hold of his dark vision.

In his finest work, Conrad's dark insights and deepest affirmation are released only by means of the imaginative penetration demanded of the reader by the author's self-fragmenting form—by his difficult and complex projection of his vision. In *Nostromo*, the lighter irony and greater simplicity of the second half draw what power they have from the difficult vision of the first half, and cannot undercut its brilliant and demanding intensity. In that first part, as in *Heart of Darkness*, Conrad enables the reader to confront and imaginatively to dominate a dark and subversive vision of the anarchic malevolence innate to man's experience—and, in so doing, to affirm in himself the endurance and the power of the imagination.

V

Let me turn again to *Heart of Darkness*, and more fully and closely identify the strategy and morality of Conrad's imagination in it. Here, in a work written at the turn of the century and four years before *Nostromo*, the order—the controlling illusion—of civilization seems to disintegrate, leaving the reader with a vision of anarchic darkness in the mind of the central 'anti-hero' Kurtz and menacing, as we saw, the mind of the central narrator, Marlow. The journey Marlow takes, of course, echoes in part Conrad's own Congo trip, his physically and spiritually exhausting final command; and in his subsequent writing career, Conrad was obsessed by the vision of darkness embodied in Marlow's journey. The two central consciousnesses the reader encounters in the work are not made merely nihilistic by their experience of the Congo darkness. On the contrary, to consider Kurtz before we focus again on Marlow, he meets his final destruction as a sort of idealist.

Kurtz entered the Congo service with the "highest" ideals and brilliant qualifications. He is motivated by a sense of pontifical superiority to the 'savage' nature of Africa and Africans. Experiencing the seemingly absolute indifference of the African social and physical 'darkness,' Kurtz's will knows no bounds; and it grows monstrous on its abstract fare of Western imperialistic ideals. A man of destructive illusions, he is without any realistic perception of human decencies or of the human condition before him. Of African natives, he thus can write "exterminate the brutes"; he has himself been worshipped in a moral obscenity as a savage god; and he attempts to act like one. Kurtz's experience is a symbolic revelation of the passionate destructiveness beneath the surface of Western ideals (to which he is committed), and his revelation of evil is designed to implicate the reader and indeed civilization itself. Conrad does not directly present the heart of darkness within Kurtz; he suggests and symbolizes its anarchic existence by means of its effect on Marlow. Yet Kurtz does at one point directly and profoundly speak out to involve us; that is when he himself becomes conscious of the meaning of his experience. Kurtz's pontifical voice is hollow and without self-awareness except for the single self-condemning insight of his final utterance: "the horror, the horror." This is as far as Conrad takes us into the particular center of Kurtz's experience.

Kurtz's fate reveals the destructive reality beneath the apparent order in human experience. In contrast, Marlow's narration reveals the vulnerability of a man's personal and communal identity to that inner reality. Marlow is a thoughtful man, sensitive to both the good and the evil in his and other men's acts, a truthful observer, a dedicated mariner. It is through his eyes that the reader encounters Kurtz, through Marlow's narrative of his journey up the Congo to contact Kurtz on behalf of their imperialist employer. From the start, the reader is struck by the honesty, maturity, and imaginative sensitivity of Marlow's observations. Blinded by neither pettiness nor idealism he perceives the reality of the human condition before him—whether it be the "insanity" of the anchored French man-of-war shooting into the African continent, the dying African slaves in the grove of death, the human restraint of his hungry cannibal crew, or the unrestrained meanness of the European pilgrims in the Congo.

The values of duty and decency which are sometimes said to sustain Marlow would be shallow and vulnerable if they were not the outgrowth of his maturity and truthfulness of *perception*. When, for example, his decency compels him to tell Kurtz's beloved a merciful "white lie," it is not out of habitual morality; it is because the "altogether too dark" spectre of Kurtz and his final whisper possess and mortify his imagination. Marlow's painful and incisive perception is that this illusion-bound woman could not understand or accommodate the knowledge of Kurtz's last words that he, Marlow, labors under and endures. Marlow's mature decency is based finally on the quality of his imagination which, in a desperate paradox, is also the basis of his final awareness of the darkness at the heart of human experience.

As he nears Kurtz's station in the novel, the moral depth and emotional maturity of Marlow's identity as an observer are severely tested. On first hearing of Kurtz's idealistic and authoritative voice, Marlow identifies with him; and as he penetrates deeper into the darkness of the Congo, he sustains his sense of himself in part by means of that sympathetic identification. When he gains his final knowledge of Kurtz's actual corruption, Marlow says: "it is his extremity I seemed to have lived through," an extremity revealing a negation at the heart of human ideals and the human voice itself—that is to say, communication itself.

Marlow's attempt to communicate this self-challenging, indeed self-disintegrating insight is the crucial source of the work's assaulting power. As he emphasized the affirmative value of Kurtz's sole *voicing* of the nature of his situation, Marlow is actually suggesting the embattled power of his own most significant qualities, the perceptive sympathy and severe honesty of his narration. Without those qualities, his story would be the simple and insignificant one of the single-minded fortitude of a mariner on a dangerous mission. At times, the tone of the narrative does, in fact, seem to mix the desperately rigid piety of his appeal to simple values ("faithfulness" and "devotion to work") with his obsessive anxiety about the ominous nature of his experience. Both the piety and the anxiety are, however, defenses against the inner heart of darkness, his own, Kurtz's, and mankind's. The process of self-defense in him accompanies that of self-discovery.

Both processes are clear in the following quotation; Marlow here seeks terms which can voice his self-challenging perception of Kurtz.

> "Since I had peeped over the edge myself, I understand better the meaning of his stare, that could not see the flame of the candle, but was wide enough to embrace the whole universe, piercing enough to penetrate all the hearts that beat in the darkness. He had summed up—he had judged. 'The horror.' . . . [This cry] was an affirmation, a moral victory paid for by innumerable defeats, by abominable terrors, by abominable satisfactions."

Here the reader encounters a flux of ambiguity unlike any found in earlier novelists. The ambiguities of metaphor and tone are not fluidly, masterfully ironic, but desperately grasping and evasive. Marlow comprehends a stare "piercing enough to penetrate" to the heart of a darkness which is "evanescing," "mysterious," and "impenetrable." The anxiously ambiguous and evasive prose attempts to convey the dimensions of the menace and to heighten the sense of the risk and moral value of perception and judgment. Conrad's reader is placed in a position to observe both processes of self-defense and discovery at work in the narrative. That position is similar to, but far more strategic and self-conscious than, the symbolic position of the listener-narrator of the novel's frame. In essence, Conrad is placing us in a position to carry and affirm Marlow's imaginative viewpoint beyond the limits of his expression of it.

A key effect achieved here is that the reader himself is never made to perceive the central "horror" but only the husk of ambiguities surrounding and suggesting it, a husk of implication which the novel's framing narrator says characterizes Marlow's tales generally. That characteristic effect is the most significant feature of the novel itself; for not the particular horror in Kurtz but, instead, the act of penetrating and exploring a potential darkness in the self is the novel's subject and its informing symbol. Marlow's narrative offers the reader not a particular discovery but the form itself of discovery, the means which enable and indeed challenge him—with and beyond Marlow—to explore the abyss of the self. That form of discovery with the reader's imaginative penetration at its center makes *Heart of Darkness* a seminal and most forceful achievement in modern fiction.

The image of Marlow's journey of discovery is, then, a crucial and revealing one for the role of the reader himself who in imagination penetrates to the "heart of darkness," who comprehends both the achievement of Mar-

low's penetration and its limits, his defensive piety and obscurity. A refinement and extension of Marlow's role, the reader's final responsibility is to see
the subversive and malevolent reality underlying both man's nature and his
experience, to oppose to this his own consciousness, his capacity deeply to
penetrate an ambiguous and menacing vision of experience, and so to affirm
with Conrad the enduring power of that rich and courageous form of imagination. This reliance of the author on the reader to see beyond the negations
of *Heart of Darkness* expresses the desperation of his view of life and art; the
final effect of this desperation is to place the reader in the position of the
novel's ultimate hero.

VI

Of the novels Conrad wrote before and after the publication of *Nostromo*
in 1904, *Heart of Darkness* is his finest. *Lord Jim*, also an earlier work, is a
compelling but imperfect extension of the patterns set in *Heart of Darkness*; its
vision of evil is less far-reaching, its complex use of narrators, including Marlow, less sharply revealing and significant, yet the essential basis of Conrad's
aesthetic and ethic, his crucial reliance on the reader, does remain. The later
novels, like *The Secret Agent* and *Under Western Eyes*, reveal a partial decline in
his imaginative hold of his dark vision. What is meant by such a decline in
these two fine novels? In his greatest works, *Nostromo* and *Heart of Darkness*,
Conrad seems to be obsessed by elemental threats to man's attempt to order
reality and to secure his human identity, threats arising from the very nature
of man and of external reality. And, finally, Conrad's only faith is in the order
that the imagination of author and reader together can give reality. No single
character is made fully to embody a commitment to their crucial use of the
imagination; even Marlow, his finest character, does not have a controlled and
secure vision. Conrad's affirmation of the imagination is intentionally atten-
uated and desperate, expressed only through the experience of fiction itself:
only the reader of the novels can achieve a rich and affirming awareness. In
the best of the later novels, however, Conrad withdraws in two directions
from the desperate affirmation and difficult vision of the earlier works. First,
he creates an ironic distance, contrived rather than revealing, between the
anarchy at the center of vision and the reader. Second, he affirms the value of
sentiment in place of the imagination.

The withdrawal into cynicism or sentimentality is the result of a confusion in Conrad's work between two attitudes toward the darkness at the
heart of experience. The attitude I have explored is, in a sense, aesthetic: only
the imagination can effectively oppose the revealed darkness. The imagination,

as the reader is made actively to use it, is man's highest, richest, most purely human quality. The other attitude is, simply put, conservative: only the orderly and humane continuity of social and moral processes can oppose the darkness in reality. Disorder and excess are contemptible. This view is related to the English character of Conrad's repatriation. In his earlier works, the vision of darkness was placed in the focus of the imagination partly because Conrad's own human identity was sustained through such perception, not only by his commitment to the code of the English seaman. However, as his identity as an Englishman became more fixed and narrowed his perceptions, he relied on that conservative and relatively moralistic identification to sustain his vision; paradoxically, as a result he was secure enough to examine explicitly now in later works the "dark" side of his new and his original homelands, of English and Eastern European life—that is, in *The Secret Agent* and *Under Western Eyes*. As the power of Conrad's imagination to dominate his vision declined, the conservative attitude in desperate reaction began to take precedence.

In *Under Western Eyes*, for example, Conrad's imaginative resistance is both a withdrawal into cynicism and a movement towards a form of sentimentality. The novel unites qualities found in two other of his finest later works, the satiric brilliance—the black comedy—of *The Secret Agent*, and the carefully formed triumph of sentiment over skepticism in *Victory*. Conrad's achievement in the novel of Russia is for the last time to create a vision which offers the reader the truth not alone of the cynical mind or of the conservative heart but of the penetrating imagination. This he does in spite of the obtuse and conservative attitude on the part of the narrator-language teacher. Yet, by putting into the narrator's voice all the bitterness and sentimentality of imaginative withdrawal, Conrad effectively reveals the limitations of such withdrawal while at the same time he suggests his increasing reliance on it. The content of the novel remains, however, a dark and mysterious vision of the anarchy and evil in man. Though Razumov is in part shallow like Lord Jim and then sentimental in his desperate love for Nathalie Haldin, still the novel presents in flawed form the morality of imaginative perception toward which Razumov tragically strives.

After *Heart of Darkness* and *Nostromo*, Conrad increasingly withdraws from the difficult task of embodying the morality of his imagination. Despite the fine craftsmanship and power of *Under Western Eyes*, the novel contains only a glimpse of the profound and complex vision which—in the brilliant, powerful strategy of the earlier novels—challenges the reader to perceive the menacing darkness at the heart of man's nature and experience, and to affirm the ethical value not of cynical or sentimental reaction but of the reader's own imaginative penetration, his rich and courageous awareness, as Conrad conceives of and relies on it. The morality of Conrad's finest vision is based on the power of the reader's imagination to explore and to sustain the self—man's consciousness and humanity—in the face of the malevolent nature of reality.

ADAM GILLON

Under Western Eyes, Chance, *and* Victory

Under Western Eyes (1911) is a political novel dealing primarily with betrayal, but it is a very different book . . . [from *The Secret Agent*]. Here are a few of the main points of difference. First, though the subject of Russian politics appears in *The Secret Agent* with the satirical portrayal of Mr. Vladimir and the other members of the Embassy, it is only in this novel that we have Conrad's truly "Russian" story. Second, it is, in Albert Guerard's words, "a great tragic novel," and *The Secret Agent* is essentially a comic one. Third, the latter is told from the omniscient point of view, while the former employs the detached, Marlovian teacher of foreign languages as the narrator. Well, perhaps not quite Marlovian, except in the most general sense; the Marlows of *Lord Jim*, "Youth," and *Heart of Darkness* are all active men of the sea, concerned with a quest for self-knowledge in their respective commitment to Jim, a younger romantic self and Kurtz, a commitment largely dictated by a fondness. The language teacher, on the other hand, does not pursue any occupation. His own life is uneventful and dull, his outlook on life that of a conventional Englishman of a liberal political persuasion who rather dislikes and resents Razumov, whom he professes not to understand. Fourth, the nature of betrayal and punishment therefore is different in each of the novels. Though Verloc and Winnie both die and Comrade Ossipon suffers a delayed shock at his betrayal of Winnie, there is no real moral conflict in them or in any other characters, and no real questioning of one's own conscience. In

From *Joseph Conrad*. © 1982 by Twayne Publishers, a division of G. K. Hall & Co. Originally entitled "The Desperate Shape of Betrayal: An Intimate Alliance of Contradictions" and "How to Love."

Under Western Eyes, however, Conrad returns to his early interest in the "destructive element" of a man's moral sensibility which, as . . . in Jim's case, may also be his redemption from guilt.

Once again Conrad has selected a young man to be his hero; he is Kirylo Sidorovitch Razumov, a student at the University of St. Petersburg, and the illegitimate son of Prince K———. Like Jim, Razumov is put through an unexpected test which will reveal his character and his moral nature. One day Victor Haldin, a revolutionist who has just killed a hated Minister of State, comes to his room, seeking shelter and assistance. Razumov's dilemma cannot really be solved satisfactorily. He does not sympathize with the revolution and is preoccupied with the writing of a prize essay in order to gain a silver medal. Haldin has been merely a casual acquaintance who mistakenly assumes that Razumov shares his views and will offer him full support. Razumov, it is reiterated a number of times, inspires confidence in people. Having locked Haldin in his room, Razumov goes to the peasant Ziemianitch to make arrangements for Haldin's escape; he finds him in a drunken stupor and beats him mercilessly. Then, walking the streets, he is beset by doubts. He is overwhelmed by a sense of helplessness: "I am being crushed—and I can't even run away. . . . He had nothing. He had not even a moral refuge—the refuge of confidence. To whom could he go with this tale—in all this great, great land?"

Razumov takes his tale to Prince K———, who does not quite acknowledge him as a son yet indicates a measure of recognition by secretly pressing his hand. The Prince's carriage brings them to the house of General T———, where Razumov again tells his story without, however, mentioning his visit to Ziemianitch. While he is being praised for the moral soundness of his action, Razumov begins to feel great revulsion for the General. Now that he has betrayed Haldin, he begins to identify with him, to imagine him lying in his room, waiting to be arrested. He returns to his room and after a lengthy discussion leaves Haldin alone once more. He then waits for the clock to strike twelve, his mind hovering "on the borders of delirium. He heard himself suddenly saying, 'I confess,' as a person might do on the rack. 'I am on the rack,' he thought . . ."

Haldin is tortured and hanged. Razumov is sent to Geneva to spy on Russian revolutionaries there. He falls in love with Nathalie Haldin, Victor's sister who is living in exile with her mother. She believes Razumov to be a fellow revolutionary who worked with Victor. Like Jim, Razumov must be the agent of his own humiliation. He confesses the whole truth to Miss Haldin and later on to a group of the revolutionists. Nikita Necator, a fellow revolutionary but also a double agent for the Russian police, punishes him in a symbolic fashion: he shatters Razumov's eardrums, plunging him to a world of silence for the rest of his life. Later on, Razumov is run over by a tramcar. He must live out his days in Russia, nursed by Tekla, a humble woman who has served Peter Ivanovitch, the self-styled feminist revolutionary. When Nathalie's mother dies, she too goes back to Russia to live in obscurity as a charitable helper of the poor and the convicts.

Initially, Conrad began the novel as a story called *Razumov,* as he had started the first draft of *The Secret Agent* under the title *Verloc.* In a letter to John Galsworthy in 1908, the author promised to render "the very soul of things Russian." In the first version Razumov marries Haldin's sister and only after their child begins to look like the betrayed revolutionist does Razumov reveal the truth to his wife. Conrad puts the emphasis on the psychological problem of the young man rather than on the political theme. The finished product, however, is a remarkable novel about Russia, remarkable because of Conrad's anti-Russian sentiments.

As one could surmise from the caricatural treatment of the Russians in *The Secret Agent,* Conrad regarded them as basically inscrutable and cynical or corrupt people, savoring of Slavo-Tartar Byzantine barbarism, incapable of any form of government except despotism. Conrad's Russophobia, however, has not prevented him from creating an essentially sympathetic hero, though there are satirical and caricatural presentations as well. The successful depiction of Russians in this novel is achieved despite Conrad's often professed ignorance of Russia (like that of the teacher-narrator) and his reluctance to deal with them.

That is why it is worthwhile to examine the correspondence between *Under Western Eyes* and *Crime and Punishment.* Dostoevsky's student-killer is Raskolnikov (*rasskol* means split, dissent), whose best friend and alter ego is Razumikhin (*razum* means reason, intelligence). Razumov and Raskolnikov are both fatherless students who consider themselves superior to ordinary mortals. Having committed a major transgression, they attempt to analyze it and then to explain it away. Each will be surprised at the discovery that he has a conventional conscience; each will suffer terrible pangs of remorse; each will go through a period of hallucination, dreamlike sequences, and masochistic self-torment; each will engage in a psychological duel with a fatherlike superior, representing the authorities; each will demonstrate the necessity for a moral purification to be obtained only by means of a public confession; each must remain totally alone and isolated; each ultimately finds his redemption through a young woman's sympathy, faith, and devotion. In both novels, there is a mother and daughter; both mothers go mad. Razumov's encounters with Councillor Mikulin and General T—— parallel the meetings of Porfiry with

Raskolnikov; in each case, the older interviewers are father figures. The faithful Tekla of Conrad reminds us of the humble Sonia; both, moreover, serve as doubles to the men under their care. Nathalie recalls Dunya. Sophia Antonovna shares her first name with Sonia, a diminutive of Sophia. The latter, though a prostitute and not, like Sophia Antonovna, a revolutionary reformer, is actually the principal reformer of the young sinner.

A startling similarity lies in the conclusion reached by the two student-transgressors. Raskolnikov asks, "Was it the old hag I killed? No, I killed *myself* and not the old hag." [All italics are mine unless otherwise indicated.] Razumov, too, identifies with his victim: "It's *myself* whom I have given up to destruction . . ." "In giving Victor Haldin up, it was *myself*, after all, whom I have betrayed most basely." There are other similarities, such as the doubling of characters, the accusation of an innocent man, and the surge of people toward the confessor. But perhaps the most telling correspondence is the devastating realization of the young heroes that they are trapped, that they have nowhere to go. Raskolnikov recalls Marmeladov's question, "Do you realize, do you realize, sir, what it means when you have nowhere to go? . . . For every man must have at least somewhere to go." When Mikulin's questioning becomes intolerable to Razumov, he declares his intention to retire and is stopped dead by the dramatic though softly spoken challenge of the bureaucrat: "Where to?" Later on, Razumov will explain to Nathalie why he came to her: "It is simply because there is no one anywhere in the whole great world I could go to. Do you understand what I say. No one to go to. Do you conceive the desolation of the thought—no-one-to-go-to?"

Such similarities do not imply a slavish imitation of *Crime and Punishment*. What might have begun as a parody of the Russian book eventually developed into an original Conradian psychological novel. The influence of other writers upon Conrad does not detract from his fictional achievement; on the contrary, the literary allusiveness broadens the fictional scope (at least for those readers who can recognize the conscious or unconscious sources) by enriching the texture of the narrative. Thus, one can find echoes from Adam Mickiewicz's *Forefathers' Eve* in Conrad's description of Russia as a "monstrous blank page."

There are also pronounced echoes from Shakespeare, especially from *Macbeth* and *Julius Caesar*, two tragedies of betrayal. The common dramatic and psychological situation of the novel and of *Macbeth* is the betrayal of a trusting guest. As Macbeth's reputation of nobility and valor is established before his deed, so, too, Razumov's trustworthiness is reiterated. Haldin explains to the bewildered Razumov why he has come to him in one word: "Confidence." The phrase "He inspires confidence" is repeated in several variants until it becomes almost comic when Razumov thinks dully and irascibly: "They all, it seems, have confidence in me . . ." Like Verloc's, however, Razumov's trustworthiness is deceptive. He too will become a spy, a secret agent. As in the two Shakespearean tragedies, there is the evocation of symbolic darkness; there is the problem of living a shamed life, and there are the supernatural phenomena accompanying severe guilt.

It is this interest of Conrad in the problem of living a shameful existence that links *Under Western Eyes* with *Lord Jim* and *Nostromo*; for both Jim and Decoud share with Razumov his desperate longing for moral support; both have experienced the terror of loneliness. Razumov "was as lonely in the world as a man swimming in the deep sea. The word Razumov was the mere label of a solitary individual." And Razumov feels that "no human being could bear a steady view of moral solitude without going mad."

Despite his "Western detachment" the professor manages to put together a story of great passion and great moral complexity, as he unfolds, quite sympathetically, it must be noted, the tale of Razumov's woes. But though he has assured the reader that he is merely presenting documentary evidence, the actual manner in which the story is told is, in effect, that of an omniscient narrator whose attention to dramatic and gory details (as in the account of the assassination of Minister de R., the President of the notorious Repressive Commission) recalls Conrad's "objective" description of Stevie's death in *The Secret Agent*.

As the action develops, it becomes apparent that we actually have two basic stories fused together by the omniscient narrator; the professor's and Razumov's diary. To attain an even greater degree of detachment, Conrad introduces additional points of view. Thus, for instance, Razumov's confession, perhaps the most dramatic event of the novel, is thrice removed from Conrad: the teacher's narrative provides two accounts of the confession, one by Julius Laspara and the other by Sophia Antonovna. She, incidentally, reports that her story comes from Razumov himself. The narrator fills in all the missing details from Razumov's diary.

The involuted time sequence and the multiple points of view, gathered by a principal "objective" narrator, result in a story of considerable dramatic potential that is, however, not fully realized because the sheer multiplicity of views at the end of the novel lessens the impact of Razumov's confession. While the symbolic and ironic density of the text indicates that Conrad still possessed great creative vigor and the clarity of vision, some readers may question the need for such involved treatment of what could have been a single, central dramatic pivot in a psychological drama. The narrator's function in this novel is that of a chorus and an intermediary between the reader and the several sources of information. On the other hand, it can be argued that the very indirectness and the interposition of the narrator in the story enable Conrad to provide a selection of events, arranged to achieve the maximal ironic thrust.

A satirical stance is evident in the portrayal of some of the "international conspirators," the Dickensian exaggeration of *The Secret Agent* turning into a more subtle parody of Dostoevsky, as in the admirable piece of caricature in the person of Peter Ivanovitch. Like the murderous Nikita, he is burly, a man who had "one of those bearded Russian faces without shape, a mere appearance of flesh and hair with not a single feature having any sort of character." Conrad pokes fun at this pretentious fugitive from Russian justice, whose exploits were celebrated in a story of his life "written by himself and translated into seven or more languages." He goes on ridiculing Peter Ivanovitch and his strident feminism, for he is actually an exploiter of women and, to use a contemporary "classification," a "male chauvinist."

Nathalie, however, is not a woman to be exploited, for she has her own mind. She believes that reform "is impossible. There is nothing to reform. There's no legality; there are no institutions. There are only arbitrary degrees. There is only a handful of cruel—perhaps blind—officials against a nation." This view has a contemporary ring; it could have come from the pen of Aleksandr Solzhenitsyn in his frequent condemnations of Soviet tyranny. Her discussion with the teacher turns to the subject of a violent revolution and its aftermath. The revolution is started by the unselfish and the intelligent, the teacher argues, "but it passes away from them. They are not the leaders of a revolution. They are its victims: the victims of disgust, of disenchantment— often of remorse. Hopes *grotesquely betrayed*, ideals caricatured—that is the definition of revolutionary success." The charitable old gentleman, who is truly fond of beautiful Nathalie, does not want her to become a victim, but she refuses to think of herself and cries out for liberty "from any hand."

Nathalie Haldin is Conrad's favorite, too, for he has chosen her words to serve as an epigraph to the novel though he usually drew on a great variety of sources for this purpose. The epigraph reads: "I would take liberty from any hand as a hungry man would snatch a piece of bread . . ." Suppose, however, that the liberty she longs for comes from the hand of a Razumov, a betrayer? Her conviction that "the right men are already amongst us," the men her brother's letter described as "unstained, lofty, and *solitary existences*" strikes a hollow note since we know that the man Haldin mentions, carrying the letter of introduction from Father Zosim, is Razumov, the very person responsible for her brother's arrest and execution. Her strange notion of a "concord" to be enacted in Russia is an echo of Conrad's own words, "an alliance of contradictions." The narrator knows her scorn for all the practical forms of "political liberty known in the Western world." He is puzzled by what he calls "Russian simplicity, a terrible corroding simplicity in which mystic phrases clothe a naïve and hopeless cynicism." Nathalie naïvely hopes that antagonistic ideas shall be reconciled. When the narrator protests with some irritation that such concord is inconceivable, she retorts: "Everything is inconceivable. . . . The whole world is inconceivable to the strict logic of ideas. And yet the world exists to our senses, and we exist in it. . . . We Russians shall find some better form of national freedom than an artificial conflict of parties—which is wrong because it is a conflict and contemptible because it is artificial. It is left for us Russians to discover a better way."

This utopian vision defies and insults the narrator's Western sense of rationality. Nathalie's mystic and logically misty ideas smack of cynicism which will not admit the truth. The teacher sums up the difference between them thus: "I think sometimes that the psychological secret of the profound difference of that people consists in this, that they detest life, the irremediable life of the earth as it is, whereas we westerners cherish it with perhaps an equal exaggeration of its sentimental value." Razumov's political ideas are the very opposite of Nathalie's—at least in his initial stage as a student. He is calm and logical. Haldin refers to his "frigid English manner" and to his being "Collected—cool as a cucumber. A regular Englishman." He is politically conservative and he wants to rise in the ranks of society. He enunciates his philosophy in five lines, scribbled in a large hand which becomes "unsteady, almost childish": "History not Theory. / Patriotism not Internationalism. / Evolution not Revolution. / Direction not Destruction. / Unity not Disruption." Symbolically, he stabs the paper with his penknife to the wall. This political credo is penned after the deed of betrayal is done, and he feels he is on a rack, and even says to himself, "I confess." He then goes to sleep and wakes several times that night, "shivering from a dream of walking through drifts of snow in a Russia where he was as *completely alone* as any *betrayed* autocrat could be . . ." Much later, however, in a verbal duel with Peter Ivanovitch, Razumov rejects the notion that he is an extraordinary person. Peter Ivanovitch senses some affinity with Razumov: "You are a man out of the common. . . . This taciturnity . . . this something inflexible and *secret* in you. . . . There is something of a Brutus . . ." Brutus, of course, is a man who betrays his Caesar. Peter Ivanovitch adds, "But you, at any rate, are *one of us*" [Conrad's italics]. This echo from *Lord Jim* is painfully ironic because the *us* here does not represent any tradition of loyalty and trust but its very opposite. Both men stand for a degree of fraud, moral and intellectual. Razumov refuses to accept Peter Ivanovitch's notion that he aims at stoicism: "That's a pose of the Greeks and the Romans. Let's leave it to them. We are Russians, that is *children*; that is—*sincere*; that is—*cynical*, if you like." The *us* means, therefore, us, the Russians.

This exchange is no longer in the manner of caricature. Rather, the narrator reveals the philosophical and psychological contradictions of the protagonists. His own reservations about Nathalie's views, despite his obvious affection for her, his skeptical assessment of the revolutionist's aim and practice; his caustic view of the Swiss; his disclaimers about his ignorance of the Russians while making pejorative statements about them—all these also add to "the alliance of contradictions" which seems to render the elderly teacher an unreliable narrator. But it is precisely because his motives and his veracity may be suspect that this method achieves its most telling effect: the reader is forced to take sides, as in *Lord Jim*. The reader, in fact, is forced to identify not only with Nathalie, who is the language teacher's "pet," but also, and perhaps to an even greater extent, with Razumov and the revolutionists as well.

It is, indeed, difficult not to feel a sense of profound sympathy for Razumov and also for the revolutionists whose cause Conrad rejects but whose proponents by and large have not been reduced to caricature, as in *The Secret Agent*. The understanding and pity some of them show to the crippled young man enhance their humanity and thereby their psychological verisimilitude. As Conrad points out in his Author's Note, his greatest anxiety was "to strike and sustain the note of scrupulous impartiality." There is little doubt that the "obligation of absolute fairness" imposed upon him "historically and hereditarily" was adhered to. Conrad avers that he "had never been called before to a greater effort of *detachment*: detachment from all passions, prejudices and even from personal memories." He is gratified that the book "had found recognition in Russia and had been re-published there in many editions." This effort of detachment was most taxing for Conrad, for he suffered a nervous breakdown after the completion of the novel, as if the identification with Russia was more than his mind and heart could stand. As if, moreover, he had seen a dark vision of the future.

For in no other political novel of Conrad do we find such profound and prophetic insights into the nature of men and women living under an autocratic regime and rebelling against it; especially insights into the men practicing political violence. Take, for example, his comment on Nikita, whom he calls "the perfect flower of the terroristic wilderness." What troubled Conrad most in dealing with him "was not his monstrosity but his *banality*." How remarkably familiar this sounds today when we think of Hannah Arendt's book about Adolph Eichmann, entitled *The Banality of Evil*. The most terrifying reflection, Conrad concludes in his Author's Note, speaking for himself and possibly for our age, "is that all these people are not the product of the exceptional but of the general—of the normality of their place, and time, and race." Writing this in 1920, Conrad was able to predict the futility of revolutionary action to alter human nature. His words carry an uncanny contemporary resonance:

> The ferocity and imbecility of an autocratic rule rejecting all legality and in fact basing itself upon complete moral anarchism provokes the no less imbecile and atrocious answer of a purely Utopian revolutionism encompassing destruction by the first means to hand, in the *strange conviction* that a fundamental change of hearts must follow the downfall of any human institutions. These people are unable to see that all they can effect is merely a change of names. The oppressors and the oppressed are all Russians together, and the world is brought once more face to face with the truth of the saying that the tiger cannot change his stripes nor the leopard his spots.

As mentioned before, Conrad dedicated *The Secret Agent* to "H. G. Wells. . . . The Biographer of Kipps and the Historian of the Ages to Come." Perhaps this dedication reveals the underlying philosophical intent in both *The Secret Agent* and in *Under Western Eyes,* two novels which span the comic and the tragic views of mankind. Though Conrad and Wells were good friends at one time, the latter's views on social utopia were anathema to Conrad, as Chernyshevsky's *What Is to Be Done?* had been to Dostoevsky. "You don't care for humanity," Conrad wrote to Wells, "but think they are to be improved. I love humanity, but know they are not. . . ."

Though Critics are divided in their appraisals of the relative merits of *Chance* (1913) and *Victory* (1915), some preferring the former and others the latter, they generally agree that both suggest a decline in Conrad's powers as a novelist. Betrayal, the leitmotiv of *The Secret Agent* and *Under Western Eyes,* still looms large in these two novels, but they are, like most of Conrad's late fiction, devoted primarily to the exploration of the flawed human heart. They are about love but also about sex or, as in the case of poor Captain Anthony, the abstinence thereof with his wife, Flora. "All of it," said Conrad, is "about a girl and with a steady run of references to women in general all along. . . . It ought to go down." Well, it did. *Chance* is Conrad's first financial success which is due to a number of factors: its serialization in the *New York Herald*; a clever and energetic promotion by Alfred Knopf, newly arrived at Double-

day; a simple and popular title, catchy headings for chapters (not used before
or again) and the two parts; an ample dose of sentimentality and pseudo-
philosophy, mostly on the subject of women; and, of course, mere chance.

The titles of the novel's two parts imply that Conrad treated the story
as a kind of fairy tale, for Part I is called "The Damsel" and Part II "The
Knight." In the past, Conrad subtitles usually suggested the author's intent,
but here the subtitle "A Tale in Two Parts" is rather perfunctory; at best, it
invites the reader's caustic response that only one of the two parts (the first)
is any good. The epigraph by Sir Thomas Browne alludes to all things being
governed by Fortune, thus echoing the title, *Chance*: "Those that hold that all
things are governed by Fortune had not erred, had they not persisted there."

The plots of both novels stress the impact of blind chance and the helplessness of the protagonists overtaken by it. Indeed, Flora de Barral, the
damsel in distress of *Chance*, is the victim of blind fate. Without a mother,
the only child of a gullible swindler who preys on others' gullibility, she
attempts suicide after her father's bankruptcy. She is betrayed and insulted
by an evil governess and she languishes in a state of a profound, moral shock
and isolation. Like Lena in *Victory*, who is pinched by Mrs. Zangiacomo and
hounded by the gross Teutonic hotelkeeper Schomberg, she is also pursued
by the head of a German household. She is completely alone, at the mercy of
the world. Fate (or chance) brings a "knight" to rescue the forlorn maiden,
and each proves to be a hermitlike man who has withdrawn from a wicked
world, and who is emotionally crippled. Both "knights" are offspring of literary men: Anthony is the son of a "delicate" poet, and Heyst is the son of a
pessimistic philosopher. Like Conrad's literary father, Apollo Korzeniowski,
these fathers have exercised a most damaging influence upon their sons by
contributing to their sons' pain and inflicting psychic wounds upon their
minds. Anthony's father gave him an overrefined sense of delicacy, so much
in contrast to his sister's feminist toughness; Heyst's philosopher father, the
author of *Storm and Dust*, has bequeathed to *his* son a deadly creed of doubt
which results in a Hamletian paralysis of will, and the inability to act or to
be committed to anyone or anything.

Another basic similarity in the two novels is Conrad's interest in sen-
suality, more specifically of the homosexual variety. Thus, in *Chance*, the
aggressively feminist Mrs. Fyne exhibits all the traits of a lesbian. Flora's
elopement with Roderick provokes her wrath. Although she herself is married,
she does not want women to be women; she believes that women should "turn
themselves into unscrupulous sexless nuisances." The effeminate, pistol-pack-
ing Jones is described by his "secretary" Ricardo as a *freakish* gentleman who

hates women: "Yes, the governor funks facing women." Eventually, the "governor" will shoot Ricardo for his involvement with a woman.

The plot of *Chance* centers on the plight of Flora, whose father is sentenced to a seven-year term in jail. Abominably treated by her governess and relatives, she finds a haven with the Fynes; Mrs. Fyne's brother, Captain Anthony, falls in love with Flora after she attempts to throw herself over a precipice. Ironically, Mrs. Fyne now turns against Flora and tries to prevent her marriage to Roderick. Under her influence Flora writes a letter to her in which she states that she does not love Roderick but will marry him for convenience. Roderick, however, will not give her up since he wants to shield Flora. He takes her and her father, who has been released from prison, on a voyage on the *Ferndale* which he commands. Marlow is right when he doubts that the isolation of the sea would help the young couple. For the ex-convict de Barral the ship is another jail, and he regards Captain Anthony not as a charitable soul but as another jailer. As in *Nostromo,* Conrad isolates these three people on a ship. All three are torn by conflicting emotions of love or hate.

Anthony refuses to have sex with his wife in the belief that she does not love him; Flora, on the other hand, thinks that Roderick has married her merely out of pity. "But who would have suspected Anthony of being a heroic creature," Marlow wonders, exasperated by his sublime delicacy. "That's your poet. He demands too much from others. The inarticulate son had set up a standard for himself with that need for embodying in his conduct the dreams, the passions, the impulses the poet puts into arrangement of verses." Lord Jim dies celebrating a wedding with a shadowy ideal of conduct. Captain Anthony's conduct, like Jim's, tears him away from the arms of a woman who loves him, and whom he also loves. His inarticulateness does not permit him to break through the barrier of estrangement between himself and Flora. "Chance had thrown that girl in his way . . . this eager appropriation was truly the act of a man of *solitude* and *desire* . . . a man of long and ardent reveries wherein the faculty of sincere passion matures slowly in the *unexplored recesses of the heart.*"

In *An Outcast of the Islands* Conrad first explored the destructive impact of the untrammeled sexual passion on Willems. Here, though he defines Roderick's passion as "dominating or tyrannical," and being close to "folly and madness," he does bring the lovers together after a prolonged period of mental and, presumably physical, agony. Anthony, unlike Willems, is not destroyed by his lover. On the second voyage of the trio, de Barral, driven by jealousy, attempts to poison Anthony. Upon being discovered, he takes his own life.

At this point, the lovers finally overcome their estrangement. Yet, though Conrad avowedly begins the story as a kind of fairy tale, there is no "happily ever-after" for Flora and Roderick. Anthony drowns, but at least young Powell gets his Flora.

A lively critical debate has been waged for decades as to whether *Chance* (and for that matter, *Victory*) is a lesser novel because of Conrad's difficulty to deal adequately with love. Perhaps Conrad was reluctant or unable to deal with intimate details of sex; unable to present sexual complications as vividly as some of the novelists of the 1960s or 1970s have done. Still, he managed to convey some fairly convincing portraits of men and women, especially women: Flora, her governess, and Mrs. Fyne. The latter, to be true, is somewhat "overdone" in Marlow's zeal to define her feminism.

Similarly, the resolution of the novel suggests a weakening of Conrad's customary concern with verisimilitude. The mysterious disappearance of a carving knife from the mess room of the *Ferndale*, the poison which de Barral unaccountably brings to the ship, and, finally, the presentation of Powell as a cardboard prince—these suggest indeed the melodramatic or romantic stuff of a fairy tale. Conrad himself defines this aspect of the book: "I suppose that to him [Mr. Powell] life . . . was something still in the nature of a fairy-tale with a 'they lived happily ever after' termination. . . . Powell felt in that way because the captain of a ship at sea is a *remote, inaccessible* creature, something like a *prince of a fairy-tale*, alone of his kind . . ."

Moreover, Conrad is only partially successful in his narrative method. The story is told by Marlow to the nameless author of the novel who argues with him about his opinions and impressions. Marlow's story draws upon the information of the Fynes, Powell, and Flora, who in turn convey their impressions of things and people. Conrad's return to Marlow as a narrator is less felicitous since it is a different Marlow, somewhat misogynous, garrulous, and, frankly, a bore. Unlike Dowell, the pathetic narrator in Ford Madox Ford's *The Good Soldier,* whose dullness serves a distinctly ironic purpose since he tells us more than he knows or understands himself, this Marlow is one of the three speakers in the novel, the other two being the "I" and young Powell. Nevertheless, the narrative method of *Chance* is often regarded as Conrad's most Jamesian work, and a good example of his innovative approaches to fiction by presenting his story without the conventional limitations of chronology.

The principal narrator rambles on, and instead of telling us what actually happened, he tells what he *imagines* to have happened: "And we may conjecture what we like. I have no difficulty in imagining that the woman . . . must have raged at large." The narrator is thus deeply interested in the tale, but given his temperament, he can maintain an ironic distance from what he is reporting on.

The sense of unreality in *Chance* reappears with a vengeance in *Victory*. The word which Conrad uses to describe Schomberg's psychology, "grotesque" (in a Note to the First Edition), constitutes a key to the novel's tonality. *Victory* is not merely a melodramatic novel of Conrad's decline, as critic after critic suggested. While not an artistic tour de force, it is still an effective novel whose highly allusive literary frame, rich texture, and comic invention have been largely ignored hitherto. Conrad's preoccupation with Calderón's *La Vida es Sueño* [Life is a Dream], translated into Polish by Conrad's favorite Romantic poet, Juliusz Słowacki, is one of the central elements in Conrad's often contradictory and paradoxical statements about the human existence. It appears in many of his works but it is in *Victory* that it reaches its climax, as Heyst, immobilized by his crippling philosophy, is fascinated by Jones, "this skeleton in a *gay* dressing-grown, jerkily agitated like a grotesque toy on the end of an invisible string"; Heyst is bewildered and it seems to him "that all this was *an incomprehensible dream*." In fact, for Heyst life becomes a grotesque dream or, more accurately, a terrifying nightmare. Camille R. La Bossière suggests that Conrad's view of life comes both from Calderón and from Cusa's principle of *coincidentia oppositorum*, or an allegorical conflict of opposing forces, "a circular logic of contraries. . . . Conrad struggles to *see* the 'Inconceivable' by the light of this synthetic logic and to translate into verbal analogies the 'unspeakable' truth of man and universe. The truth eludes surface logic and the language of affirmation."

Indeed, *Victory* is based on this allegorical conflict of opposing forces, with Conrad once again delving into the problem of human alienation. As we follow the fortunes of the two lovers isolated on their island of Samburan, the physical nature of their universe has shrunk yet it contains the whole gamut of human passions. The moral problems of the protagonists are no less complex than their lovemaking and, ultimately, survival. Even the villains have a certain kind of morality, and they assume the stance of the devil's disciple. For example, Ricardo keeps harping on the alleged betrayal by Heyst of his friend Morrison. Until Lena comes along, Ricardo displays a certain loyalty to his master, the "governor." As in other novels, only the extreme, the final existential test, can reveal the meaning of life to the hero, and by that time it is too late.

Heyst skims the surface of the world. He is not fully alive; though he has a chance to defend himself against the villains who are about to take Lena from him, and even his own life, he will do nothing until the very last moment. Only when everything is lost does he begin to understand the true

nature of his own life and emotions. Only when Lena is dying does he understand finally that he has been in love with her. He is not merely disgusted
with the world, he is disgusted with himself. And that, as in the case of
Hamlet, makes it impossible for him to act.

Heyst believes that a man is lost if he forms a tie. He is a man of universal
scorn and *unbelief*, "the most detached of creatures in this earthly captivity,
the veriest *tramp* of this earth, an *indifferent stroller* going through the world's
bustle." Yet he is essentially a rather naïve and a good man who is suspected
of foul play against his associate Morrison when, in fact, he has proved most
charitable toward him. Ironically, echoing Jim's ambivalence at the Court of
Inquiry, Heyst's action, when he does choose to act, will prove him both
right and wrong. His voluntary commitment to Lena's welfare—or the forming of a tie—will prove his undoing; on the other hand, his distrust of life
and his fatalism make him impotent and thereby nullify his genuine concern
with Lena's safety. He cannot and will not fight back.

The original name Conrad chose for this man was "Berg" (or mountain
in German), which, like Kurtz in *Heart of Darkness*, was to be symbolic,
suggesting perhaps a man larger than life, a strong, towering personality. In
the final version, however, Heyst won. But this name is closer to *heist* or *theft*.
Is it too farfetched to assume that Conrad did not notice the correspondence,
for, after all, Heyst does steal his little Lena (Magdalen and Alma) from the
lecherous Schomberg? The trace of the original conception remains, to some
extent, since Heyst is of noble parentage and is referred to as "a puffect
g'n'lman . . . but he's a ut-uto-utopist" or a dreamer living in a state of
unreality.

As in *Chance*, this sense of unreality pervades the novel and estranges the
two lovers from each other. "The girl was to him like a script in an unknown
language, or even more simply mysterious, like any writing to the illiterate."
In *Chance*, we have "psychological wilderness" and Marlow becomes an expert
in it; here we face the wilderness of a godforsaken island along with the cultural
and moral gap between the two lovers. In *Chance* Flora suffers from a "mystic
wound"; in *Victory* Heyst is the victim of this injury, both intellectual and
psychic. Lena is a mystery to Heyst, who in turn is a mystery to her. She
knows him so little that she, too, like his enemies, is at first convinced that
he may have murdered poor Morrison; and when she decides to save her lover
and obtain Ricardo's knife, she stoops to deception and becomes so intoxicated
with her dream of self-sacrifice that, in effect, she is partially responsible for
the final catastrophe. Thus, in each case, we see an extreme form of solipsism,
not too far removed from Jim's "exalted egoism" in psychological terms.

But while Lena is granted the triumphal gesture of self-sacrifice, Heyst is left in despair. The unpredictable decree of destiny (chance) has caught up with him and exposed the utter futility of his unbelief. Even a short moment before her death, Heyst was capable of believing her infidelity as if "paying her back for her doubts about him." She speaks to him "in accents of wild joy," but he looks at her "with a *black, horror*-struck curiosity." In this final melodramatic scene, Lena resembles Jewel who is trying to hold on to her lover and also to send him away, to save him: "I have done it! . . . Never get it back. Oh, my beloved!" Whereupon the refined Heyst bows his head gravely and speaks in his polite Heystian tone: "No doubt you acted from instinct. Women have been provided with their own weapon. I was a *disarmed man*. I have been a *disarmed man* all my life, as I see it now. You may glory in your resourcefulness—your profound knowledge of yourself; but I may say that the other attitude, suggestive of *shame*, had its charm. For you are full of charm!"

I suppose one can say that Conrad fails here stylistically. Would any man speak like this to his dying lover? But the point is that Heyst cannot *see* the truth because he is too wrapped up in his own detached view of things to be able to *see anything*. He even turns his back on her as her enchanting voice cuts deep into his heart. Only when her voice begins to falter does he spin around and finally go to her, snatching her up bodily out of her chair and becoming aware of her limpness as the knife drops to the floor with a metallic clatter. Like Othello in the moment when he perceives that he has killed an innocent Desdemona, Heyst cannot utter a word, but must "let out a groan . . . the heavy plaint of a man who falls clubbed in the dark." The melodramatic and, unfortunately, somewhat sentimental scene between the lovers reaches its climax, yet it contains the familiar ring of Conrad's bitter irony.

" 'O my beloved,' she cried weakly, 'I've saved you! Why don't you take me into your arms and carry me *out of this lonely place?*' " But Heyst is now afraid to touch her as he bends low over her, "cursing his fastidious soul, which even at that moment kept the true cry of love from his lips in its *infernal mistrust* of all life." Heyst has brought Lena to the illusory paradise in Samburan with the intent of saving her from a menacing world. But it has proven both lonely and destructive. Lena breathes "her last, triumphant, seeking for his glance in the shades of death." *His* last words indicate a measure of enlightenment: "woe to the man whose heart has not learned while young to hope, to love—and to put its trust in life!"

Heyst's suicide by means of the purifying *Flammentod* ("death by fire") and Lena's death from Jones's bullet both symbolize their respective failures and ironic triumphs. The thunderous and melodramatic ending of the novel (seen by some critics as a typically Victorian tying-up of loose ends) is also Shakespearean. It recalls the storms of the major tragedies like *King Lear*,

Macbeth, and *Julius Caesar* and the romance *The Tempest*. The upheaval of nature mirrors the storm within men's souls. As the violent struggle on the island of Samburan comes to its pathetic close, the thunder over it ceases "to growl at last." All the principal combatants are dead: Ricardo, appropriately "shot neatly through the *heart*"; Pedro, the Caliban-like servant, shot by Wang, the unfaithful servant of Heyst, with the revolver he has stolen from his master; Jones, the strange alter ego of Heyst, tumbles into the water and drowns in what may be another "purifying" death in the novel. The story is over, and Heyst's assessment of his unreal situation on the island has been confirmed by the events. When he was held prisoner by Jones he had a feeling that it was all "an elaborate *other-world joke*, contrived by that *specter* in a gorgeous dressing grown." As the story opens with Heyst's *enchantment* with the islands, with Lena's voice, so the enchantment develops gradually into a macabre nightmare, a grotesque vision of human existence.

Although Conrad's epigraph for *Victory* is drawn from Milton's *Comus*, the subtitle "An Island Tale," the apparent parallel with Villiers de L'Isle-Adam's *Axël*, the numerous Shakespearean echoes, and the main allegorical thrust all point to an analogy with *The Tempest*. The islands of Prospero the enchanter, and Axel Heyst, the Enchanted, are invaded by sinister people who are vanquished in the end, but each of the elder men, the real and the surrogate father, must sustain the loss of his young ward, and be left in a mood of despair.

In some ways Conrad goes back to *Lord Jim* in his presentation of Heyst as a "*thoroughly white man*," always immaculately attired in white apparel, even wearing white shoes. His appearance, like that of Jim, is misleading. Heyst *seems* virile and strong and cuts a martial figure with his flaming red moustaches and glowing cigar. Yet there is that same infernal alloy in his metal. Neither man's mother appears to have played any part in the shaping of Heyst's or Jim's personalities, while each of the two fathers exercised a profound and lasting influence. And as Jim fails in his confrontation with Gentleman Brown, so Heyst is taunted by "Gentleman" Jones (as he is called by Ricardo), who explains the meaning of his being a *reckoning*: "I, my dear Sir . . . I am the world itself come to pay you a visit. In another sense I am an *outcast*— almost an *outlaw*. If you prefer a less materialistic view, I am a sort of *fate*— the *retribution* that waits its time." Both men are outcasts *and* doubles.

Despite its flaws, *Victory*, in my view, is not a simple pseudo-Victorian novel; nor does it signify a complete decline of Conrad's artistic powers, as suggested by Albert Guerard or Thomas Moser. Upon closer scrutiny, the novel reveals an impressive tonal richness: from black comedy to sentimental melodrama; from philosophical meditation to romantic twaddle; from static descriptions to scenes of brutal violence; from delicate, almost prudish depictions of sexuality to riotously comic aspects of fetishism and voyeurism.

For all the stylistic lapses, Conrad's conception of Jones and Ricardo justifies their language. The latter's utterance, according to Guerard, is too effeminate. But Ricardo, with his knife strapped to his leg and frequently exhibited, *is* effeminate *and* a fetishist to boot, whose central passion, it appears, is focused on Lena's foot: " 'Give your *foot*,' he begged in a *timid* murmur. . . . She advanced *her foot* forward a little from under the hem of her skirt; and *he threw himself on it greedily.* She was not even aware of him." This is not awkward prose; it makes excellent comedy. Conrad continues with a straight face: "Ricardo, *clasping her ankle,* pressed his *lips* time after time to the *instep, muttering gasping* words that were like *sobs,* making *little noises* that resembled the *sounds of grief and distress.*"

Lest one consider this unintentionally humorous or an expression of Conrad's own subconscious sexual patterns, one must note the somewhat caustic authorial comment on the psychological condition of Jones, which also anticipates Ricardo's own strange tastes. When Ricardo explains his governor's rabid hatred of women, "he paused to reflect on this psychological phenomenon, and as no philosopher was at hand to tell him there is no strong sentiment without some terror, as there is no real religion without *a little fetichism,* he emitted his own conclusion."

Well, there is more than a little fetishism and voyeurism in *Victory* and, as Dr. Bernard Meyer repeatedly observed, a tendency to blur the distinctions between the masculine and the feminine, and to endow women with phallus-like characteristics of solidity, hardness, and the power of thrust and penetration: "Suddenly Ricardo felt himself *spurned* by the *foot* he had been *cherishing*—spurned with a *push* of such *violence* into the very *hollow* of his throat that it swung him back into an upright position *on his knees.* He read his danger in the *stony* eyes of the girl." There is a great deal of comic-serious business with Ricardo's slipper, as it is missed, found, tossed out the window by Lena, then triumphantly retrieved by Ricardo. "As soon as it *passed the opening,* it was out of her sight. . . . It had gone clear." She stood "as if turned into *stone.*" Lena reels forward and momentarily finds support in yet another fetishist object by "embracing with both arms one of the tall, *roughly carved posts* holding the mosquito net above the *bed,*" thereby saving herself "from *a fall.*" She clings to it for a long time, her forehead leaning against the wood. Her sarong slips and reveals part of her naked body, the long brown tresses falling in lank wisps. "Her *uncovered flank,* damp with the *sweat of anguish* and *fatigue* gleamed *coldly* with the *immobility* of polished *marble.*"

I offer these examples of prose that is neither sentimental nor awkward.

Perhaps there *are* passages of pure melodrama in *Victory,* as there are in Dickens's *Bleak House,* beloved of Conrad. But as the death of little Jo works despite the overwhelming sentimentality of the scene, so does the scene of Lena's death. It is not surprising that Conrad's American audience was moved to tears when he read it aloud. *Victory* is, thus, its alleged and real flaws notwithstanding, a novel of allegorical and tragic dimensions. Its treatment of sexuality, of women in general, is in my view, more complex than in the early works such as *Lord Jim* or *Heart of Darkness.*

It has been suggested that *both* Jones and Heyst are homosexuals and that the "powerful theme" of the novel is "that homosexuals, who represent a withdrawal from normal relations and a denial of life, are doomed and damned beyond redemption." If one accepts this thesis, it is possible to argue that Jones's bullet, intended for Ricardo to punish him for his betrayal, reaches Lena's breast because Jones now acts on Heyst's behalf. He must rid himself of Lena so that he can have Heyst, his alter ego, to himself. Ironically, Lena saves Ricardo by kicking him in his throat, in a sense justifying his faith in her. Only he thought she would kill *Heyst.* One wonders whether with her final gesture in handing Ricardo's phallic knife (the symbol of his manhood) to Heyst she thereby unwittingly delivers his death sentence. Indirectly, she does drive Heyst to his death with her own act of sacrifice.

On another level, the novel is a microcosm reflecting the less than perfect society of prewar Europe. Its title, tagged on, as it were, after its completion (the book appeared in 1915), represents not merely Lena's ambivalent victory but also the dubious victory scored by the Allies in World War I. Peace was imposed on the smoldering volcano of the European continent. The smoking volcano is a constant reminder of the ironically paradisiac island of Samburan. The volcano's glow is compared to the end of a gigantic cigar, and the reader does not fail to make the connection between the cigar-puffing Heyst of martial appearance and the dormant volcano. The safety offered by the island and Heyst's looks are as deceptive as the deck of the *Patna* and Jim's impressive mien. The unexpected strikes with murderous fury as the unholy trio of bandits lands on the island. There is no security in this strange Eden. There is only the inevitable disaster, the terrible, meaningless, and absurd carnage at the end, no more absurd, however, than the carnage of the battlefields of France that erupted in 1914. Davidson sums up the story by a reference to warfare: "there are more dead in this affair . . . than have been killed in many of the battles of the last Achin war."

But though Davidson echoes Marlow's question at the end of *Lord Jim,* "Who knows?" the ending of *Victory* is in some ways more poignant and effective than that of *Lord Jim.* Let us examine the final word of the novel,

"Nothing," a word which has been used repeatedly to create a sense of dramatic irony, reminiscent of King Lear's shock at Cordelia's "Nothing." The word-frequency table of the concordance to *Victory* indicates that not counting auxiliary words and proper names, *nothing* is one of the most often used words (160 times) after *man* (293 times) and *eyes* (233 times). Could one draw a corollary from this that man is *nothing*? Perhaps, but with some qualifications. Heyst repeats the word, thereby underlining the illusory quality of his and Lena's retreat. His assurances ring hollow: "Is your mind turning towards the future . . . because if it is so there is *nothing* easier than to dismiss it. In our future, as in what people call the other life, there is *nothing* to be afraid of." "*Nothing* can break in on us here." "*Nothing* whatever was to be *seen* between the point and the jetty." "*Nothing* was to be *seen*. . . . The civilization of the tropics could have *nothing* to do with it."

The frequency of Shakespearean allusions in the novel leaves no doubt of the final word's connotation. Lear's "*Nothing* can be made of *nothing*," is not unlike the elder Heyst's skeptical philosophy. The point of *King Lear* is, in my view, that everything comes from *nothing*. Lear gives his two evil daughters everything in the material sense—but he gets nothing in return. Cordelia gives him a word, "Nothing," and gets *nothing* in return. Lear gives Cordelia nothing but actually gets everything from her. Love is not to be measured by words of flattery or by real estate. It is spiritual; it is not quantitative at all. That is why it comes from *nothing* material. Heyst's resolution to do *nothing* in this world is a transgression not different from Jim's egotistic "*Nothing* can touch me." Heyst has broken Conrad's code of human solidarity. He must learn, as other Conradian heroes have, that no man is an island unto himself.

Heyst's exit from the turbulent stage of Samburan implies that though he has negated the world, the world has not negated him. If there is any logic in his suicide after Lena's passionate affirmation of her love for him, it is his paradoxical acceptance of himself as a responsible man in the real world of men and women. Yes, Heyst has learned, too painfully, perhaps, the lesson that man must put his trust in life. So now he finally decides to act, to acknowledge Lena's life and his responsibility therefor, while denying life itself. Once more, as in Conrad's view of anarchistic violence in *The Secret Agent*, it is the logic of perverse unreason. It is absurd.

RUTH NADELHAFT

Women as Moral
and Political Alternatives
in Conrad's Early Novels

As recently as 1973, critics of Joseph Conrad were still writing such mis-guided lines as "Conrad could no more have conceived of a woman hero than could Dickens." Carolyn G. Heilbrun, author of this rather typical misstate-ment, went on to write that Conrad was a creator "of artistic worlds in which women have no part, or no continually essential part." In fact, Heilbrun is just one in a long parade of critics who have not understood that women are, and always were, central to Conrad's vision as a political and moral novelist. For Conrad's novels and tales are about political morality, particularly the morality of imperialism and colonialism, a theme at least partially recognized by Jonah Raskin, who wrote of Conrad, in a study of imperialism in the works of late nineteenth-century authors, that he "fought against his society. He is most representative of his time because he stands in the sharpest opposition to it."

In his earliest novels, *Almayer's Folly* (1895) and *An Outcast of the Islands* (1896), Conrad embodies his already-formed ambivalent and searching criti-cism of the colonialism that makes up much of the books' real subject matter. Women, frequently half-breeds, represent the clearest means of challenging and revealing Western male insularity and domination. These first two novels, like the women who embody many of their insights, are frequently overlooked by critics, who prefer to concentrate on the more central revelations of the acknowledged great middle novels of Conrad's career. Conrad's questioning

From *Theory and Practice of Feminist Literary Criticism.* © 1982 by Bilingual Review/ Press.

and pessimistic analysis of the colonial relationship finds expression through the complex dependency of character revealed in character doubling, a technique usually understood to function between men in the middle and late novels. In fact, in the early novels European society is projected through white men and half-caste women on whom such men are halfway dependent. The continuum ranges from the bluff (and destructive) confidence of Tom Lingard, through the hesitating and torn Almayer or Willems, to the half-caste Nina (also represented by Mrs. Willems and Mrs. Almayer with their strikingly similar stories), and ends in Aissa, a brilliantly militant woman and an outspoken hater of whites. Women are shown to be especially vulnerable to white colonialism; unable to force white men to take them seriously (the goal of women everywhere), they resort to cunning and subversion to destroy the identity of the very men who enslave them. In these two books, the complex relationship between men and women, designed to confirm the identity of men, results instead in limiting the effect of white power, in revealing the liberating potential of native vitality, and in projecting the doom of male European colonialism.

From the outset of both these early novels, whose plots concern the early rise and subsequent disintegration of white European men, it is the protagonist's good opinion of himself that hangs in the balance; for Conrad a man's vision of himself is ordinarily the ironic stillpoint upon which the action turns. In these books, as in others to follow, that vision is largely determined by the piercing evaluation of women. These women, protagonists in their own right, have been largely ignored by their own society and by literary critics, most of whom have been male. The observant women provide a sort of gallery—whistling, catcalling, weeping—to comment on the action and to insist that action goes on offstage as well. Nina in *Almayer's Folly* and Aissa in *An Outcast of the Islands* are tautly imagined and described, full-fledged characterizations complete with all the ambiguity of Conrad's traditionally ambiguous men. Further, they possess character doubles as well, traditionally a measure of the complexity of the male central character. Character doubles, usually physically similar to the psychologically divided central characters, serve to personify in their own lives the possible alternatives imperfectly understood by the protagonists. In these early novels, it is significant that the women are projected through their doubles (for Nina, the slave girl Taminah, as an example); in such classic works as *Lord Jim* and "The Secret Sharer," character doubles project and embody crucial moral dilemmas and complex personalities for central male characters. A remarkable use of character doubling in these two novels is the projection of alternatives for the men through the women they fear and misuse. So doubling is central in at least two respects: the complexity of the women is presented through the use of paired female characters, and the central women (Nina in *Almayer's Folly*, Aissa in *An Outcast of the Islands*) embody the personal, moral, and political possibilities of the male protagonist.

Kaspar Almayer's good opinion of himself, so central to the opening chapters of *Almayer's Folly*, rests in fact on the approbation first of his wife (whom he misunderstands) and then of his daughter, Nina (of whom his apprehension is totally incorrect). White culture exists in the persons of Almayer, Lingard, and the white officers (themselves differing in temperament and response to Nina); the natives in both *Almayer's Folly* and *An Outcast of the Islands* are a complex presentation as well. Nina chooses between the culture of her father and that of the natives, who range from her lover, Dain, to the cunning and opportunistic Babalatchi; the subtlety and range of characterizations ensure that the choice for Nina is a real one. Ideally, such a central character opts for fusion, reconciliation. In fact, as the closing chapters of *Almayer's Folly* make clear, there has been too much history; Almayer is the end of colonialism and Nina its inevitable product.

Through the characterization of Nina's mother, Almayer's wife, and using the image of kidnapping (for Mrs. Almayer was a pirate's daughter snatched from her culture by Almayer's mentor, Captain Lingard), Conrad succeeds in dramatizing the imposition of imperial history upon private sensibility. As much as Almayer, his wife is the creation of Lingard, the embodiment of bluff, well-intentioned English imperialism. (It was, after all, George Orwell who said that of all colonialism he would choose the British variety.) Lingard's capture of the young fighting girl and his placement of her in a cool, repressive convent are the symbolic core of women's experience in this book. Lingard has captured Almayer as well and placed him in as confined an existence as that of the wild and savage woman who is to become his wife. Blindly, meaning the best, he has forced together white and native. The future that results is called Nina.

Conrad, in juxtaposing white and Malay cultures, uses the flawed characters of Almayer and his wife to plead their cases before Nina, a scrupulous and sorrowful judge. At the end of the book, in their lengthy conversation on the beach, Almayer and Nina at last touch with language the real struggle between his culture and what is to be hers. "Did you not see me struggling before your eyes," Nina asks him. "I have listened to your voice and to her voice. Then I saw that you could not understand me; for was I not part of that woman? Of her who was the regret and shame of your life. I had to choose—I hesitated." In this speech, and throughout the long dialogue with her father that surrounds it, Nina shows clearly that she understands the imposition of the past upon the present, understands her parents' inability to think and feel beyond their historical context. "What is there to forgive," Nina asks, "as if arguing with herself." Her father's rigid ambitions for her are paralleled by the limits of her mother's insight; Nina must create a complete future of her own duality. For what her mother offers, what Conrad drily describes as "the lost possibilities of murder and mischief," cannot satisfy the more humane and complex nature of the daughter. Neither can the pathetic and subservient love of Taminah, the slave girl, express the future adequately for Nina. Taminah, physically almost identical to Nina, possesses no self-knowledge, no self-consciousness; paradoxically, though self-consciousness may paralyze Europeans, it is also their great advantage over the least civilized native when properly fused with resolution.

In both these novels, which are dramas of choice expressed through male-female relationships, the native Babalatchi may represent the human ideal; a superb go-between, Babalatchi is a perfectly rational animal who expresses physically his instinctive and reasonable adaptation to his surroundings. To Mrs. Almayer's ravings, her taunts about his age and lack of courage, Baba-latchi answers in terms of survival: "A man knows when to fight and when to tell peaceful lies. You would know that if you were not a woman." The issue is here joined, fittingly enough between two Malays; it is never entirely to be resolved, but it is always clear. The women, taken seriously by neither white men nor natives, must find subtle, often misunderstood means to live beyond history, to alter culture. Even her mother's parting advice to Nina makes such a commitment clear. "When I hear of white men driven from the islands, then I shall know that you are alive, and that you remember my words." Indirection, subtlety, the use of love to achieve power, are the message of Nina's mother; having failed through direct conflict, she perceives that history must be imposed on individual lives. "Do not let him look too long in your eyes, nor lay his head on your knees without reminding him that men should fight before the rest." The use of the past to change the future lies with women; it is to Nina's self-awareness, coupled with her instinctive pas-sion, that both her parents appeal. In turn, Nina offers to them the chance to escape their own cultural prisons. "No woman is worth a man's life," says Babalatchi, the cynical go-between, speaking from his own historical limita-tion. In fact, through Nina, Conrad portrays an equality between men and women that denies Babalatchi's cynicism as well as her mother's subtle vio-lence. The sentimental information, after the conclusion of the story, that Nina's male child has been safely born may encourage speculation at the end of *Almayer's Folly*. However, even though the child is male, it is clear that through the complex introspective figure of the half-caste woman Conrad has explored the process and future of colonialism. Almayer's exhaustion contrasts with the self-conscious and articulate portrait of Nina, who shows understanding both of the man and of the historical process that shaped and then abandoned him. Her awareness, in fact, is far greater than his.

Thus, the creation of a subtle, self-conscious, and developing woman was possible for Conrad very early in his career. Nevertheless, it is the character of Aissa in his second book, *An Outcast of the Islands*, which shows even better the role of women in expressing, altering, and creating historical individuality. Just as Nina represents aspects of Almayer, as he clearly perceives in his moment of choice, so Aissa in *An Outcast of the Islands* is the central representation of the inner Willems. The two early novels, having the same location and many of the same characters, share as well the theme of colonialism and the disintegration of the men who exemplify it. The pitting of one sex against the other, which in these novels serves also to pit race against race, serves only to destroy; ordinarily, as character doubling functions, it splits rather than reconciles aspects of characters. In fact, as *Almayer's Folly* is the first to show, only through a reconciliation and identification between man and woman can wholeness of character, of civilization, even be attempted.

From the beginning of *An Outcast of the Islands*, the self-deluded Willems looks only to men for models; he relegates his wife to abject posturing and approval of his fantasies. (Like Almayer he does not perceive his wife as fully human.) The significance of the native Aissa, as a character and as a projection of the possibilities open to Willems as her lover, lies in her being a woman who consciously rejects the tradition from which Willems comes and to which he blindly determines to return. Native culture (which he equates with savagery) as a deliberate alternative to European culture always terrifies Willems. But as in *Almayer's Folly*, it is usually the natives who act with caution, with reason, and with adherence to understandable rules and traditions. The real savagery, as Conrad shows in both these books, comes from the thoughtless and impetuous imposition of the powerful personalities of white men. Almayer and Willems act out the colonial fantasies of their superiors, Hudig and Lingard. Native women are orphaned, their identity stripped from them, and then married to white men to carry out the paternalism of their real or adoptive fathers. The revenge of such women is slow and vicious; their competition and concern for their half-caste children are obsessive and immediately understandable. As Mrs. Almayer shows most clearly, the child is used to reject and destroy the culture with which the men mistakenly claim their identification. Only through an acceptance of native culture, paradoxically, can the white man forge a real identity, but such acceptance is literally out of the question for him; in Willems' life, it drives him mad.

The native woman Aissa, who captivates and terrifies Willems, represents in *An Outcast of the Islands* not only a love affair but also a personification of native culture in all its wildness and its passionate self-consciousness. Fleeing failure, Willems confronts in Aissa both himself and his history. As a character, Aissa suffers from overwriting and from some fairly hysterical prose cadences. But her grandeur (greater than Nina's) ultimately emerges, particularly toward the end of the book in her confrontation on the island with the appalling and horrified Captain Lingard. Her estimate of herself and of the men around her strikingly parallels the understanding reached earlier by Mrs. Almayer. The deviousness of white men holds no appeal for such women. Both are nostalgic for direct and courageous action, and both remember their own secret success in battle in the roles of men. The challenge such women offer, even in their own cultures, is often resented. To the white man, Lingard, Aissa is frightening.

This encounter between Aissa and Captain Lingard, while the exhausted and terrified Willems sleeps, is the crucial point of *An Outcast of the Islands*. Conrad has traditionally been judged incapable of creating viable women characters; "overwriting and rhetorical excess" according to one critic are the major limitations of Conrad's attempts in *Almayer's Folly*. For his psychoanalytical biographer, Bernard C. Meyer, the only explanation for any success in depicting the love relationship between Aissa and Willems rests on its parallel to Conrad's own developing relationship with Jessie George. The power, the self-consciousness that distinguish and illuminate Aissa have been ignored, except when they have been studiously judged as "overwrought," by critics and Captain Lingard alike. Her rejection reflects more upon the culture and expectations of our critics than upon Captain Lingard; the accusation Aissa levels at him is one that affronts us all. "That was my life. What has been yours?"

For the apprehension—the fear—that Aissa creates in Lingard and in Willems (who repeatedly imagines his soul vanishing under her steady gaze, in the classic double experience) is not merely fear of herself; it is rather that anxiety before a powerful, integrated personality, a thoroughly alive woman who silences captains and critics alike. From the earliest moments of their relationship, Willems perceives himself as facing annihilation. Half asleep, he often has fleeting dreams of his figure vanishing. "He had a notion of being lost among shapeless things that were dangerous and ghastly." A moment before, he was fearful for his civilization; thus his ego and his whiteness are inextricably entwined. Paradoxically, of course, it is always the woman who surrenders, and that very willingness to lose herself constitutes a threat so grave that he clutches at himself and rejects the very concept of surrender. Only a character certain of his own role, his own manhood, and his own identity can risk surrender to a relationship that will result in two new people, a new dual identity. Ironically, Dain in *Almayer's Folly* possesses that kind of inner security, coming as he does from a royal family to which he will certainly return. Both Almayer and Willems have only Captain Lingard to look to for security; having failed in the white world, they have been adopted as his surrogate sons. Lingard's certainty is often described by Conrad in terms of the deceptive surface of the river, "that river whose entrances only himself knew." Baffled by depths, inevitably Lingard is wrecked by the passionate river he has pretended to master and which he has claimed to own. He is bluff, hearty, and has a captivating stupidity, and he is all Almayer and Willems have before them as a model male. Thus, his terrified response to Aissa's direct challenge is a revelation of what she threatens to less secure men such as Willems.

Clearly, what Conrad describes is the defensiveness common to all the male characters in *An Outcast of the Islands*, but the lucid understanding of Lingard's involuntary response takes us a good deal further. For in his involuntary shudder, Tom Lingard is one of us. Generations of readers and critics have responded to Aissa as did Lingard, and for precisely the same reason. Leo Gurko is just one of those who equate Aissa with savagery, with a retreat from the blessings of civilization; in this novel, he says, "Willems' journey . . . is from man to animal." It is "a steep psychological descent." Willems' fear of what is not himself, of the other, contrasts starkly with Aissa's desire to know, her consuming need to understand others. Looking at Lingard,

> she gave him the look that was like a stab, not of anger but of desire; of the intense, overpowering desire to see in, to see through, to understand everything: every thought, emotion, purpose; every impulse, every hesitation inside that man . . .

This desire to know, the conscious cultivation of probing sensitivity, is not only characteristic of Aissa. It is true of all the women in these first two books and, in general, it remains true of Conrad's women up to Winnie Verloc's reasoned defensiveness in *The Secret Agent*, her stolid awareness that things do not bear too much looking into.

Early Conradian white men are distinguished by their lack of knowing, their determined ignorance. Almayer, Willems, and Lingard are all men of the surface, all self-deluded. In fact, the self-deluded protagonist is a recognizable constant in Conrad's work. The crisis of identity comes as it does only to a protagonist wrapped in delusion. In sharp contrast, these women of the early books are distinguished by their passionate apprehension of knowledge— about themselves and about the white men who use them. The natives have to be passionately intelligent to survive the white men. Not sex but intelligent sex is what frightens Willems; the grace and beauty of the natives are only appalling when they are seen to cover the intelligent mystery.

It is interesting that strong emotion brings consciousness to the women of these early novels; even Taminah, the slave girl in *Almayer's Folly*, comes to a crushing sense of the reality of her slave's life through the desire for Dain that abruptly enters her awareness. None of the women fears this consciousness; none resists it. Consciousness comes as a threat to the white man and they reject it. Almayer's great desire is forgetfulness, even at the cost of losing both his daughter and himself. Both Almayer and Willems, who are remarkably similar in their preoccupation with status, with whiteness, with the figures they cut, instinctively reject the kind of self-knowledge that passionate apprehension of a woman involves. They attribute it to savagery and sharply contrast this savagery with what they call Europeanism. Willems says frantically, "I did not know there was something in me she could get hold of. She, a savage. I, a civilized European, and clever. She that knew no more than a wild animal! Well, she found out something in me."

When one compares Willems' assessment of Aissa with Conrad's account of her consuming desire to know, to understand, the discrepancy between Willems' rationalization and the reality of her humanity is startling. Even in a letter to his early mentor, Edward Garnett, Conrad wrote evenly of the two: "they both long to have a significance in the order of nature or of society." In the books, the white men's consistent explanation of the women's incomprehensible behavior has to do with their savagery, with their instinctive acts that must not derive from any mutually intelligible source. In fact, the women (as well as their native male counterparts) act out of deliberate and skeptical assessments of white men; they observe, they wonder, they calculate. All the white men act impetuously and irrationally, blaming the predictable consequences on the natives in general and the women in particular. It is a familiar pattern. What has not been so clear before is the way in which sex and sexual doubling function in these books to show a departure route from the pattern. Nina and Dain, somewhat sentimentally, represent a future to *Almayer's Folly*. More graphically, more realistically, and more unhappily, Aissa offers such a departure to Willems in *An Outcast of the Islands*.

It is usual in these early books for Conrad to create a rounded character of action out of the combination of two or three less completely drawn fragments. Thus, Taminah and Mrs. Almayer round out the portrait of the half-caste of which the central figure is Nina. Both Mrs. Almayer and Taminah illustrate the bitter resolution possible to the kind of submissive relationship traditionally experienced by native and white women. Conrad's awareness of the unhappy and shattering possibilities finds expression through Mrs. Almayer's bitterness and Taminah's vulnerability and eventual death. Against these two tentative doubles, Nina emerges more clearly and without sentimentality. Her physical resemblance to Taminah is so extraordinary that the description of one stands perfectly for the other. "In that supple figure straight as an arrow, so graceful and free in its walk, behind those soft eyes that spoke of nothing but of unconscious resignation, there slept all fears, the curse of life and the consolation of death." This description of Taminah parallels the accounts of Nina, whose inner division and anxiety are quite invisible to her father and eventually to her lover as well. Taminah "shrank from Nina as she would have shrunk from the sharp blade of a knife cutting into her flesh, but she kept on visiting the brig to feed her dumb ignorant soul on her own despair." These traditional character doublings serve several purposes; not only do they delineate the potential of each character but they intensify what ultimately happens to each. They provide, as well, an opening toward the more complex doubling which, juxtaposing as it does a man and a woman, provides the most telling means of simultaneously defining and showing the limits of consciousness of the male identity.

Almayer, Dain, Lingard, and Willems all resist and are threatened by the full identification of self through a woman. Only Dain has the security of his tribal hierarchy behind him that allows his complete identification with Nina. He is the only male in these early books who is not terrified by the implications of a woman's submission. Nina, acting out her mother's advice, perceives in Dain's moment of triumph his real submission. The account of their crucial meeting and of their final commitment to one another is strikingly similar to the initial description of Aissa's surrender to Willems. What is remarkable is the difference between the reactions of the men. Of Nina, Conrad writes:

> She drew back her head and fastened her eyes on his in one of those long looks that are a woman's most terrible weapons, a look that is more stirring than the closest touch, and more dangerous than the thrust of a dagger, because it also whips the soul out of the body, but leaves the body alive and helpless, to be swayed here and there by the capricious tempests of passion and desire; a look that enwraps the whole body, and that penetrates into the innermost recesses of the being, bringing terrible defeat in the delirious uplifting of accomplished conquest. It has the same meaning for the man of the forests and the sea as for the man threading the paths of the more dangerous wilderness of houses and streets.

Significantly, at this moment Dain responds with a shout of joy; falling at her feet, he experiences his triumph. The contrast with Willems, who reacts with terror to Aissa's surrender, could not be more clear.

> And . . . look at her . . . she took me as if I did not belong to myself. She did. I did not know there was something in me she could get hold of. She, a savage. I, a civilized European, and clever! She that knew no more than a wild animal! Well, she found out something in me. She found it out, and I was lost. I knew it. She tormented me. I was ready to do anything. I resisted—but I was ready.

Dain's sense that with Nina he has the strength to accomplish everything has its tortured counterpart in Willems' terror that Aissa will, in her surrender, bring out his latent powers for what he calls savage action. What the women possess, what they offer, is the same. The key lies rather in the response found within the men who represent the varieties of colonial experience. And, in the remarkable difference between the responses of whites and Malays, there is visible the corrupting effect of the colonial relationship. Like Charles Gould, who responds inadequately to Emilia in *Nostromo*, the white men have been in some sense reduced, lessened as men, through their dependence upon European civilization and materialism.

The ambiguity inherent in a complex relationship is not ignored by Conrad even in the romanticism of Nina and Dain's relationship. Aware of the triumph inherent in surrender, Conrad describes with great ambiguity the smile hovering about Nina's mouth. "Who can tell in the fitful light of a camp fire? It might have been a smile of triumph, or of conscious power, or of tender pity, or, perhaps, of love." These relationships offer an expansion of self, a redefining of self. The men are defined not only through their similarities and identification with other men, as is usual, but through their ability to identify themselves with these "savage" or half-caste women. And because these men represent the colonial empires both literally, as their agents, and figuratively, as their products, their inability to achieve identification with the native women is a serious reflection upon the nature and future of their colonial civilization.

Many of these elements of Conrad's early work have been separately considered and understood. But there has been a tendency, easily understandable in light of the society we represent, to view aspects of Conrad's work in fragments. Character doubling has been considered as a device, as a psychological mechanism for exploring character, occasionally as a revelation of Conrad's psychic inadequacies. In these early works it seems clear that it is far more than any of these fragmentary means. It is instead the full-fledged expression of the juxtaposition of men and women, culture and culture, through which lies the only possibility for resolution of difference and active creation of a new life. Consistently, the men identify themselves, just as do Almayer, Willems, and Lingard, with Western imperialism (in the guise of "civilization") and against savagery. And, just as consistently, it remains for the women to offer in their characterization the humanity that goes beyond Western civilization.

In these early novels, customarily judged to be interesting but naturally inferior to the later, more accomplished creations, it is clear that Conrad has already mastered the complex art of making each element of the novel serve simultaneously on several levels. The love relationship, which successive waves of criticism have judged badly wrought, actually works convincingly in these early novels, not only personally but historically as well. Further, it is important to consider Conrad's entire novelistic production as a unified entity, one in which elements juxtaposed with one another provide in some sense new meanings and new insights which, considered singly, are not readily apparent. These early works, especially as they use characters jointly, need to be considered together. And, particularly, the parallel relationship between Nina and Dain, Aissa and Willems, is a revelation when seen in this dual light.

These early women are neither inarticulate nor unaware of the critical value of their lives and their perceptions set against white men and white society. Their comments are lucid and important. Nina's awareness of submission as potential triumph emerges clearly in her thoughts as she contemplates Dain's figure huddled at her feet. "As she glanced down at his kneeling form she felt a great pitying tenderness for that man she was used to calling— even in her thoughts—the master of life." Aissa is more lucid than Nina, more despairing in the face of Willems' determination to return to Europe despite her. "She was appalled, surprised and angry with the anger of unexpected humiliation; and her eyes looked fixedly, sombre and steady, at that man born in the land of violence and evil wherefrom nothing but misfortune comes to those who are not white." A moment later she arrives at her conscious and deliberate resolution to keep him with her, "a slave and a master." Unlike Nina, Aissa cannot turn to positive use the dual slave-master relationship that they both so accurately assess. The nature of colonialism, its spreading contamination, demands of each human being a choice; in the end, Willems chooses to be white and Aissa kills him for that.

The dual relationship of master and slave offers the threat of destruction only to the insecure white colonialist. Native men, even those who distrust

the strength of Aissa, take for granted the subtle shifts and interchanges marking the total exchange of affection between man and woman. Babalatchi's
respect for Aissa sharply contrasts with Lingard's distaste and revulsion from
her intense questions. And yet, even in her ferocious desire for knowledge
and her sense of her own value, she instinctively falls at Lingard's feet and
leaves him appalled by her willingness to abase herself. The ability to express
contradictions, to admit opposites within one nature, baffles and revolts a
single-minded white man. The challenge that Aissa hurls at Lingard is the
one these women hurl at us all. "Get out of my path," Lingard tells Aissa.
"You ought to know that when men meet in daylight women must be silent
and abide their fate."

> "Women!" she retorted, with subdued vehemence. "Yes, I am a
> woman! Your eyes see that, O Rajah Laut, but can you see my
> life? I have also heard—O man of many fights—I have also heard
> the voice of firearms; I also have felt the rain of young twigs and
> of leaves cut up by bullets fall down about my head; I also know
> how to look in silence at angry faces and at strong hands raised
> high grasping sharp steel. I also saw men fall dead around me
> without a cry of fear and of mourning; and I have watched the
> sleep of weary fugitives, and looked at night shadows full of men-
> ace and death with eyes that knew nothing but watchfulness.
> And," she went on with a mournful drop in her voice, "I have
> faced the heartless sea, held on my lap the heads of those who died
> raving from thirst, and from their cold hands took the paddle and
> worked so that those with me did not know that one man more
> was dead. I did all this. What more have you done? That was my
> life. What has been yours?"

Even Lingard is stunned into silence. But even more telling than this super-
lative tirade is the line that follows, a line that is the essence of what these
women represent as potential identities for these shells of men. "And I have
knelt at your feet! And I am afraid!" Lingard can only reject her in his self-
satisfied role as Rajah Laut.

That confrontation, the dramatic high point of *An Outcast of the Islands*,
epitomizes the success of Conrad's treatment of women in these two novels.
They function on so many levels simultaneously that they testify to the maturity of the author even at this early stage in his career. The native and half-
caste women do not blur into one another. Rather, they are sharply drawn
facets of a complex portrayal of strong and self-conscious women. They speak
clearly of a historical awareness, a sense of lost time and rapidly vanishing

possibilities for redemption. Through the personal relationship, in which identities merge and reform, they offer the possibility of transcending history. Sadly, only their own doomed kind are capable of accepting this gift of identity with its master-slave ambiguity. The white men, those who might have gained most humanity from such a doubling, have not the humanity to accept it.

J. HILLIS MILLER

Lord Jim: *Repetition as Subversion of Organic Form*

Lord Jim, like most works of literature, contains self-interpretative elements. Much of it is an explication of words and signs by means of other words, as narrator follows narrator, or as narration is inserted within narration. The critic who attempts to understand *Lord Jim* becomes another in a series of interpreters. He enters into a process of interpretation in which words bring out the meaning of other words and those words refer to others in their turn. No literary text has a manifest pattern, like the design of a rug, which the eye of the critic can survey from the outside and describe as a spatial form, but the intricacies of multiple narrators and time shifts in *Lord Jim* make this particularly evident. The textuality of a text, a "yarn" spun by Conrad, is the meshing of its filaments as they are interwoven in ways hidden from an objectifying eye. The critic must enter into the text, follow its threads as they weave in and out, appearing and disappearing, crisscrossing with other threads. In doing this he adds his own thread of interpretation to the fabric, or he cuts it in one way or another, so becoming part of its texture or changing it. Only in this way can he hope to identify the evasive center of ground which is not visible as a fixed emblem around which the story is spun, but is paradoxically, as Wallace Stevens says in "A Primitive Like an Orb," a "center on the horizon," a center which is outside and around rather than within and punctual.

Samuel Taylor Coleridge, that brilliant manipulator of the metaphors of

From *Fiction and Repetition: Seven English Novels.* © 1982 by J. Hillis Miller. Harvard University Press, 1982.

Occidental metaphysics, presents an image of the work of art in its rounded
unity corresponding to the assumption that there is such an interior center.
Aesthetic wholeness in a narrative, he says, must be copied from the wholeness
of a universe which circles in time around the motionless center of a God to
whose eternal insight all times are copresent:

> The common end of all *narrative*, nay, of *all*, Poems is to convert
> a *series* into a *Whole*: to make those events, which in real or imagined
> History move on in a *strait* line, assume to our Understandings a
> *circular* motion—the snake with it's Tail in its mouth. Hence in-
> deed the almost flattering and yet appropriate Term, Poesy—i.e.
> poiesis-*making*. Doubtless, to his eye, which alone comprehends
> all Past and all Future in one eternal Present, what to our short
> sight appears strait is but part of the great Cycle—just as the calm
> Sea to us *appears* level, tho' it indeed [be] only a part of a *globe*.
> Now what the Globe is in Geography, *miniaturing* in order to
> *manifest* the Truth, such is a Poem to that Image of God, which
> we were created with, and which still seeks Unity or Revelation
> of the *One* in and by the *Many*.

The concept of the organic unity of the work of art, as this passage
shows, cannot be detached from its theological basis. Nor can it separate itself
from mimetic theories of art. Far from asserting the autonomy of the artwork,
its way of being self-sufficiently rounded in on itself, Coleridge here describes
the poem as an image or a representation, even the representation of a representation. Its globular roundness miniatures not God in his relation to the
creation, but the image of God created in our souls which drives us to seek
the one in the many. The poem is the image of an image. Moreover, the
oneness revealed in and by the many is not intrinsic but extrinsic. It is the
center of a circle made up of a series of events which move in sequence but
are curved back on themselves, like the fabled snake with its tail in its mouth,
by the attraction of that center, just as the soul "in order to be an individual
Being . . . must go forth *from* God, yet as the *receding* from *him* is to *proceed*
towards Nothingness and Privation, it must still at every step turn back toward
him in order to *be* at all—Now, a straight Line, continuously retracted forms
of necessity a circular orbit." The creation, the soul, the work of art—all
three have the same shape, the same movement, and the same relation to a
generative center. They are related in a descending series of analogical equiv-
alences, each a copy of the one above and all able to be defined by the same
geometrical or zoological metaphors.

In place of this kind of doubling, twice removed, of God's universe by

the little world of the work of art, Conrad presents for both cosmos and work
of literature a structure which has no beginning, no foundation outside itself,
and exists only as a self-generated web:

> There is a—let us say—a machine. It evolved itself (I am severely
> scientific) out of a chaos of scraps of iron and behold!—it knits. I
> am horrified at the horrible work and stand appalled. I feel it ought
> to embroider—but it goes on knitting . . . And the most withering
> thought is that the infamous thing has made itself; made itself
> without thought, without conscience, without foresight, without
> eyes, without heart. It is a tragic accident—and it has happened
> . . . It knits us in and it knits us out. It has knitted time, space,
> pain, death, corruption, despair and all the illusions—and nothing
> matters. I'll admit however that to look at the remorseless process
> is sometimes amusing.

One way of looking at the remorseless process is by way of a novel, but
a novel is not for Conrad an *image* of the horrible knitting machine and its
work. It is part of the knitting, woven into its web. The infamous machine
has made human beings and all their works too, including language and its
power of generating or of expressing all the illusions. Works of art, like man's
other works, are what they are "in virtue of that truth one and immortal
which lurks in the force that made [the machine] spring into existence." Product of the same force which has knit the rest of the universe, a work of art
has the same kind of structure. A novel by Conrad, though it invites the
reader to hope that he can find a center of the sort Coleridge ascribes to the
good work of art, has nothing certainly identifiable outside itself by which it
might be measured or from which it might be seen. It has no visible thematic
or structuring principle which will allow the reader to find out its secret,
explicate it once and for all, untie all its knots and straighten all its threads.
The knitting machine cannot be said to be the origin of the cloth it knits,
since what the machine knits is itself, knitter and knitted forming one indistinguishable whole without start or finish, continuously self-creating. The
cloth exists as the process of its knitting, the twisting of its yarns as they are
looped and knotted by a pervasive "force." This force is the truth one and
immortal everywhere present but nowhere visible in itself, an energy both of
differentiation and of destruction. "It knits us in and it knits us out."

A familiar passage in Conrad's *Heart of Darkness* describes the indirection
characteristic of works of literature like *Lord Jim*. The passage uses a variant
of the image of the knitted fabric in the letter to Cunninghame Graham. "The
yarns of seamen," says the narrator, "have a direct simplicity, the whole mean-

ing of which lies within the shell of a cracked nut. But Marlow was not typical
(if his propensity to spin yarns be excepted), and to him the meaning of an
episode was not inside like a kernel but outside, enveloping the tale which
brought it out only as a glow brings out a haze, in the likeness of one of those
misty halos that sometimes are made visible by the spectral illumination of
moonshine." Though the meaning is outside, it may only be seen by way of
the tale which brings it out. This bringing out takes place in the interaction
of its different elements in their reference to one another. These the critic
must track, circling from one word or image to another within the text. Only
in this movement of interpretation does the meaning exist. It is not a central
and originating node, like the kernel of a nut, a solid and pre-existing nub. It
is a darkness, an absence, a haze invisible in itself and only made visible by
the ghostlike indirection of a light which is already derived. It is not the direct
light of the sun but the reflected light of the moon which brings out the haze.
This visible but secondary light and the invisible haze create a halo of "moonshine" which depends for its existence on the reader's involvement in the play
of light and dark which generates it. Does this invitation to believe that there
is an explanatory center, without positive identification of that center or even
certainty about whether or not it exists, in fact characterize *Lord Jim*? I shall
investigate briefly here a series of ways the novel might be interpreted.

The theme of *Lord Jim* is stated most explicitly toward the end of
chapter 5, in Marlow's attempt to explain why he concerns himself with Jim:

> Why I longed to go grubbing into the deplorable details of an
> occurrence which, after all, concerned me no more than as a mem-
> ber of an obscure body of men held together by a community of
> inglorious toil and by fidelity to a certain standard of conduct, I
> can't explain. You may call it an unhealthy curiosity if you like;
> but I have a distinct notion I wished to find something. Perhaps,
> unconsciously, I hoped I would find that something, some pro-
> found and redeeming cause, some merciful explanation, some con-
> vincing shadow of an excuse. I see well enough now that I hoped
> for the impossible—for the laying of what is the most obstinate
> ghost of man's creation, of the uneasy doubt uprising like a mist,
> secret and gnawing like a worm, and more chilling than the cer-
> titude of death—the doubt of the sovereign power enthroned in a
> fixed standard of conduct.

Jim is "one of us," an Englishman, son of a country clergyman, a "gentleman," brought up in the British traditions of duty, obedience, quiet faithfulness, and unostentatious courage. Nevertheless, he has committed the

shockingly dishonorable act of deserting his ship and the helpless pilgrims it carried. Jim's desertion seems especially deplorable to Marlow because Jim looks so trustworthy, so perfect an example of an unassuming nobility of the tradition from which he has sprung. "He had no business to look so sound," says Marlow. "I thought to myself—well, if this sort can go wrong like that . . . and I felt as though I could fling down my hat and dance on it from sheer mortification"; "He looked as genuine as a new sovereign, but there was some infernal alloy in his metal" (ch. 5). The descrepancy between what Jim looks like and what he is puts in question for Marlow "the sovereign power enthroned in a fixed standard of conduct." He does not doubt the existence of the standard, the seaman's code of fidelity, obedience, and obscure courage on which the British empire was built. He comes to question the power installed behind this standard and within it. This power, as its defining adjective affirms, justifies the standard as its king—its principle, its source, its law.

If there is no sovereign power enthroned in the fixed standard of conduct then the standard is without validity. It is an all-too-human fiction, an arbitrary code of behavior—"this precious notion of a convention," as Marlow says, "only one of the rules of the game, nothing more" (ch. 7). Nothing matters, and anything is possible, as in that condition of spiritual anarchy which takes over on the ship's boat after Jim and the other officers have deserted the *Patna* and left her to sink with eight hundred men, women, and children. "After the ship's lights had gone," says Jim, "anything might have happened in that boat—anything in the world—and the world no wiser. I felt this, and I was pleased. It was just dark enough, too. We were like men walled up quick in a roomy grave. No concern with anything on earth. Nobody to pass an opinion. Nothing mattered. . . . No fear, no law, no sounds, no eyes—not even our own, till—till sunrise at least" (ch. 10). Marlow interprets Jim's words in a way which gives them the widest application to the derelict condition of a man who has lost faith, conviction, his customary material surroundings—whatever has given his world stability and order by seeming to support it from outside. "When your ship fails you," says Marlow, "your whole world seems to fail you; the world that made you, restrained you, taken [*sic*] care of you. It is as if the souls of men floating on an abyss and in touch with immensity had been set free for any excess of heroism, absurdity, or abomination. Of course, as with belief, thought, love, hate, conviction, or even the visual aspect of material things, there are as many shipwrecks as there are men . . . Trust a boat on the high seas to bring about the Irrational that lurks at the bottom of every thought, sentiment, sensation, emotion" (ch. 10).

Marlow's aim (or Conrad's) seems clear: to find some explanation for Jim's action which will make it still possible to believe in the sovereign power. Many critics think that in the end Marlow (or Conrad) is satisfied, that even Jim is satisfied. The circumstances of Jim's death and his willingness to take responsibility for the death of Dain Waris ("He hath taken it upon his own head"; ch. 45) make up for all Jim has done before. Jim's end re-enthrones the regal power justifying the fixed standard of conduct by which he condemns himself to death.

Matters are not so simple in this novel. For one thing, there is something suspect in Marlow's enterprise of interpretation. "Was it for my own sake," he asks, "that I wished to find some shadow of an excuse for that young fellow whom I had never seen before?" (ch. 5). If so much is at stake for himself, he is likely to find what he wants to find.

Marlow attempts to maintain his faith in the sovereign power in several contradictory ways. One is to discover that there are extenuating circumstances. Perhaps Jim is not all bad. Perhaps he can be excused. Perhaps he can ultimately redeem himself. At other times Marlow suggests that in spite of appearances Jim has a fatal soft spot. He cannot be safely trusted for an instant. If this is so, then he must be condemned in the name of the kingly law determining good and evil, praise and blame. At still other times Marlow's language implies that Jim is the victim of dark powers within himself, powers which also secretly govern the universe outside. If there is no benign sovereign power there may be a malign one, a principle not of light but of blackness, "a destructive fate ready for us all" (ch. 5). If this is the case, there are indeed extenuating circumstances, precisely the "shadow of an excuse." To act according to a fixed standard of conduct which is justified by no sovereign power, as perhaps Jim does in his death, is the truest heroism. It is defiance of the shadowy powers which would undermine everything man finds good. If this is so, Jim's death is nevertheless in one sense still a sham. It is a sham in the sense that it is valued by no extrahuman judge. It is only one way of acting among others.

Perhaps, to pursue this line a little further, the source of all Jim's trouble is his romanticism, that childish image of himself as a hero which has its source in fraudulent literature and sticks with him all his life: "He confronted savages on tropical shores, quelled mutinies on the high seas, and in a small boat upon the ocean kept up the hearts of despairing men—always an example of devotion to duty, and as unflinching as a hero in a book" (ch. 1). Perhaps it is Jim's confidence in this illusory image of himself which is the source of his inability to confront the truth about himself and about the universe. Perhaps this confidence even paradoxically explains his repeated acts of cowardice. It may be that Jim's death is no more than the last of such acts, his last failure to face the dark side of himself which is so rudely brought back before him in the person of Gentleman Brown. His death may be no more than his last attempt to act according to a fictional idea of heroic conduct. Certainly the final paragraphs of the novel show Marlow by no means "satisfied." The ending is a tissue of unanswered questions in which Marlow affirms once more not that Jim is a hero or that Jim is a coward but that he remains an indecipherable mystery:

> And that's the end. He passes away under a cloud, inscrutable at heart, forgotten, unforgiven, and excessively romantic.. . . . He goes away from a living woman to celebrate his pitiless wedding with a shadowy ideal of conduct. Is he satisfied—quite, now, I wonder? We ought to know. He is one of us—and have I not stood up once, like an evoked ghost, to answer for his eternal constancy? Was I so very wrong after all? Now he is no more, there are days when the reality of his existence comes to me with an immense, with an overwhelming force; and yet upon my honour there are moments, too, when he passes from my eyes like a disembodied spirit astray amongst the passions of this earth, ready to surrender himself faithfully to the claim of his own world of shades.
>
> Who knows?
>
> (Ch. 45)

The ending seems to confirm Marlow's earlier statement that the heart of each man is a dark forest to all his fellows and "loneliness" a "hard and absolute condition of existence": "The envelope of flesh and blood on which our eyes are fixed melts before the out-stretched hand, and there remains only the capricious, unconsolable, and elusive spirit that no eye can follow, no hand can grasp" (ch. 16).

On the other hand, all that seems problematic and inconclusive about *Lord Jim* when it is approached from the point of view of explicit thematic statements and by way of Marlow's interpretation of Jim may be resolved if the reader stands back from Marlow's perspective and looks at the novel as a whole. The detached view may see the truth, according to that proverb Marlow recalls which affirms that "the onlookers see most of the game" (ch. 21). Seen from a distance, *Lord Jim* may turn out to be a pattern of recurrent motifs which reveals more about Jim than Marlow comes to understand. Jim's feeling at his trial that "only a meticulous precision of statement would bring out the true horror behind the face of things" (ch. 4) may be the clue to the aesthetic method of the book. The episodes Marlow and others relate, the language they use, may reveal to the readers of the novel a secret hidden from

Marlow, from Jim, and from all the characters, a secret known only to Conrad. He may have chosen this way to show forth the truth because only as a participant in its revelation can the reader understand it.

When *Lord Jim* is approached from the perspective of its narrative structure and its design of recurrent images it reveals itself to be not less but more problematic, more inscrutable, like Jim himself. I have elsewhere argued that temporal form, interpersonal relations, and relations of fiction and reality are three structuring principles fundamental to fiction. *Lord Jim* is an admirable example of the tendency of these in their interaction to weave a fabric of words which is incapable of being interpreted unambiguously, as a fixed pattern of meaning, even though the various possibilities of meaning are rigorously delimited by the text.

To begin with the structure of interpersonal relations: Victorian novels were often apparently stabilized by the presence of an omniscient narrator, spokesman for the collective wisdom of the community, though . . . such a narrator never turns out to be unequivocally the basis of the storytelling when a given Victorian novel is interpreted in detail. Such a narrator, if he were ever to exist, would represent a trustworthy point of view and also a safe vantage point from which to watch the hearts and minds of the characters in their relations to one another. Conrad, as many critics have noted, does not employ a "reliable" narrator. In *Lord Jim* no point of view is entirely trustworthy. The novel is a complex design of interrelated minds, no one of which can be taken as a secure point of reference from which the others may be judged.

The first part of the story is told by an "omniscient" narrator who seems like the narrator of a novel by Trollope or by George Eliot. This first narrator of *Lord Jim* has the same superhuman powers of insight, including direct access to the hero's mind, that is possessed by those earlier Victorian narrators. He relinquishes that access early in the story, as though it could not provide a satisfactory avenue to the truth behind Jim's life. He then returns in chapter 36, after Marlow's narrative to his almost silent auditors is over. He returns to introduce the man who receives the letter which is Marlow's "last word" about Jim. The bulk of the novel is made up of Marlow's telling of Jim's story to the group of listeners in the darkness who are the reader's surrogates. Those listeners stand between the reader and Marlow's telling. "He existed for me," says Marlow, "and after all it is only through me that he exists for you. I've led him out by the hand; I have paraded him before you" (ch. 21).

Many sections of the story are told to Marlow by Jim. In these the reader can see Jim attempting to interpret his experience by putting it into words.

This self-interpretation is interpreted once more by Marlow, then by implication interpreted again by Marlow's listeners. The latter appear occasionally
as intervening minds, as when one of them says: "You are so subtle, Marlow"
(ch. 8). This overlapping of interpretative minds within minds is put in question in its turn, at least implicitly, by the "omniscient" narrator. He surrounds
all and perhaps understands all, though he does not give the reader the sort
of interpretative help provided by the narrator of *Middlemarch* or of *The Last
Chronicle of Barset*. Even so, this narrator may have been brought back briefly
near the end of the novel to suggest that the reader might be wise to put in
question Marlow's interpretation of Jim, even though the narrator cannot or
will not provide the reader with any solid alternative ground on which to
stand.

Within Marlow's narrative there are many minor characters—Captain
Brierly, the French lieutenant, Chester, Stein—who have their say in the story.
They are irreplaceable points of view on Jim within Marlow's point of view.
They are sources of parts of his story and offer alternative ways of judging it.
Their own stories, moreover, are analogous to Jim's story, though whether in
a positive or in a negative way is often hard to tell. Just as the crucial episodes
in Jim's life echo one another, the jump from the *Patna* repeating his failure
to jump in the small boat when he was in training and being repeated again
by his jump over the stockade in Patusan ("Patusan" recalling *Patna*), so Captain Brierly's suicide is a jump ambiguously duplicating Jim's jumps (was it
cowardly or an act of heroism following logically from a shattering insight into
the truth of things?), while the French lieutenant's courage shows what Jim
might have done on the *Patna*, and Stein's strange history echoes Jim's either
positively or negatively. Stein appears to be either an unreliable narrator or a
trustworthy commentator, depending on one's judgment of his life and personality. Is he a man who has bravely immersed himself in the destructive
element to win an ultimate wisdom, or has he withdrawn passively from life
to collect his butterflies and to give Marlow and the readers of the novel only
misleading clues to the meaning of Jim's life?

Lord Jim is made up of episodes similar in design. In each a man confronts
a crisis testing his courage, the strength of his faith in the sovereign power
enthroned in a fixed standard of conduct. In each case someone, the man
himself or someone else, interprets that test, or rather he interprets the words
which the man's reaction to the test has already generated. There is even a
parody of this pattern early in the novel, as if to call attention to it as a
structuring principle or as a universal way in which men are related to one
another. Just as Marlow seeks out the chief engineer of the *Patna* in the hospital
"in the eccentric hope of hearing something explanatory of the famous affair

from his point of view," so the doctor who is tending the engineer after his brandy debauch says he "never remember[s] being so interested in a case of the jim-jams before." "The head, ah! the head, of course, gone, but the curious part is that there is some sort of method in his raving. I am trying to find out. Most unusual—that thread of logic in such a delirium" (ch. 5). The reader of *Lord Jim*, like the doctor, must seek the thread of logic within a bewildering complexity of words. With these words Conrad attempts to express a truth beyond direct expression in words, "for words also belong to the sheltering conception of light and order which is our refuge" (ch. 33), our refuge from the truth hidden in the darkness. In the sequence of discrete episodes which makes up the novel, no episode serves as the point of origin, the arch-example of the *mythos* of the novel, but each is, by reason of its analogy to other episodes, a repetition of them, each example being as enigmatic as all the others.

A similar complexity characterizes the temporal structure of the novel. Jim says of his memory of watching the other officers struggle to get the *Patna*'s boat in the water: "I ought to have a merry life of it, by God! for I shall see that funny sight a good many times yet before I die" (ch. 9). Of an earlier moment before the officers desert the ship he says: "It was as though I had heard it all, seen it all, gone through it all twenty times already" (ch. 8). Each enactment of a given episode echoes backward and forward indefinitely, creating a pattern of eddying repetition. If there are narrators within narrators there are also times within times—time-shifts, breaks in time, anticipations, retrogressions, retellings, and reminders that a given part of the story has often been told before. Marlow, for example, like the Ancient Mariner, has related Jim's story "many times, in distant parts of the world" (ch. 4). The novel is made up of recurrences in which each part of the story has already happened repeatedly when the reader first encounters it, either in someone's mind, or in someone's telling, or in the way it repeats other similar events in the same person's life or in the lives of others. The temporal structure of the novel is open. *Lord Jim* is a chain of repetitions, each event referring back to others which it both explains and is explained by, while at the same time it prefigures those which will occur in the future. Each exists as part of an infinite regression and progression within which the narrative moves back and forth discontinuously across time seeking unsuccessfully some motionless point in its flow.

It might be argued that the sequence of events as the reader is given them by Conrad, in a deliberately chosen order, is a linear series with a beginning, middle, and end which determines a straightforward development of gradually revealed meaning moving through time as the reader follows word after word and page after page, becoming more and more absorbed in the story and more and more emotionally involved in it. This sequence, it might be argued, generates a determinate meaning. It is true that this linear sequence is shared by any reader and that it establishes a large background of agreement about what happens and even about the meaning of what happens. That Jim jumps from the *Patna* and that this is a morally deplorable act no reader is likely to doubt. But it is also true that the linear sequence of episodes as it is presented to the reader by the various narrators is radically rearranged from the chronological order in which the events actually occurred. This could imply that Conrad, the "omniscient narrator," or Marlow has ordered the episodes in such a way that the best understanding by the reader of a total meaning possessed by one or another of these narrators will be revealed. Or it may imply, as I think it does, that the deeper explanatory meaning behind those facts open to the sunlight, about which anyone would agree, remains hidden, so that any conceivable narrator of these facts or interpreter of them is forced to move back and forth across the facts, putting them in one or another achronological order in the hope that this deeper meaning will reveal itself. The narration in many ways, not least by calling attention to the way one episode repeats another rather than being clearly a temporal advance on it, breaks down the chronological sequence and invites the reader to think of it as a simultaneous set of echoing episodes spread out spatially like villages or mountain peaks on a map. *Lord Jim* too, to borrow the splendid phrase Henry James uses in his review of Conrad's *Chance*, is "a prolonged hovering flight of the subjective over the outstretched ground of the case exposed." Insofar as the novel is this and not the straightforward historical movement suggested by Aristotle's comments on beginning, middle, and end in the *Poetics*, then the sort of metaphysical certainty implicit in Aristotle, the confidence that some *logos* or underlying cause and ground supports the events, is suspended. It is replaced by the image of a consciousness attempting to grope its way to the hidden cause behind a set of enigmatic facts by moving back and forth over them. If the "facts" are determinate (more or less) the novel encourages the reader to seek the "why" behind the events, some "shadow of an excuse." It is here, I am arguing, that the text does not permit the reader to decide among alternative possibilities, even though those possibilities themselves are identified with precise determinate certainty.

The similarities between one episode and another or one character and another in *Lord Jim* no doubt appear to be deliberately designed (whether by Conrad or by Marlow), like most of the cases of repetition discussed in this book. Such repetitions differ from those which are accidental or merely contingent, perhaps even insignificant, although the reader would do well not to be too sure about the existence of insignificant similarities. Moreover, the fact that Conrad probably consciously intended most of the repetitions I discuss here (though certainty about that is of course impossible) may be trivial compared to the way the novel represents human life as happening to fall into repetitive patterns, whether in the life of a single person, as Jim repeats variants of the same actions over and over, or from person to person, as Brierly's jump repeats Jim's jump. The question the novel asks and cannot unequivocally answer is "Why is this?" To say it is because Conrad designed his novel in recurring patterns is to trivialize the question and to give a misplaced answer to it.

Nor can the meaning of the novel be identified by returning to its historical sources, however helpful or even essential these are in establishing a context for our reading. The "source" of *Lord Jim*, as Conrad tells the reader in the Author's Note, was a glimpse of the "real" Jim: "One sunny morning in the common-place surroundings of an Eastern roadstead, I saw his form pass by—appealing—significant—under a cloud—perfectly silent. . . . It was for me, with all the sympathy of which I was capable, to seek fit words for his meaning." Norman Sherry, in *Conrad's Eastern World*, and Ian Watt, in *Conrad in the Nineteenth Century*, have discussed in detail the historical events which lie behind the novel. *Lord Jim* can be defined as an attempt on Conrad's part to understand the real by way of a long detour through the fictive. To think of *Lord Jim* as the interpretation of history is to recognize that the historical events "behind" the novel exist now as documents, and that these documents, too, are enigmatic. They are as interesting for the ways in which Conrad changed them as for the ways in which he repeated them exactly. The novel is related to its sources in a pattern of similarity and difference like that of the episodes inside the novel proper. The facts brought to light by Sherry and Watt, for example the "Report of a Court of Inquiry held at Aden into the cause of the abandonment of the steamship 'Jeddah,' " do not serve as a solid and unequivocal point of origin by means of which the novel may be viewed, measured, and understood. The documents are themselves mysterious, as mysterious as the Old Yellow Book on which Browning based *The Ring and the Book* or as the dry, factual account of historical events included at the end of Melville's *Benito Cereno*. In all these cases knowledge of the historical sources makes the story based on them not less but more inscrutable, more difficult to understand. If there are "fit words" for Jim's "meaning" they are to be found only within the novel, not in any texts outside it.

Perhaps, to turn to a last place where an unambiguous meaning may be found, the pattern of images in its recurrences somehow transcends the complexities I have discussed. It may constitute a design lying in the sunlight, ready to be seen and understood. It will be remembered that Conrad attempts above all, as he says in the Preface to *The Nigger of the "Narcissus,"* to make us *see*. Matching this is the recurrent image in *Lord Jim* according to which Marlow gets glimpses of Jim through a rift in the clouds. "The views he let me have of himself," says Marlow, "were like those glimpses through the shifting rents in a thick fog—bits of vivid and vanishing detail, giving no connected idea of the general aspect of a country" (ch. 6). The metaphorical structure of the novel may reveal in such disconnected glimpses a secret which cannot be found out by exploring its narrative, temporal, or interpersonal patterns, or by extracting explicit thematic statements.

A network of light and dark imagery manifestly organizes the novel throughout. It is first established insistently near the beginning in the description of the *Patna* steaming across the calm sea: "The *Patna*, with a slight hiss, passed over that plain luminous and smooth, unrolled a black ribbon of smoke across the sky, left behind her on the water a white ribbon of foam that vanished at once, like a phantom of a track drawn upon a lifeless sea by the phantom of a steamer" (ch. 2). Black against white, light against dark—perhaps the meaning of *Lord Jim* is to be found in Conrad's manipulation of this binary pattern.

This metaphorical or "symbolic" pattern, too, is systematically ambiguous, as may be seen by looking at two examples, the description of Jim's visit to Marlow's room after his trial and the description of Marlow's last glimpse of Jim on the shore. The juxtaposition of light and dark offers no better standing ground from which what is equivocal about the rest of the novel may be surveyed and comprehended than any other aspect of the text. The "visual aspect of material things" and the clues it may offer to the meaning of man's life sink in the general shipwreck which puts in doubt the sovereign power enthroned in a fixed standard of conduct:

> He remained outside, faintly lighted on the background of night, as if standing on the shore of a sombre and hopeless sea.
>
> An abrupt heavy rumble made me lift my head. The noise seemed to roll away, and suddenly a searching and violent glare fell on the blind face of the night. The sustained and dazzling flickers seemed to last for an unconscionable time. The growl of the thunder increased steadily while I looked at him, distinct and black, planted solidly upon the shores of a sea of light. At the moment of greatest brilliance the darkness leaped back with a culminating crash, and he vanished before my dazzled eyes as utterly as though he had been blown to atoms.
>
> (Ch. 16)

He was white from head to foot, and remained persistently visible with the stronghold of the night at his back, the sea at his feet, the opportunity by his side—still veiled. What do you say? Was it still veiled? I don't know. For me that white figure in the stillness of coast and sea seemed to stand at the heart of a vast enigma. The twilight was ebbing fast from the sky above his head, the strip of sand had sunk already under his feet, he himself appeared no bigger than a child—then only a speck, a tiny white speck, that seemed to catch all the light left in a darkened world. . . . And, suddenly, I lost him.

                                                                          (Ch. 35)

In one of these passages Jim is the light that illuminates the darkness. In the other he is the blackness that stands out against a blinding light which suddenly reveals itself from its hiding place and then disappears. Light changes place with dark; the value placed on dark and light changes place, as light is sometimes the origin of dark, dark sometimes the origin of light. Each such passage, moreover, refers to the others by way of anticipation or recollection, as the first of the texts quoted prefigures the second, but when the reader turns to the other passage it is no easier to understand and itself refers to other such passages. No one of them is the original ground, the basis on which the others may be interpreted. *Lord Jim* is like a dictionary in which the entry under one word refers the reader to another word which refers him to another and then back to the first word again, in an endless circling. Marlow sitting in his hotel room ceaselessly writing letters by the light of a single candle while Jim struggles with his conscience and the thunderstorm prepares in the darkness outside may be taken as an emblem of literature as Conrad sees it. A work of literature is for him in a paradoxical relation to a nonverbal reality it seeks both to uncover and to evade in the creation of its own exclusively verbal realm.

I claim, then, that from whatever angle it is approached *Lord Jim* reveals itself to be a work which raises questions rather than answering them. The fact that it contains its own interpretations does not make it easier to understand. The overabundance of possible explanations only inveigles the reader to share in the self-sustaining motion of a process of interpretation which cannot reach an unequivocal conclusion. This weaving movement of advance and retreat constitutes and sustains the meaning of the text, that evasive center which is everywhere and nowhere in the play of its language.

Marlow several times calls explicit attention to the unendingness of the process by which he and the readers of the novel go over and over the details of Jim's life in an ever-renewed, never-successful attempt to understand it completely and so write "Finis" to his story. "And besides," affirms Marlow apropos of his "last" words about Jim, "the last word is not said,—probably shall never be said. Are not our lives too short for that full utterance which through all our stammerings is of course our only and abiding intention? . . . There is never time to say our last word—the last word of our love, or our desire, faith, remorse, submission, revolt" (ch. 21). The reader will remember here those "last words" of Kurtz ("The horror! The horror!") which Marlow in another story hears and ironically praises for their finality, their power to sum up. If this theme is repeated within *Lord Jim*, these repetitions echo in their turn passages in other novels by Conrad. If *Heart of Darkness* leads to Marlow's recognition that he cannot understand Kurtz as long as he has not followed Kurtz all the way into the abyss of death, the "ending" of *Lord Jim* is Marlow's realization that it is impossible to write "The End" to any story: "End! Finis! the potent word that exorcises from the house of life the haunting shadow of fate. This is what—notwithstanding the testimony of my eyes and his own earnest assurances—I miss when I look back upon Jim's success. While there's life there is hope, truly; but there is fear, too . . . he made so much of his disgrace while it is the guilt alone that matters. He was not—if I may say so—clear to me. He was not clear. And there is a suspicion he was not clear to himself either" (ch. 16). Nor can he, I am arguing, ever be clear to us, except with the paradoxical clarity generated by our recognition that the process of interpreting his story is a ceaseless movement toward a light which always remains hidden in the dark.

Let there be no misunderstanding here. The situation I have just described does not mean that the set of possible explanations for Jim's action is limitless, indeterminate in the sense of being indefinitely multiple and nebulous. The various meanings are not the free imposition of subjective interpretations by the reader, but are controlled by the text. In that sense they are determinate. The novel provides the textual material for identifying exactly what the possible explanations are. The reader is not permitted to go outside the text to make up other possible explanations of his own. The indeterminacy lies in the multiplicity of possible incompatible explanations given by the novel and in the lack of evidence justifying a choice of one over the others. The reader cannot logically have them all, and yet nothing he is given determines a choice among them. The possibilities, moreover, are not just given side by side as entirely separate hypotheses. They are related to one another in a system of mutual implication and mutual contradiction. Each calls up the others, but it does not make sense to have more than one of them.

MARTIN PRICE

The Limits of Irony:
Lord Jim *and* Nostromo

LORD JIM

Conrad's *Lord Jim* is a work that explores and profoundly questions romanticism, and it takes the form of a meditation on the romantic hero. To Jim
falls the burden of action and to Marlow that of reflection. Marlow can fully
exercise his powers of thought because, within the novel, nothing else is
required of him. There is no action for his consciousness to block or disable.
And while in a real sense Marlow's own fate—or his conception of himself—
is tied to his reflections on Jim, still we recognize in Marlow a power to
subsist without certitudes. Marlow is not "romantic" to the same degree as
Jim, but the memory of having been romantic has great importance for him.
He is in that respect not unlike the narrator of Byron's *Don Juan*, disabused
and critical of youthful folly but at the same time envious of its capacity for
passion and of the grandeur of its illusions. Marlow has, one can say, unfinished business with romantic dreams. We know little about what has inter-
vened between the time of such dreams and the moment of his meeting Jim,
but it is clear that the enormity of Jim's failure and the tortured incomprehension with which Jim tries to evade his guilt have the power to unsettle
Marlow like a painful memory of his own. He must hold unremittingly to
what he knows is reality lest Jim's imagination somehow contaminate his own.

Jim has come out of a peaceful life where no issues were raised, much
less met; his father, a parson, "possessed such certain knowledge of the un-

From *Forms of Life: Character and Moral Imagination in the Novel.* © 1983 by Yale University. Yale University Press, 1983. Originally entitled "Conrad: The Limits of
Irony."

knowable as made for the righteousness of people in cottages without disturbing the ease of mind of those whom an unerring Providence enables to live in
mansions." Like his father, Jim can overlook difficulties: if he is immobilized
by danger, he can believe that his superior courage disdains the vanity of
display. As a young officer, Jim makes his choice without awareness that he
has done so. He sails as chief mate on the *Patna*—having chosen to remain in
the East—and we see its remarkable cargo of eight hundred passengers, Mos-
lems from all kinds of life, joined together by "the call of an idea," as "pilgrims
of an exacting faith."

In the transition from the close of the second chapter to the third Conrad
gives two pictures of the *Patna* traversing Eastern waters. In the first, we see
it from the outside in its fragility under the eye of the merciless sun, the
identical hot days "falling into an abyss forever open in the wake of the ship."
The ship holds on "her steadfast way black and smouldering in a luminous
immensity, as if scorched by a flame flicked at her from a heaven without
pity." But in the calm amidships, where the five white officers live, there is
only the "assurance of everlasting security." Jim, as he stands a watch on the
bridge, feels "the great certitude of unbounded safety and peace that could
be read on the silent aspect of nature, like the certitude of fostering love upon
the placid tenderness of a mother's face." In his undemanding tasks Jim is
free to entertain dreams of "valorous deeds." They have "a gorgeous virility"
and "the charm of vagueness," and he imagines there is "nothing he cannot
face."

Conrad gives us only the shallow surface of dreams that Jim indulges;
their imagery, based in part on "light holiday literature," is not drawn from
the private world and local scenes Jim inhabits. The very generality is appropriate enough, for it represents at once withdrawal from the actual, the in-
definite solitude of a gentle narcissism, and the triteness of a conventional
mind. Jim has not yet begun to live. He is sufficiently defined for himself by
his contrast with the passengers and the rest of the officers. The latter are
grotesquely ugly, particularly the captain, who looks "like a clumsy effigy of
a man cut out of a block of fat." But their grossness and obscenity only confirm
Jim's belief in his privileged world: "They could not touch him; he shared
the air they breathed, but he was different . . ."

The novel begins in medias res with Jim as a ship-chandler, a customer's
man, persuading ships' captains to trade with the dealer whose profits he
promotes. But, apart from that brief glimpse of Jim, we come to know him
most clearly at the official hearings after the *Patna* disaster, where he alone of
his ship's officers presents himself, and in his dinner and conversation with
Marlow. The note of all that is to follow is given in the painful exposure Jim

makes of his self-contempt. When he hears someone say "Look at that wretched cur," he takes for granted that the words have been directed at him. He spins about, ready to fight Marlow or whoever else may have spoken. For a moment Jim has the opportunity to attribute the feelings he has about himself to someone else and to fight them in some external and immediate way. But even that sad consolation is denied him by the sight of an actual dog. All that remains is Jim's open avowal, a new source of shame, of his expectation that he will be thought a cur. When Marlow overtakes him and taxes him with running away, Jim is instantly defiant and proud: "From no man—from not a single man on earth." But there is, of course, one man he doesn't consider; it is from himself that he is running away.

The long scene in the dining room and on the verandah of the hotel is a fine study of Jim's desperate evasion of the painful truth of his role on board the *Patna*. Here, for the first time, he has a history with which he is concerned and we are involved, and he begins to acquire identity. We learn in this scene what has not been established earlier, that the *Patna* has survived the officers' desertion and has been towed to port by a French vessel. The crime, therefore, has become a pure instance of the failure to observe the code of duty. It has unrelieved ugliness rather than any of the spurious grandeur it might have acquired from horror. And Marlow finds Jim's manner confusing at first: "He talked soberly, with a sort of composed unreserve, and with a quiet bearing that might have been the outcome of manly self-control, of impudence, of callousness, of a colossal unconsciousness, of a gigantic deception. Who can tell! From our tone we might have been discussing a third person, a football match, last year's weather." The unreality of the talk persists; for Jim seems to exhibit "some conviction of innate blamelessness," and he exhibits it, contradictorily, in the severe judgments he makes of his action. He achieves simultaneously a specious honesty of self-accusation and a specious severity of judgment. The judge and the defendant are mingled in one man, the judge gaining the sympathy the defendant exacts, the defendant gaining the honor due to the judge.

Marlow sees through this spectacle of Jim's self-deception: "I didn't know how much of it he believed himself. I didn't know what he was playing up to—if he was playing up to anything at all—and I suspect he did not know either; for it is my belief no man ever understands quite his own artful dodge to escape from the grim shadow of self-knowledge." At moments the delusion becomes so outrageous that Marlow must respond with an irony that is a mixture of the therapeutic and the vindictive. For every fall into painful self-awareness Jim finds a "fresh foothold" on self-justification. He is most painfully transparent as he thinks with incredulity of the fact that the threatened

bulkhead held. He is soon well beyond that fact into a vision of the ship
sinking ("My god! what a chance missed!") and seems lost in a "fanciful realm
of recklessly heroic aspirations." As Jim becomes absorbed in a vision of the
heroism he might have achieved, his face betrays "a strange look of beatitude."
Marlow's reply is an angry defense of the actual: "If you had stuck to this
ship, you mean!" And Jim is shocked into awareness, "as though he had
tumbled down from a star."

Jim's sophistry converts a moral sanction, which must be absolute for
the man who ackowledges a duty, into the calculus of probability. He thinks
back to the thin bulkhead, which should, by all expectation, have given.
"There was not the thickness of a sheet of paper between the right and wrong
of this affair." To that Marlow can reply only with the grim irony of one who
insists upon these necessary distinctions that constitute our moral life: "How
much more did you want?" Jim goes on obliviously lamenting the unfairness
of his plight: "Not the breadth of a hair between this and that," and Marlow
responds with vicious point, "It is difficult to see a hair at midnight." Marlow's feelings are important here: "I was aggrieved against him as though he
had cheated me—me!—of a splendid opportunity to keep up the illusion of
my beginnings, as though he had robbed our common life of the last spark
of its glamour." "And so," he adds savagely, "you cleared out—at once."

Jim's imagination is quite different from the subtle awareness which Marlow displays. His imagination has no room for sympathetic regard for others'
feelings; it is too busy with fantasies, whether wishful or defensive. When he
speaks of his peculiar unreadiness to act, it is as if he were still in the midst
of irrevocable disaster; his fancy overleaps the actual and plunges him into the
horror that seems once more to be ahead. In retrospect Jim's panic and hys-
teria have disguised from him the fears he did have and lead him to swear
that it was not death he feared. Not death perhaps, Marlow reflects, but "he
was afraid of the emergency. . . . He wanted to die without added terrors,
quietly, in a sort of peaceful trance." And one is led to think back to those
moments of easy languor aboard the untroubled *Patna*, when nothing could
seem very threatening, and at worst one would die a glorious hero, even
watching with an indulgent but superior glance the posthumous ceremonies
that honored one's achievement.

Marlow sees from the outside what must be Jim's fierce internal conflict,
his struggle "with an invisible personality, an antagonistic and inseparable
partner of his existence—another possessor of his soul." Marlow feels a kind
of vertigo in watching the process: this experience of Jim's "subtle unsoundness" opens into a deeper sense of what all of us share with Jim, and Jim's
desperate efforts recall the occasions when the truth is so intolerable that we

can survive only by transforming it into some saving illusion. Jim's own helpless surrender to what he needs to believe is at once "fabulously innocent" and "enormous." He can ignore the Malay helmsmen who remained unquestioningly fast at their post in the face of calamity; "there had been no order," one of them testified, "he could not remember an order; why should he leave the helm?"

The bestiality of the other officers and the gross farce of their clumsiness seem an affront to any conception of human dignity. Jim can only feel "an element of burlesque in his ordeal." It is robbed of whatever grandeur danger and resistance might have attained; his disdain loses its import in the muddle of chance events and of traduced intentions. Jim can only see himself as wronged, maligned, mocked: "as though he . . . had suffered himself to be handled by the infernal powers who had selected him for the victim of their practical joke." He cannot bring himself to take responsibility for either his action or his inaction. He can only remember himself as the well-meaning victim of cruel disgrace. "The infernal joke was being crammed devilishly down his throat, but—look you—he was not going to admit of any sort of swallowing motion in his gullet." And so Jim crosses the impossible gap between his intention and his act: "I had jumped . . . it seems."

Conrad so manipulates the narrative that it introduces a series of counterparts and contrasts to Jim. The most striking is Brierly, a captain who is one of the board of inquiry. Brierly is a man of proven courage and confident superiority, a man who has risen to command without indecision or self-doubt. But the case of Jim—whose family is known to Brierly's—has not aroused Brierly's usual contempt and impatience. It has suddenly, by its disclosure of Jim's "subtle unsoundness," awakened Brierly to whatever in himself has remained unexamined or hidden from his consciousness. Brierly tries to persuade Jim to run out; he is even willing to pay Jim to escape this needless public disgrace, a disgrace which (for reasons we cannot know) threatens Brierly's own vision of himself. Finally, making careful arrangements for his first mate to succeed him, weighting his body with belaying pins, a week after Jim's inquiry has ended, Brierly suddenly jumps overboard. Marlow describes his suicide as "the posthumous revenge of fate for that belief in his own splendour which had almost cheated his life of its legitimate terrors." Or does not that belief triumph after all? "Who can tell what flattering view he had induced himself to take of his own suicide?"

The case of Brierly is one of several to which Jim's is related. There is the French lieutenant who remained aboard the *Patna* for thirty hours while a gunboat towed it into port. There is the case of little Bob Stanton, "the shortest chief mate in the merchant service," who died trying to rescue a large

woman who had fallen overboard. As one spectator remarks, "It was for all
the world, sir, like a naughty youngster fighting with his mother." Both the
lieutenant and Bob Stanton are figures without any superficial show of heroic
dignity; they provide a sharp contrast with Jim's promising and deceptive
appearance.

These counterparts or alternatives might be seen, in Peter Ure's phrase,
as "enemies of the story, enemies of the imagination." It may be also apt to
call them enemies of the romantic. For they accommodate the claims of the
imagination in different ways, but they do not inhabit a dream with the
tenacity and wholeness of faith that Jim—for want, perhaps, of greater wisdom—does. In one sense, Jim's persistence is the result of weakness. As the
center of this novel, Jim's imagination is all the better for its innocence. What
Conrad once said of himself applies as well to his treatment of Jim. It is "not
my depth," he wrote to Edward Garnett, "but my shallowness that makes me
so inscrutable." Jim's inability to understand himself—his failure even to guess
what forces are at work within him—frees his power to act out his beliefs,
and the puzzle he presents through his very simplicity is what a sophisticated
witness like Marlow needs. Our interest in Jim derives from Marlow's meditation upon him.

Stein is the full romantic of the novel, a man who has lived freely and
dangerously, who has loved deeply, and who has become a scholar and at last
a collector of beetles and butterflies. Marlow sees in him a peculiar power,
like that of the artist:

> I respected the intense, almost passionate, absorption with which
> he looked at a butterfly, as though on the bronze sheen of these
> frail wings, in the white tracings, in the gorgeous markings, he
> could see other things, an image of something as perishable and
> defying destruction as these delicate and lifeless tissues displaying
> a splendour unmarred by death.

Stein seems to preserve in imperishable form what comes into being through
the perishable; the lifeless creatures in his collection embody "beauty, accuracy, harmony, the balance of Nature's colossal forces, the perfect equilibrium
of the mighty Kosmos."

The most striking instance of this process occurred on the remarkable
day when Stein shot himself out of an ambush and found, as he looked for
signs of life in one of the three bodies, the shadow of a rare and beautiful
butterfly, one he had always dreamed of catching. There is some implicit
connection between his deep love for his family, his brave and shrewd facing
of his enemies, and this rare prize, the butterfly "sitting on a small heap of

dirt." What Stein achieves is an abstraction of form from living matter; and, when he turns his attention to Jim he is, inevitably, interested in Jim as a problem. For one can say that man's form exists less in his physical structure than in his dream, his guiding motive and vision. Stein is fully aware of the precariousness of all life; he has lost his wife and daughter and begun a new career after their death. Man, unlike the butterfly, "will never on his heap of mud keep still." He is, instead, consumed by conflicting dreams: "He wants to be a saint, and he wants to be a devil—and every time he shuts his eyes he sees himself as a very fine fellow—so fine as he can never be."

As Stein contemplates the problem, he, too, seems to lose substance and to hover "noiselessly over invisible things," to dissolve into a world of idea. And he comes to his well-known statement:

> A man that is born falls into a dream like the man who falls into the sea. If he tries to climb out into the air as inexperienced people endeavor to do, he drowns—*nicht war?* . . . No, I tell you! The way is to the destructive element submit yourself, and with the exertions of your hands and feet in the water make the deep, deep sea keep you up.

Man, as Stein has remarked, comes "where he is not wanted, where there is no place for him"; the sea is the destructive element because it is not the element to which man is naturally adapted, and yet it is the only one in which he can live. Or one can take the sea as the realm of idea—always evanescent, always exacting—in which alone man can live; the realm of "fact," the world of land and air, will kill more surely than the other. But to keep alive in the water is to commit oneself to unceasing effort and ambition: "To follow the dream, and again to follow the dream—and so—*ewig—usque ad finem*. . . ." Marlow imagines before him "a vast and uncertain expanse, as of a crepuscular horizon on a plain at dawn—or was it, perchance, the coming of the night." He recognizes Stein's own obduracy and boldness, following his dream "without faltering, and therefore without shame and without regret."

Marlow has earlier described Stein's courage as "like a natural function of the body—say, good digestion, for instance—completely unconscious of itself." Marlow cannot attain the unconscious rightness that is given only in action. He has come to mistrust the crepuscular light as less charming than deceptive and to see the expanse as a desolate plain, its bright edge indicating only "an abyss full of flames." The vision of Stein turns under Marlow's eyes from benign to terrible.

Stein himself recognizes the problem as he speaks of Jim: "He is romantic—romantic. . . . And that is very bad—very bad. . . . Very good, too."

To Marlow's doubts he replies with a full sense of the terror and the value of consciousness: "What is it by that inward pain makes him know himself? What is it that for you and me makes him—exist?" Stein becomes for Marlow a man who has achieved "all the exalted elements of romance." And Jim's "imperishable reality" (rather than the actual man) gains "irresistible force" in a realm where "absolute Truth . . . floats elusive, obscure, half submerged, in the still silent waters of mystery."

Conrad leaves Marlow in a half-mesmerized state, his mind excited by mystery and hope, the world of idea curiously close, even visible in the seemingly disembodied forms of Stein's half-darkened rooms. Marlow is haunted, moreover, by the intensity of life that is achieved through following the dream; intensity—or one may call it authenticity, since it makes all other moments seem so unreal as to become betrayals of our proper nature. Marlow can speak with raillery to his listeners, but he is trying to convey the power of what they may not sense:

> I could be eloquent were I not afraid you fellows had starved your imaginations to feed your bodies. I do not mean to be offensive; it is respectable to have no illusions—and safe—and profitable— and dull. Yet you, too, in your time must have known the intensity of life, that light of glamour created in the shock of trifles, as amazing as the glow of sparks struck from a cold stone—and as short-lived, alas!

This evocation of a life that achieves intensity, that commands the self in the name of an idea and wrests from torpor or mediocrity the momentary illusion, is clearly a romantic conception of experience, where brief intensity so thoroughly transcends the cool, dull succession of the quotidian as to become a higher reality. And yet, granted the power of such moments, is all life to be found in them? Perhaps only for those who are "imaginative" in the full and ambiguous sense of that term. Marlow professes to have no imagination, and we take that to mean that he is neither the victim nor the master of imagination, not so much the fantasist or the hero as the man of acute perception.

Marlow presents our world as a tissue of imagined relationships. From our travels, as he says, we return to "our superiors, our kindred, our friends," and those who have no person waiting for them "have to meet the spirit that dwells within the land, under its sky, in its air, in its valleys . . .—a mute friend, judge, and inspirer. Say what you like, to get its joy, to breathe its peace, to face its truth one must return with a clear consciousness." The spirit of the place is made up of the feelings, affections, loyalties we have known there, and we can find renewed communion with it only if we have not betrayed those sentiments that have become grounded in the remembered or imagined place itself. Those who return, Marlow says (speaking, one assumes, for himself), "not to a dwelling but to the land itself, to meet its disembodied, external, and unchangeable spirit—it is those who understand best its severity, its saving power, the grace of its secular right to our fidelity, to our obedience." Each of us is "rooted to the land from which he draws his faith together with his life." And Marlow is sure that Jim felt "the demand of some such truth or some such illusion—I don't care how you call it, there is so little difference, and the difference means so little"; and "those who do not feel do not count."

But it is only a small step from this conception of a land as the source and locus of our sentiment—of men tied to each other by the countless ligatures of kinship, loyalty, faith, and love—to the more oppressive image of those ranks in which we march together: "Woe to the stragglers! We exist only in so far as we hang together. He had straggled in a way, he had not hung on; but he was aware of it with an intensity that made him touching, just as a man's more intense life makes his death more touching than the death of a tree." Jim remains, then, "a straggler yearning inconsolably for his humble place in the ranks." Much later, when Marlow has seen Jim's apparent regeneration in Patusan, he all but scorns his own place in the ranks: "I felt a gratitude, an affection for that straggler whose eyes had singled me out, keeping my place in the ranks of an insignificant multitude. How little that was to boast of, after all!" Jim's intensity has elicited from Marlow an intensity of a different kind, a somewhat frightening sense of how much that we take as the ground of our existence is a convention we have created for ourselves. And all such creations, if they have no other ground in reality, must of necessity be arbitrary, illusory, a necessity only of our imagination rather than of nature itself. Those ranks we keep become a somewhat humiliating image of our jealously preserved interdependence, and our fear of those who may awaken us to the rigid artifice of our cadence and our files.

In the views ascribed to the "privileged man" who receives Marlow's letter, all the narrow and rigid assertions of class, color, and race are assumed as if they were necessary structures:

> "We want its strength at our backs," you had said. "We want a belief in its necessity and its justice to make a worthy and conscious sacrifice of our lives. Without it the sacrifice is only forgetfulness, the way of offering is no better than the way to perdition."
> In other words, you maintained that we must fight in the ranks or our lives don't count.

This final phrase evokes a debasing conformity, especially if the ranks are

formed by those who share "a firm conviction in the truth of ideas racially
our own, in which name are established the order, the morality of an ethical
progress." We do not need to know much about Conrad's criticism of Kipling
or his views of the Spanish-American or Boer wars to recognize the dangers
implicit in the mind of the "privileged man," a counterpart of the American
banker Holroyd in *Nostromo*.

The problems that are awakened here cannot be easily put by. There *is*
a confidence we gain from knowing that our beliefs are shared, there *is* a
peculiar strength that men gain from a common faith and from the deep
sentiments that tie them to their land. All of these are important bonds, and
they may be essential—or almost so—to man's imaginative existence. He gains
a moral existence from accepting these claims upon him, from a sense of duty
or obligation and from the recognition that these are claims upon others and
recognized as such. And yet, as we contemplate our lives, the demands we
make upon ourselves often seem factitious and corrupt: a mixture of coercion
and dependence, a nightmare of unrealizable hopes and impoverishing ideals.
Conrad uses Jim himself as the crux of such problems; we may admire his
moral redemption in bringing order and light to Patusan, we may pity the
intolerable and unassuageable shame he feels at any thought of the *Patna*, but
we must be troubled by the extravagant expectations he uses to test himself.

The portion of the novel that deals with Patusan is different in form but,
I think, a necessary realization of the earlier part. There Jim struggled against
truth, trying to retreat into his dream. In the second part Jim follows his
dream *usque ad finem*, as Stein proposed. He gains tremendously in self-confidence, and he earns that confidence by unequivocal actions. And yet, he
remains to the last "a straggler yearning inconsolably for his humble place in
the ranks." Jim's feelings are divided even at the time of his greatest triumph.
"You have had your opportunity," Marlow says, but Jim is less certain:

> "Had I? . . . Well yes. I suppose so. Yes. I have got back my
> confidence in myself—a good name—yet sometimes I wish . . .
> No! I shall hold what I've got. Can't expect anything more." He
> flung his arm toward the sea. "Not out there anyhow." He stamped
> his foot upon the sand. "This is my limit, because nothing less
> will do."

This last phrase conveys the imperious egoism, the demand for respect that
is only the obverse of his profound self-distrust.

Conrad surrounds the scene of Patusan with a sense of the imaginative
force that has carried the pepper traders into the Eastern seas, their "blind
persistence in endeavor and sacrifice." In contrast to their fierce endeavor is

the miserable Rajah Allang, who nominally rules the territory: a "dirty, little, used-up old man with evil eyes and a weak mouth, who swallowed an opium pill every two hours." We see Jim in the Rajah's compound, self-possessed, diplomatic, but austerely reserved: "his stalwart figure in white apparel, the gleaming clusters of his fair hair, seemed to catch all the sunshine that trickled" into the Rajah's dim hall. Jim "appeared like a creature not only of another kind but of another essence." This is an evocation of those simple contrasts we might expect of boys' stories, the romances which Conrad is often deliberately reinterpreting and undercutting. Patusan is a "totally new set of conditions" for Jim's "imaginative faculty to work upon." It is in effect the scene of romance. But this triumph can happen only because, like Jim himself, Patusan is beneath notice, a country "not judged ripe for interference" by European or Asian powers.

All the internal conflicts of Patusan have revolved about "trade"; the Rajah Allang has claimed a monopoly, "but his idea of trading was indistinguishable from the commonest forms of robbery." In contrast, a more legitimate power is exercised among the Malayans by Doramin and his son, Dain Waris—almost figures of heroic legend. As an introduction to Doramin, Stein has given Jim a ring that is a token of an old friendship. "It's like something you read of in books," Jim remarks in the midst of his boyish "elated rattle." It is at the top of the hill he first captured from the Rajah's forces that Jim is seen by Marlow:

> He dominated the forest, the secular gloom, the old mankind. He was like a figure set up on a pedestal, to represent in his persistent youth the power, and perhaps the virtue, of races that never grow old, that have emerged from the gloom. I don't know why he should always have appeared to me symbolic. Perhaps this is the real cause of my interest in his fate.

Marlow's concern has been with providing a refuge, and he is offended by Jim's easy romantic dream of it as a great chance. Offended but understanding: "Youth's insolent; it is its right—its necessity; it has got to assert itself, and all assertion in this world of doubts is a defiance, is an insolence." Jim's insolent hopes are simply the bright side of his unforgiving memory of his disgrace. "It is not I or the world who remember," Marlow shouts at him. "It is you—you, who remember." But, as Jim observes, Marlow does too.

Yet there follows once more the boyish defiance of reality: "Don't you worry, by Jove! I feel as if nothing could touch me. Why! This is luck from the word Go. I wouldn't spoil such a magnificent chance!" It is no wonder that Marlow concludes, "I am fated never to see him clearly."

The adventures on Patusan during the two years before Marlow's visit establish Jim as the arbiter and source of order in Patusan. They win him the friendship of Dain Waris and the love of Jewel, the daughter of the Portuguese trader Cornelius. In an episode which resembles Stein's own story, Jim is warned by Jewel of an ambush and shoots his way out, killing a man in the process. In that act, Jim's imagination serves his courage as it had his cowardice earlier. He holds his shot deliberately:

> He held it for the tenth part of a second, for three strides of the man—an unconscionable time. He held it for the pleasure of saying to himself, that's a bad man! He was absolutely positive and certain. He let him come on because it did not matter. A dead man, anyhow. He noticed the dilated nostrils, the wide eyes, the intent, the eager stillness of the face, and then he fired.

Afterward, Jim "found himself calm, appeased, without rancour, without uneasiness, as if the death of that man had atoned for everything." And, once he has brought peace to Patusan and gained command of the imagination of its people, he can speak to Marlow with "dignity" if not eloquence, with "a high seriousness in his stammerings," even a solemn "certitude of rehabilitation." "That is why," Marlow concludes, "he seemed to love the land and the people with a fierce egoism, with a contemptuous tenderness." It is almost as if Jim cannot yet so fully believe in that rehabilitation as to be free of the egoism which it should appease. For clearly that egoism is a strenuous defiance of doubt. And Jim seems unable to respect, even while he loves, the people of Patusan for the trust they show him.

Marlow is teased and teases himself at every point; there can be no repose in his view of Jim. The precariousness of Jim's achievement is caught in what is perhaps the strongest passage in the novel. Jewel is afraid that Jim will leave her. She recalls the sadness of her mother's life. "I don't want to die weeping," she says to Marlow, and her remarks summon up all the "secular gloom" that Jim has seemed to dispel from Patusan. She presents a vision of "passive unremediable horror," and Marlow records its force:

> It had the power to drive me out of my conception of existence, out of that shelter each of us makes for himself to creep under in moments of danger, as a tortoise withdraws within its shell. For a moment I had a view of a world that seemed to wear a vast and dismal aspect of disorder, while, in truth, thanks to our unwearied efforts, it is as sunny an arrangement of small conveniences as the mind of man can conceive. But still—it was only a moment: I went back into my shell directly. One *must*—don't you know—

though I seemed to have lost all my words in the chaos of dark thoughts I had contemplated for a second or two beyond the pale. These came back, too, very soon, for words also belong to the sheltering conception of light and order which is our refuge.

And it is as part of that sheltering conception that Marlow last sees Jim. That final view is the romantic ending the novel seems to earn:

> For me that white figure in the stillness of the coast and sea seemed to stand at the heart of a vast enigma. The twilight was ebbing fast from the sky above his head, the strip of sand had sunk already under his feet, he himself appeared no bigger than a child—then only a speck, a tiny white speck, that seemed to catch all the light left in a darkened world.

Everything in the image is open to symbolism: gathering darkness that frames Jim's figure—childlike as it seems, standing on no visible firmness but on sheer groundlessness, surrounded by the infinity of sky and sea—and, concentrating within itself all our faith, the illusory light that one does not dare surrender.

But, of course, Conrad's novel does not end there. For immediately upon this follows the account of Gentleman Brown, the last of Jim's counterparts. Brown, who has turned his own act of desertion into a career of terror, almost a didactic "demonstration of some obscure and awful attribute of our nature," has had his rifleman kill a man from a great distance; and by that action— arbitrary, absurd, terrifying—he has threatened to destroy the fabric of order Jim has created.

When Jim returns, Brown offers to negotiate; but he is enraged by all that Jim seems to stand for, in effect all that Brown has devoted his life to rejecting with a peculiar hatred. Brown angrily tries to cut Jim down to his own size, to shock him out of his cool superiority. "I came here for food. . . . And what did *you* come for?" Brown thinks the answer is wealth, but he has found his way into Jim's own terrors; Brown has a "satanic gift for finding out the best and weakest spot in his victims." And so he plays upon their common guilt: "I am here because I was afraid once in my life. Want to know what of? Of a prison. That scares me, and you may know it—if it's any good to you. I won't ask you what scared you into this infernal hole, where you seem to have found pretty pickings." There runs through Brown's talk ("as if a demon had been whispering advice in his ear") a "vein of subtle reference to their common blood, an assumption of common experience; a sickening suggestion of common guilt, of secret knowledge that was like a bond of their minds and of their hearts."

The effect, clearly, is to disable Jim, to make him unready to take the measures that judgment might propose. Jim does not try to disarm Brown; he allows him "a clear road or else a clear fight." Jim's servant, Tamb' Itam, can only feel in this response a "saddened acceptance of a mysterious failure." Jim offers to answer with his life to the people of Patusan for any harm that should come to them "if the white men with beards were allowed to retire." He knows that Jewel and Tamb' Itam would have killed Brown and his crew just as he, with neither doubt nor regret, killed the man who held him in ambush (or as Stein had before him). He is unable to take any effective action because of the compromising sense of being no better than, no different from, Brown. As he says of Brown (and clearly of himself) to Jewel, "Men act badly sometimes without being much worse than others."

The outer world has entered Patusan, offered its reminder of his failure, reduced him once more to self-doubt and hesitation; and, by reaction, to exalted pride. "He was inflexible, and with the growing loneliness of his obstinacy his spirit seemed to rise above the ruins of his existence." Jewel can scarcely believe in his failure to act, and when the consequences of that failure cost the life of Dain Waris, she pleads with Jim to save himself by escaping. But he refuses. "I should not be worth having," he tells her. " 'For the last time,' she cried menacingly, 'will you defend yourself?'" " 'Nothing can touch me,' he said in a last flicker of superb egoism." And as he leaves, asking her forgiveness, she calls back "Never! Never!" Jim offers himself to Doramin, accepting full responsibility for his son's death, and the old man shoots him. "They say that the white man sent right and left at all those proud faces a proud and unflinching glance. Then with his hand over his lips he fell forward, dead."

The true ending splits apart those forces that for a moment find balance in Stein's butterfly. Jim passes away "under a cloud, inscrutable at heart, forgotten, unforgiven, and excessively romantic." Two themes are brought to the surface here—one is the proud, contemptuous, and desperate defiance Jim has expressed so often: "Nothing can touch me." The other is his infidelity not only to Jewel but to life as he pursues the sublime opportunity "which like an Eastern bride had come veiled to his side."

We see him "tearing himself out of the arms of a jealous love at the sign, at the call of his exalted egoism. He goes away from a living woman to celebrate his pitiless wedding with a shadowy ideal of conduct. Is he satisfied—quite, now, I wonder? We ought to know. He is one of us. . . ."

We have a last view of Jewel leading a "soundless inert life" in Stein's house. And as for the romantic collector—he has aged, and waves his hand sadly at his butterflies.

Conrad has forced apart the heroic and the authentic; the shadowy ideal becomes the successful rival of the living woman. The heroic is made a proud assertion of the ego, but of a self-distrustful ego which gains spurious strength from acts of unsparing self-judgment. The heroic, finally, seems childish and wistful, the bluster of the straggler who wants nothing more than to be taken into the ranks. And on the other hand, the ranks themselves are scorned by Marlow, who is fully aware of the narrowness and rigidity of the principles that hold them together. Conrad remains both romantic and skeptic, each opposing the other, but neither quite controlled or limited. It is a book without balance or repose, and it seems to me Conrad's greatest work because of the generosity with which each alternative is imagined.

NOSTROMO

In *Nostromo* Conrad's irony becomes more inclusive, enfolding the political history of a nation as well as the motives of individuals. The central irony is that of "material interests." They alone seem to possess the power to bring order to Costaguana. They require stability for their profitable operation, and they bring peace through their great financial power, through bribery or an improved standard of living. The danger of "material interests," in turn, lies in their use of the power they acquire, making men instruments of an institution and sacrificing them when they fail to be useful.

The story of the Gould concession opens in Italy, where Charles and Emilia meet. She is staying with an old aunt, the widow of an Italian nobleman who gave his life in Garibaldi's cause. The *marchesa* now leads "a still, whispering existence" in a part of "an ancient and ruinous palace, whose big empty halls downstairs sheltered under their painted ceilings the harvests, the fowls, and even the cattle, together with the whole family of the tenant farmer." It is there that Charles brings the news of his father's death. The death has been caused by the torment of the unworked silver mine, whose ownership Mr. Gould has not been allowed to relinquish and for which he has been forced to pay a stiff annual fee. It has been a grotesque but fatal farce. Charles and Emilia meet "in the hall of the ruined *palazzo*, a room magnificent and naked, with here and there a long strip of damask, black with damp and age, hanging down on a bare panel of the wall. It was furnished with exactly one gilt armchair, with a broken back, and an octagon columnar stand bearing a heavy marble vase ornamented with sculptured masks and garlands of flowers, and cracked from top to bottom." Charles stares at the urn as he speaks and kisses her hand. Emilia weeps in sympathy, "very small in her simple, white frock, almost like a lost child crying in the degraded grandeur of the noble hall, while he stood by her, again perfectly motionless in the contemplation of the marble urn."

Conrad uses the setting of the palazzo to suggest the world the Goulds will enter, the "degraded grandeur" comprehending both the original idealism with which their silver mine will be worked and the long history of corruptibility to which Gould's service to material interests will add another chapter. One can both recognize the Goulds' new hope as they stand in the decayed palazzo and read, in the painted ceiling above them, the grandeur of an older generation which has had to yield to fowls and cattle its uselessly large and formal spaces. Conrad does not insist upon allegorical meanings, but he exacts from his scene a high degree of initial suggestion and of ultimate relevance. Some of it is perhaps apparent at once to Charles, who stares at the cracked urn "as though he had resolved to fix its shape forever in his memory." But it is not clear what he sees. The scene, garrulous with suggestion for us, like the sounding church bells "thin and alert" in the valley below, is something of which the Goulds are perhaps touchingly, even pathetically, oblivious. They are excited now by a future "in which there was an air of adventure, of combat—a subtle thought of redress and conquest." It is a prospect which earns for Charles Gould an ironic comment which he does not hear and could hardly imagine: "Action is consolatory. It is the enemy of thought and the friend of flattering illusions. Only in the conduct of our action can we find the sense of mastery over the Fates."

The enthusiasm with which Emilia later speaks of the time, deprecating her genuine idealism with a "slight flavor of irony," charms visitors to the Casa Gould; but it does not lead them to imagine any higher end than the acquisition of wealth. The betrayal of Emilia's idealism and its faint pathos are suggested by the niche in the steps of their house where a Madonna stands "with the crowned child sitting on her arm." More visible and audible is the "big green parrot, brilliant like an emerald in a cage that flashed like gold." Like the player piano in *The Secret Agent* or its ancestor, Mrs. Merdle's derisive parrot in *Little Dorrit*, the parrot performs at irregular intervals; it sometimes screams out "Viva Costaguana," or calls the servant "mellifluously . . . in imitation of Mrs. Gould's voice," or as suddenly takes "refuge in immobility and silence."

The Goulds feel "morally bound to make good their vigorous view of life against the unnatural error of weariness and despair." In order to accomplish this, Charles Gould needs the financial support of Holroyd, an American millionaire with "the temperament of a puritan and an insatiable imagination of conquest." Holroyd wants to conquer the world for the "purer forms of Christianity" and for American business; the two goals are fused in the cant of a ruthless idealism. It is not the only idealism Charles Gould encounters outside his own. Another version is the republican eloquence and vision of freedom of Antonia's father, Don José Avellanos. Emilia Gould thinks Charles muddleheaded for equating the two forms of idealism, but Charles has the confidence of a man convinced of his own realism. Others may declaim, he says, "but I pin my faith to material interests." He has, he thinks, no illusions; he is "prepared to stoop for his weapons."

During the years of her travel in Costaguana with her husband, Emilia Gould has come to know the land beyond the coastal settlements, "a great land of plain and mountain and people, suffering and mute, waiting for the future in a pathetic immobility of patience." Everywhere she finds "a weary desire for peace, the dread of officialdom with its nightmarish parody administration without law, without security, and without justice." The history of Costaguana has been a grotesque succession of forms of power, some barbarous, some virtuous but weak, none stable for long; it is a history of contingency, of upset and overturn, with only the misery of the people a constant presence beneath the various forms that oppression may take. Charles Gould puts up with idiocy and venality; he lives within a fortress of polite silence. The land has changed as the mine has grown; the original waterfall of San Tomé survives only as a memory in Emilia Gould's watercolor sketch. Emilia keeps alive the idealism she has shared with Charles: "she endowed that lump of metal"—the first silver ingot produced by the mine—"with a justificative conception, as though it were not a mere fact, but something far-reaching and unpalpable, like the true expression of an emotion or the emergence of a principle." But Emilia becomes at last an ineffectual and lonely spectator, dismayed by the weight of power that the mine carries in the new political state of its own creation, Sulaco.

Dr. Monygham, who shares her vision, is another bitter spectator. He has learned, he thinks, to live without illusions; his self-respect had been destroyed under torture when he found himself betraying others to the dictator, Guzman Bento. Like Lord Jim, he is "the slave of a ghost," haunted by his failure. He has created "an ideal conception of his disgrace," not a false reading of the past but "a rule of conduct resting mainly on severe rejections." Dr. Monygham's "eminently loyal nature" can trust only someone so innocent and helpless as Emilia Gould. For her husband's efforts he has only scorn:

> The administrador had acted as if the immense and powerful prosperity of the mine had been founded on methods of probity, on

the sense of usefulness. And it was nothing of the kind. The
method followed had been the only one possible. The Gould
Concession had ransomed its way through all those years. It was
a nauseous process. He quite understood that Charles Gould had
got sick of it and had left the old path to back up that hopeless
attempt at reform. The doctor did not believe in the reform of
Costaguana. . . . What made him uneasy was that Charles Gould
seemed to him to have weakened at the decisive moment when a
frank return to the old methods was the only chance. Listening to
Decoud's wild scheme had been a weakness.

This passage is interesting as much for the moral confusion it embodies as
for that which it attacks. Charles Gould is blamed for pretending to high
purpose while using base means. Could he have exercised it more fully by
some other means? No, his method was "the only one possible," but we must
recognize it for what it is. Charles Gould has in fact tried to free himself of
the base methods; his very eagerness to do so led to his support of so weak
a reformer as Ribiera. Would it have been better both to practice base means
and renounce a high purpose? This would seem to Dr. Monygham more
sensible since the high purpose of reform was, in his eyes, foredoomed. And
now Dr. Monygham is troubled because Gould turns to Decoud's plan for an
independent Sulaco instead of using his silver, as he has before, to buy off
the latest would-be Caesars, the Montero brothers. As we see, Gould is more
realistic in this than Dr. Monygham.

One is left with a morality that scorns bribery but scolds Gould for
repudiating it, that questions Gould's success but fears his failure; it is a
morality that can question any action since its grounds for judgment shift
between an exacting idealism and a cynical despair. Any form of success must
be unthinkable for Dr. Monygham, and any apparent success must reveal itself
to be a new and more insidious form of failure. Only the commitment to
personal loyalty survives the larger pattern of Dr. Monygham's fatalism. The
doctor is loyal to the mine because it "presented itself . . . in the shape of a
little woman, . . . the delicate preciousness of her inner worth, partaking of
a gem and a flower, revealed in every attitude of her person." In the presence
of danger "this illusion acquired force, permanency, and authority. It claimed
him at last!" Dr. Monygham's loyalty to Mrs. Gould is as ruthless as any of
the illusions we see in the novel: it steels him "against remorse and pity." As
he undertakes deception in her cause, he feels that he is "the only one fit for
that dirty work." Like Lord Jim, Dr. Monygham feels disabled by his failure;
he "believed that he had forfeited the right to be indignant with any one—
for anything." It is only the "exaltation of self-sacrifice" that can support him.

Martin Decoud, different as he is from Dr. Monygham, shares his distrust of Charles Gould's unstable mixture of moral idealism and material interests. The distrust comes in each case, I would argue, from a deeper idealism
that each tries to disguise as (or reduce to) a personal loyalty. Decoud does
not have Monygham's shame of betrayal (or, in Dickens's phrase, his "vanity
of unworthiness"). Decoud seems, as we first encounter him, a supercilious
young expatriate, a smatterer in satiric journalism, a man who prefers the
boulevards of Paris to the barbarism of his own country. He is torn between
a despair of ever bringing order to Costaguana and the infamy of serving
interests whose motives or whose realism he can easily impugn.

Decoud suffers from a kind of spoiled idealism; he cannot admit impurity
of motive without feeling betrayed and controlled by it. Antonia, who does
not suffer from the same fastidiousness, rejects his cynicism: "Men must be
used as they are. I suppose nobody is really disinterested, unless, perhaps,
you, Don Martin." For whenever Decoud puts aside an idealistic goal (which
he nevertheless uses as a touchstone of others' actions), he reverts to a cynicism
which seems to take people at their worst. "You read all the correspondence,
you write all the papers," he says to Antonia, "all those state papers that are
inspired here, in this room, in blind deference to a theory of political purity."
But Gould's company and his mine are the "practical demonstrations" of what
is possible. "Do you think he succeeded by his fidelity to a theory of virtue?"
And yet, for all the guilt he may have incurred, Gould has been too weak to
carry bribery far enough to buy off the Monteros.

Decoud professes himself unmoved by the claims of patriotism; such
"narrowness" of belief must be "odious" to "cultured minds." But at a deeper
level, Decoud seems bitterly disappointed in his country, where patriotism
has too often been "the cry of dark barbarism, the cloak of lawlessness, of
crime, of rapacity, or simple thieving." Even as he denounces Costaguana,
Decoud is "surprised at the warmth" of his own words. Antonia picks up
that point: "The word you despise has stood also for courage, for constancy,
for suffering." Decoud cannot accede to Antonia's faith: for him a conviction
remains only a "particular view of personal advantage either practical or emotional." He rejects patriotic illusions. He claims "only the supreme illusion of
a lover." This is Decoud's form of authenticity. He can accept none of the
hypocrisy, the self-deception, or fanaticism he sees in Costaguanan patriotism;
he holds to a principle he can acknowledge as quixotic but also as personal
and sincere.

In political affairs Decoud has cultivated detachment: he "imagined himself to derive an artistic pleasure from watching the picturesque extreme of
wrongheadedness into which an honest, almost sacred, conviction may drive

a man." It seems to Decoud that every conviction, to the extent that it is
effective, becomes delusion or madness; the man who has come to accept a
belief is no longer in command of it or himself. But while he regards himself
as a connoisseur of madness, enjoying the colorful virulence of others' obses-
sions, he tries to preserve decency in skepticism. He deposits in his skeptical
better self the full awareness he must relinquish as a propagandist. His better
self preserves its integrity, and he wishes it to remain an asylum, an eventual
place of return for the activist, the ideologist and propagandist, he finds himself becoming.

Decoud can participate in action only by scorning the limitations—he
would say dishonesty—that action imposes. Yet some of his best feelings,
concealed from his ironic consciousness as they must be to survive, are at
work in his political action. Emilia Gould sees a "tremendous excitement
under its cloak of studied carelessness," betrayed in "his audacious and watchful stare, in the curve, half-reckless, half contemptuous, of his lips." Nevertheless, he mocks his own enthusiasm as he proposes that Sulaco secede and
become a new state. His devotion to the new cause is born, he insists, of love
for Antonia rather than any idealism of Charles Gould's kind. Gould, he
insists to Emilia, "cannot act or exist without idealizing every simple feeling,
desire, or achievement."

Decoud wants no such sublimation. He ascribes it to Antonia, and it
clearly has some part in her appeal for him; but he thinks he undertakes the
cause he has devised only to be able to remain with her (since, he adds
mockingly, she refuses to run away). While Decoud scorns Gould's "sentimental basis for action," he appeals nevertheless to Emilia Gould's concern
for the victims she has protected: "Are you not responsible to your conscience
for all these people? Is it not worthwhile to make another effort, which is
not at all so desperate as it looks?" Yet, having said this, Decoud must separate
himself from her husband's idealism. "I cannot endow my personal desires
with a shining robe of silk and jewels," he boasts. "Life is not for me a moral
romance derived from the tradition of a pretty fairy tale." With the supremely
ironic blindness of the self-styled realist, Decoud asserts, "I am not afraid of
my motives."

At the mention by Mrs. Gould of the banker Holroyd, Decoud comes
to a second plan—not only to create an independent state of Sulaco but to
save the next shipment of silver from capture by the Monteros. In effect, he
accepts the material interests in the simplest sense of that phrase: "This silver
must be kept flowing north to return in the form of financial backing from
the great house of Holroyd." For the task of saving the silver Decoud thinks
of Nostromo. He trusts Nostromo's self-interest; Nostromo came to Costa-

guana, by his own account, to seek his fortune. Emilia puts her trust in Nostromo's integrity; old Viola has called him "the incorruptible." "I prefer," she says to Decoud, "to think him disinterested, and therefore trustworthy." Neither of them can quite imagine Nostromo's vanity and his dependence upon others' regard.

Nostromo is neither mercenary nor idealistic in the ways that they imagine. As Teresa Viola recognizes, he is under the spell of his reputation, eager to gain distinction by being "invaluable" to people like Captain Mitchell. He is precisely opposed to old Giorgio Viola, in whom the "spirit of self-forgetfulness, the simple devotion to a vast humanitarian idea" has bred "an austere contempt for all personal advantage." Viola cries out fiercely in behalf of Garibaldi's followers: "We wanted nothing, we suffered for the love of all humanity!" Nostromo has little of this thoughtful idealism; he is the captive of an image rather than of an idea. It is a handsome image. We see it best in the swaggering performance with which he turns off the anger of a pretty *morenita* and allows her to cut the silver buttons from his coat.

Whereas Charles Gould is a captive of an idea and an institution, Nostromo becomes the captive of the literal silver. Doomed to possess it, daring to spend it only very slowly, unable to return it because of the missing bars with which Decoud weighted his body, he becomes "the slave of a treasure with full self-knowledge." He must live by stealth and suffer a disabling sense of falseness, and he feels at the last that the silver has killed him. As she comforts Giselle Viola, who loved Nostromo, Emilia Gould has the "first and only moment of bitterness in her life," and speaks in terms worthy of Dr. Monygham himself: "Console yourself, child. Very soon he would have forgotten you for his treasure." In effect, as Emilia Gould recognizes, Nostromo transposes the pattern of Charles Gould to another key. Nostromo turns out to be a far less interesting, far less complex character than he promises to be at first, and that is true of Gould as well. This has been explained by H. M. Daleski as the "thwarting of the conventional expectations" awakened by the characters and the mine itself. Just as the idealism is replaced by impoverishing obsession, so these characters have less and less life.

With studied irony, Conrad allows Captain Mitchell to introduce us to the new state of Sulaco. His naive pride in the new republic is the means by which we learn how the events initiated by the doctor and Nostromo have concluded. He provides a requiem for the heroic dead and an altogether uncritical account of how heroism and dedication have been absorbed into new institutional structures. Father Corbelán is now a cardinal-archbishop. Hernandez, who was once a kind of Robin Hood, a glorious outlaw, is now minister of war. Even Dr. Monygham has an institutional role as inspector of state hospitals. The war to free Sulaco has been ended by an "international naval demonstration" in the harbor; a United States cruiser was the first to give official recognition to the new state. Once more Conrad has forced together the heroism in which the state is conceived with the bureaucratic structure and scene of imperialist enterprise it becomes.

The next stage of Sulaco's history is suggested in the doctor's conversation with Antonia Avellanos and Father Corbelán. They are now involved in promoting a campaign to annex the rest of Costaguana to the new power of Sulaco. For Antonia this would be a means of using the wealth of the new state to relieve the oppression of fellow countrymen. Dr. Monygham ridicules this hope: "Yes, but the material interests will not let you jeopardize their development for a mere idea of pity and justice." He characteristically adds: "And it is just as well perhaps." The true support for Antonia's hope has been found in "the secret societies amongst immigrants and natives, where Nostromo . . . is the great man." Such a moment, Dr. Monygham adds, may simply exploit the appeal of "the wealth for the people." With all his cynicism about both forces, Dr. Monygham expects violence:

> "There is no place and no rest in the development of material interests. They have their law, and their justice. But it is founded on expediency, and is inhuman; it is without rectitude, without the continuity and the force that can be found only in a moral principle. Mrs. Gould, the time approaches when all that the Gould Concession stands for shall weigh as heavily upon the people as the barbarism, cruelty, and misrule of a few years back."

It will "provoke resentment, bloodshed, and vengeance, because the men have grown different." Does this mean simply that men will become disaffected with the mine or does it imply that they have now acquired higher expectations of their worth and rights?

What are we to make of Dr. Monygham and Emilia Gould? They lack the "polished callousness" or even the simple worldliness that might make for tolerance of the mixed motive or belief in its usefulness. He is a man of deep feeling, whose vulnerability creates "his sardonic turn of mind and his biting speeches." He shares Emilia's "still and sad immobility." Both accept the fatality of forces that have been released and can no longer be recalled. Mrs. Gould's nightmare vision is of an "immense desolation" in which she survives alone "the degradation of her young ideal of life, of love, of work—all alone in the Treasure House of the World." Both have the moral intensity of quietism. Emilia Gould thinks: "there was something inherent in the necessities of successful action which carried with it the moral degradation of the idea." The alternatives to the process are either unsuccessful action or none at all. There may be a grandeur of despair in such an assertion that compensates for the inability to act. Not to act is at least to commit no error and do no wrong. It leaves the realm of politics to one or another pattern of fanaticism or cynicism. In *Nostromo* there are intimations of a new radical, perhaps revolutionary, movement, emerging under the cover of Nostromo's leadership but under the real direction of "an indigent, sickly, somewhat hunchbacked little photographer, with a white face and a magnanimous soul dyed crimson by a bloodthirsty hate of all capitalists, oppressors of the two hemispheres." Rarely has a magnanimous soul been so poorly housed and so passively governed by rage.

I have tried to get at the way in which Conrad's tendency to reduce experience to the outrage of an impossible choice requires characters of a special kind. In *Lord Jim* the puzzle surrounds the hero. He is generously conceived, neither shown as master of his fate nor made a moral bankrupt. Marlow in turn is a figure of fuller consciousness, deeply concerned with the questions which Jim exemplifies but which Marlow alone can formulate. Marlow fails to save Jim; he can only observe the destiny Jim achieves once he goes to Patusan. And the initial hope gives way to something darker and enigmatic. In *Nostromo* Conrad has created characters who are victims of an idea. We see that theme announced early: the "cool purity" of the white peak of Higuerota—a "colossal embodiment of silence"—seems to fade into (Conrad is very cinematic) the white hair of the anachronistic old Garibaldino Giorgio Viola. Charles Gould pursues an idea which requires means that threaten to subvert its end; his failure lies in his uncritical commitment to "material interests," and that is in turn reflected in the dehumanization imposed upon him by the idea. His "subtle conjugal infidelity" to Emilia is like Jim's to Jewel—each man turns to an idea as to "an Eastern bride" who has come "veiled to his side." In Jim's case it is "a pitiless wedding with a shadowy ideal of conduct"; in Gould's with a sense of "redress and conquest." Conrad stresses the futility of Gould's achievement: the peace of the Sulaco we come to under the guidance of Captain Mitchell is made, like that of Geneva in *Under Western Eyes*, to seem complacent and indifferent to the claims of any idea. It is at most a superficial peace, for the promise of new violence is inherent in the dialectic of material interests.

What I miss is some intimation of men being moved by mixed motives without inevitably succumbing to the lowest. There seems at moments something rigged in Conrad's demonstration of futility, of the impossibility of Costaguana's ever achieving a government both tolerable and stable. It is not hard to be realistic if one rules out hope, and it is not hard to be ironic—it is in fact hard not to be—if all forms of political activity lead to the same inevitable futility. Unlimited irony can easily turn into fatalism.

Decoud, we are told by the author, "died from solitude and want of faith in himself and others." Solitude creates "a state of soul in which the affectations of irony and scepticism have no place." Decoud can no longer set himself against the world but is absorbed into it at the cost of his identity. "In our activity alone do we find the sustaining illusion of an independent existence as against the whole scheme of things of which we form a helpless part." The fatalism of "form a helpless part" and the skepticism of "sustaining illusion" makes one wonder whether a novelist who writes these words would succumb, or fear that he might succumb, as Decoud does. One recalls Conrad's words about writing *Lord Jim*: "Everything is there: descriptions, dialogue, reflexion—everything—everything but the belief, the conviction, the only thing needed to make me put pen to paper."

Many have felt that Conrad is trying to exorcise something by forcing himself to imagine his way into Decoud—just as there were moments in the writing of *The Secret Agent* when he was, as he tells us, an "extreme revolutionist." If Decoud is a "victim of the disillusioned weariness which is the retribution meted out to intellectual audacity," he seems a thinner character in his death than in his life. One may feel that he is not so much "swallowed up in the immense indifference of things" as sentenced and executed by his author. I wonder why so few are ready to question the propriety of Decoud's suicide, to ask, that is, whether it seems an action that follows from his nature rather than a somewhat superstitious reprisal against the irony and skepticism that the author otherwise overindulges.

But the problem of Decoud is only part of what seems to me troublesome in the novel. As I have indicated, the central characters are captivated by "illusion," with little capacity to recognize or resist it; or, if they are without illusion, they are without power or hope as well. The book achieves some tragic force. It does not achieve that force by demonstrating the inevitable corruption and the implicit blindness of all action, at least of all action that professes a purpose or an ideal. For Conrad's feelings are truer than his thought. There is more complexity in his presentation of characters than there is in his analysis; and, if we see more in what they do than Conrad's ironic handling allows for, it is because they have won their claims upon our minds and feelings in those unattended moments when Conrad's oversight allows them some freedom.

AARON FOGEL

Silver and Silence:
Dependent Currencies in Nostromo

N*ostromo* is a smaller giant novel, an oxymoron of scale, and not simply a
work of vast historical scope. Rhythmic obstacles—jerkinesses and breaks that
interrupt the expansive prose—force the reader to share a feeling of historical
disproportion with the characters, as well as tensions between force and farce.
The novel establishes a rhythm of contraction against expansion. A historical
understanding of this contradictory rhythm governing the sometimes vast and
sometimes Lilliputian Sulaco can free us at least in part from Leavis' split
evaluation of the novel as great but finally "hollow." His judgment anticipates
many other strong but slightly unfair statements about Conrad as elusive,
cold, stilted. These complaints are reasonable—anybody can see the source
of them—but they come in part from a desire to set his work tonally inside
the framework of the English "sympathetic" moral imagination and against
the background of the great nineteenth-century historical novel. These standards don't apply, or aren't entirely applicable, because Conrad has an ironic
relation to these traditions. Canonization has led to overemphasis of his historical range and blindness to his other side—his stubborn, even Menippean
dislike of greatness. *Nostromo* isn't exactly meant to have the inclusive sympathetic force of *War and Peace*, *Bleak House*, *Middlemarch*, or even *Waverly*, but
reads partly like an ironic attack on historical scope, a contracted scale model
of "the great novel"—like the model ships Conrad encouraged his son John
to build. His well-known comment, in the Note to *The Secret Agent*, that

From *Coercion to Speak: Conrad's Poetics of Dialogue.* © 1985 by the President and Fellows
of Harvard College. Harvard University Press, 1985.

Nostromo had been his "largest canvas" stands more in relation to his own fiction than to that of other writers. His largest canvas may still be less grandiose than a historical novel by, for example, Henryk Sienkiewicz. The word *canvas* itself, beneath the obvious metaphor, may even connote sailing, the grandest sailing ship being small compared to a modern steamer. Close reading will show that Conrad did not want to write a great national novel or even a great ironic provincial novel. Though Avrom Fleishman has accurately deflated what he calls "the Polish myth" about Conrad by sketching ethnic and social relations in the part of the Ukraine where he grew up, there is no doubt that Conrad shows himself as Polish. Where major works by Tolstoy, Melville, and Dickens, whatever their melancholy about scale, try to achieve a great rhythm appropriate to their great nations or cities, and where provincial novels enlarge small communities, Conrad insists on a priori confusion about scale itself, paying attention to a large community that is at the same time small, half inside and half outside, a "great world" that is somehow trivial. In *Nostromo*, paltriness and greatness often show up undecidably fused in the same person or incident. Nostromo's adventure on the lighter, for instance, is pettily grand. In the central political action, when Sulaco secedes, does secession amount to becoming larger or smaller? Is secession success? Is the newly condensed nation made practicably small (as Rousseau suggested Poland should contract to preserve freedom), or is it in fact only enslaved to a greater empire? Stylistically *Nostromo* mocks "greatness," and has a consistent strain of anti-imperial puns, dialogical fusions, and noise. It jeers at and violently contracts the scope of the great novel. Edward Said, one of the novel's most serious readers, takes up this question (for different reasons, since he argues that Conrad's motive for narrative disorder is to break with authorial intention), and writes about standard comparisons to *War and Peace*: "In sheer size, of course, the two novels are similar; but beyond that, comparing them is not valuable." Yet the two books are not similar in sheer size. He then goes on— as if looking for justification by another standard of immensity—to compare the book's epically clumsy quality to that of *Moby Dick*. The comparison is strong, but again *Nostromo* has a much more skeptically confined idiom of space—sometimes like that on a chessboard—than Melville's epic.

Politically the main theme of *Nostromo* may be the impossibility of real secession—the forced dialogue of Sulaco with the outside world. Sulaco wins independence through separation, but this effects inclusion in a larger empire. The story of *Nostromo*, then, is partly that of the attempt of one smaller but vast "place"—not clearly defined as a nation or a province—to contract for autonomy within an expansionist setting. "If the country of Poland was, curiously," Fernand Braudel writes of the sixteenth century, "a kind of free-trade area or rather an area of free passage with a minimum of duties or tolls, it was also a vast expanse, 'twice as big as France.' " As with historical Poland, we are left uncertain as to geographical and commercial status. The center of attention here is colonial dependency, in dialogue form, in imagery, and in spatialization. The snakes, the ropes and threads from which characters are suspended, the rocking chair on which Avellanos sits, the silences, the silver, the recurrent forced dialogues—images and relations are organized around the idea of forced dependency. And if we want to understand the dialogical force of *Nostromo*, both in its own form and in its relation to other writings, we have to point toward the special poetics of this ironic project, which led Conrad to reject, more than Scott, the historical novel's dialectic of inclusion, and to insist upon the falsity of any historical "dialectic" that disguises or ignores the reality of the coercive dialogic.

When Dickens begins *Bleak House*, the grim chime name "London," to make an understatement, locates the novel for his audience, and foretells the chiming prose to follow. Dickens, of course, doesn't have to supply a London map. Sulaco, by contrast, not unlike a place in Swift, is mapped for the reader in the first chapters: the shape of the harbor, the islands, the circumscribing mountain chain or cordillera, the position of the mine, the alameda. But it is done so as to implicate the reader in a problem of scale. On the one hand it is alien, a very limited stage, as was the deck of the *Narcissus*; at the other extreme, and not only to avoid making this place too small or too much like a stage for reductive satire, Sulaco is also "vast" and almost equivalent to all of nature. This is a deliberate proportional anomaly in the opening chapters. Conrad builds us not a stage but what has to be called a problem geography, in the way that we speak of Shakespeare's "problem plays," making the reader work on a dilemma of scale. The geographical question of Sulaco—a country, a province, vast, small, part of Costaguana, part of the sea—is imposed at the outset on the reader by the opening descriptions long before Decoud's secessionist plan appears.

Lawrence Graver has argued that Conrad's "shorter fictions," the novellas or long stories, are his most perfect works, but that he tended to lose his way in his novels. Graver speaks of the "longer short" pieces as the most perfect. This thesis is right to consider scale the agony of Conrad's prose, but a little too simple. Aesthetic and political proportion are not for Conrad separable issues. In his image of the world, Russian is largeness, Poland relative small-ness, Napoleonic Europe largeness, England a bleakly brilliant compromise, contract, or bargain, like his own life, between smallness and largeness. A novella might be successful in aesthetic scale, and achieve aesthetic unity, but fail to take on real quandaries of scale in the political world: its perfection is its limitation. Conrad in fact deliberately writes novellas that go on too long and large novels which are somehow abrupt, and this is a kind of historical wit. In the Author's Note to *Nostromo* Conrad describes himself as returning to his family from obsessive work on the book "somewhat in the style of Captain Gulliver"—who was of course caught up in a bathos of scale, between megalomania and insignificance—and also gives the book a carnivalesque source in José Avellanos' never-published *Fifty Years of Misrule*. These burlesques of the book's in fact agonized production remind us that for all its immensity and seriousness, it has many stops and dwarfing ironies, offered with a good deal of Bakhtin's *rire resorbé*—hints of other more comic genres, and of what the narrator calls "mock solemnity"—and is indebted to Swift, perhaps even to Rabelais, for a sense of joking about its own proportions. Conrad's well-known preference for Turgenev over Dostoevsky and Tolstoy is partly a matter of scale.

Stealing Graver's phrase to travesty it, then, we could say that even *Nostromo* is one of Conrad's "shorter fictions." Graver may be right that Conrad worked best scaling down, but he fails to see how this happens most effectively and absorbingly not in the novellas, where compression is formally typical, but in his political novels, *Nostromo*, *The Secret Agent*, and *Under Western Eyes*, all three of which put the scope of larger historical novels under an idiosyncratic and surprising contractual pressure. Some of this pressure, I will try to show, appears in the Menippean device of organizing its own information as the result of "forced dialogue." That is, pressing people to speak, inquisitorial process, yields a kind of truth, whose origin itself is in question. The result of this process, which shows the prose that we read as "forced" in its forcefulness, is a contraction of romantic prose energy. "Expansion" and "contraction," which are the problems of imperialism, are also the problems of prose form in historical narration. This conflict is simultaneously political (having to do with the reining in of the expansive rhetoric of imperialism), aesthetic (having to do with the dramatic relation of prose masses to each other as presented to the reader), and dialogical (having to do with the amount each person speaks in a dialogue).

Nostromo is in fact a dialogue with a number of energetic works usually not mentioned. Cunninghame Graham's *Mogreb-el-Acksa*, with its picture of a "sub-European" Morocco in which Muslims, Jews, and Christians are brought together into continual uneasy contact, and its mobile, traveling sentences, had a complex influence on Conrad in this period—though partly because he quarreled with its simple linguistic flamboyance and the nature of its assumptions about polyglossia. The "Italian" element in *Nostromo*—the Garibaldian politics and melodramatically "operatic" pitch—recalls the more general use of Italian settings in English tradition, from Shakespeare to Browning, to mean anarchic, Machiavellian, and therefore dramatically interesting politics, but of a kind that doesn't hit satirically home. The strongest and most similar text among all *Nostromo*'s ancestors may be *The Pelopponesian Wars*, and not the later histories which Conrad used for documentation. Conrad arguably had wide classical reading, and the counterpoint in *Nostromo* between dense realpolitik and scenes of ironically framed set speeches resembles Thucydides' version of the classical irony about speech and action. Thucydides' most famous problem scene is itself a colonial "forced dialogue," the Dialogue at Melos. *Nostromo* recalls Thucydides also in its intricate and demanding sentence style based on phrasal verbs; and in its historical context, that of a colonial world of "force" and dismal dependency, in which political speech conceals its unfreedom by rhetorical flourish. Finally, what *Nostromo* may owe to Swift is that prose masses on the page sometimes appear in visibly excessive, even scatological *dis*proportion, as a part of the satirical and political meaning. Even if we exclude the element of popular romance full of various "types" who will capture an audience, *Nostromo* has an intention which is at least double: first as a realistic, even vast, history, but second as an ingenious satiric "miniature" of the disproportions in relations that occur under imperialism. This complex intention must be held together, but *not* "unified," by a general sense of forced relation. As in the other political novels, Conrad here seems to burlesque his own unusual powers of international synthesis. He does not mean, as does Pound in the *Cantos*, to bring international variety into a unity of civilized feeling. On the contrary, he shows us, intentionally, a variegate hodgepodge, held together only by his own openly arbitrary force as a novelist, as the characters also force each other into relation.

A first sense of force as disproportion appears in the portrait of the banker Holroyd—the first figure in *Nostromo* whose speech as proportion receives specific comment. He believes expansively that he can hold the world together as one coherent empire. Holroyd's personal rhythms express the historical period *Nostromo* seeks to capture. The key word for him would be *filibuster*; though Conrad does not himself use the word, Cunninghame Graham does, again in *Mogreb-el-Acksa*, to refer to his own reputation as a rover, and Conrad later calls Peyrol a "freebooter," from which the more cynical and politically shady modern term derives. The word *freebooter*, which also appears in Scott, applies, though at a historical slant, to a whole class of Conradian postromantic heroes, from Lingard to Whalley to Nostromo to Peyrol. In each case, however, the story shows how specific historical or political "tethers" bind and contract the figure of the freebooter, so that this type of Conradian hero is another trope of coercion, the "unfree freebooter," whose gift for roving and "free piracy" is now politically under "contract." Politicized freebooting is "filibuster." The "unfree freebooter" in Conrad—the filibuster or hired man of force—acts in the field of coercive contractual politics and usually fails in some way. Nostromo himself is this figure on a ledge between the two conditions.

But *filibuster* as a dual and historically dialogized term—like *impression*—is a good metaphor for the entire novel *Nostromo* because it also links disproportion in action to disproportion in oratory. These are, the novel shows, parallel problems in a colonial setting. We should remember that as a noun *filibuster* means, first of all, "An American who in the mid-19th century took part in fomenting revolutions and insurrections in a Latin-American country"; nineteenth-century slang only secondarily and figuratively makes it the pirating of parliamentary time by a minority or dependent group. By bringing up this word, which Conrad does not use—as by bringing up Graham, Thucydides, and Swift—I am trying to reinforce our sense of the age in which Conrad and his readers felt immersed, and which he was both criticizing and representing, when he created his own narrative methods of plural filibuster. As speech, filibuster is a kind of morosely politicized sailor's yarn; the Spanish idiom *hablar de la mar* means "endless speech." A filibuster, as a personal noun, is a politicized freebooter; but as a parliamentary speech act it resembles that "temporizing," stalling, monologuing delay which has always been recognized as a key to Conrad's narrative technique, yet which has never been fully grasped as a political, as well as poetic, rhythm.

The genius of *Nostromo* in its prose rhythms is to render the emergence of filibuster as both action and speech on all sides of the colonial relation: those in power and those who are powerless all filibuster. The San Franciscan, Holroyd, for example, foments his own Latin American revolution by directive investment; visiting Gould he talks in egotistical, expansive monológues—seen on the page—about his expansionist religion in a way that Gould rejects but can't openly criticize. The representation of talkative people is an old comic device, but here we have something different from Austen's Miss Bates or Scott's pedants. The equation made on the page is clear: his talk expands to take over as his politics does. By contrast and resemblance, many other characters indigenous to Sulaco, and weaker, filibuster more secretly and pathetically, insofar as each is forced to work at his own incongruous revolution, and to make his own monologue about it. Certainly the ancestor of José Avellanos might be found in Walter Scott's loquacious old Scotsman, whose lengthy jargon, sometimes nearly unreadable, often indicates the historical pathos of speaking at length in a "dead" language, and who talks so much because he is a living encyclopedia of a group about to disappear. But Conrad's gesture, though it grows out of this tradition, seems more abstract and planned: the historical period which *Nostromo* seeks to give us via prose rhythm is one in which romantic expansive "freebooting" has turned into "filibustering," both in action and in speech—that is, in which the romantic piratical free agent, and the expansively hopeful monologuing self, are in process of losing their glamour, and have come under contraction and contract. Parliamentary coherence in aggressive debate threatens to degenerate into a "concatenation" (Eloise Knapp Hay's word) of pathetically forceful monologues. Romantic poetry, expansive about the joyous self, now seems a function of expansionism in politics. Romanticism is expansionism; that was the pivot of Marlow's self-recognition. In this context, if there were no forced dialogue to hold speech together, speech in *Nostromo* would be only anarchic pathos. Instead, "masses of words" are dramatized as imperial, not romantically free, energies.

To read *Nostromo*, then, is to have our idea of the "field" of dialogue, in both politics and aesthetics, forcibly changed, and to move out of a world of parliamentary dialogue into one of general filibuster. In both its meanings, the dialogical world of "filibuster" opposes, or subverts, the liberal parliamentary idea that energetic public speech, for all its conflict and egoism, can cohere positively, and lead to collective action. Parliaments work in nations, not for empires or colonies. "A lot of words" here is often synonymous not with parliamentary spirit but with hopelessness and the inability to be heard. Individuals act diversely to foment each his own revolution in the Americas; dilatory, powerless talk has become the self-caricaturing *essence* of an ineffective parliament. Decoud's skepticism may often be a pose, but there is no doubt that his ridicule of Parliament as a *Gran' bestia* is partly endorsed. In the true parliamentary idea of dialogue—to be found from Milton to early Dickens at the core of "English" energy—everyone heatedly but addressively tries to exert as much power over public dialogue as he can. Dickens caught this brilliantly in what are in some sense the "first" pages of his work, the description of the mutual insults of the Pickwick Club, which hilariously transform themselves into praise. There may be shouting down, interference, and denunciation, but even at its most brutal and dilatory the parliamentary image optimistically implies some communal action, and the assumption by all the speakers that they address someone and belong. "Filibuster" appears because parliamentary form collapses under the weight of imperialist and colonial disproportions. The technique of filibuster was first used in the British parliament as the strategy of the nearest colony, Ireland (think of Swift again and *A Tale of a Tub*), and in the United States the filibuster is of course the exemplary speech act of the defeated South. Personal filibuster might be one way to describe the great power of Faulkner's style in *Absalom! Absalom!* and other works. The pathos of filibuster begins as a conscious tactical subversion of the dialogue of parliament—which implies that everyone belongs—by overdoing the right to be heard to the point where the principle annihilates itself. Instead of leaving the scene, the outnumbered minority speaker, to protest a lack of actual power, gains a futile, temporary "grieving" monopoly on talk which in no way hides his powerlessness in reality or his marginality in history. Filibuster then appears as a grievance against parliamentary order itself. This creates a new image of dialogue and speech in the novel. Faulkner's liking for Conrad can be traced partly to their shared intuition of the emergence of filibuster to replace the Dickensian exuberance of the parliament. The more language the speaker produces (including the writers themselves) the more they seem defeated, "taken over" by the force of history, dependent, Faulkner as Southern, Conrad as Polish.

Nostromo tries to capture this paradoxical rhythm of colonial talk in a prose of self-defeating rhythms. Verbal "expansion" and accumulation lack expansive romantic joy. This is one reason for the book's unpopularity in spite of its virtuoso cast of romantic characters, clearly a bid to attract an audience: Conrad here makes the very technique of romantic expansiveness which he seems to be practicing deliberately joyless. This contracted expansiveness in prose style may be typical of a certain kind of poetic novel, in which condensation is ill at ease with narrative momentum. But here it "refers" rhythmically to the historical problem of expansion itself. As in the difficult prose rhythm, in politics neither contraction nor expansion is shown to be the simple answer.

As often in Conrad's best work, the alert characters are painfully conscious of the problems of speech proportion and discuss them openly but are unable to alter them. The Goulds, for example, confront together the fact that both Holroyd and Avellanos talk a lot, and find themselves suddenly disagreeing:

> They had stopped near the cage. The parrot, catching the sound of a word belonging to his vocabulary, was moved to interfere. Parrots are very human.
>
> "Viva Costaguana!" he shrieked, with intense self-assertion, and, instantly ruffling up his feathers, assumed an air of puffed-up somnolence behind the glittering wires.
>
> "And do you believe that, Charley?" Mrs. Gould asked. "This seems to me most awful materialism, and—"
>
> "My dear, it's nothing to me," interrupted her husband, in a reasonable tone. "I make use of what I see. What's it to me whether

his talk is the voice of destiny or simply a bit of claptrap eloquence? There's a good deal of eloquence of one sort or another produced in both Americas. The air of the New World seems favourable to the art of declamation. Have you forgotten how dear Avellanos can hold forth for hours here—?"

"Oh, but that's different," protested Mrs. Gould, almost shocked. The allusion was not to the point. Don José was a dear good man, who talked very well, and was enthusiastic about the greatness of the San Tomé mine. "How can you compare them, Charles?" she exclaimed, reproachfully. "He has suffered—and yet he hopes."

The working competence of men—which she never questioned—was very surprising to Mrs. Gould, because upon so many obvious issues they showed themselves strangely muddleheaded.

Charles Gould, with a careworn calmness which secured for him at once his wife's anxious sympathy, assured her that he was not comparing.

Here the Goulds between them divide up the meaning of those masses of words that challenge the reader's sense of rhythm on encountering the difficult opening movement of the novel. What are we to think of the production of "major force" by cumulative language? Is this force aesthetic or political? Is it force or farce? Is Avellanos' force the same as Holroyd's, or ethically different? Before siding too quickly with one of the speakers, we should recognize the intended dialogism: the equal case made for each side. The scene itself is framed and emblematized by the deceptively banal parrot, who screams out (in translation), "Long live the coast of bird-droppings," one instance of Swiftian satire partly hidden from the English audience by polyglossia. The slogan that comes out of a bird's mouth—its *bêtise*—will celebrate whatever comes out of its rectum or "mine." That is, the parrot is an emblem of ideological speech itself. The name Costaguana is typical of Conrad's punning—onomastic jokes being themselves allegorical coercions which the reader with an urge for freedom will usually want to resist. But that is the point: the parrot is not just the emblem of mechanically produced speech but a representative of language as not free but materially "caused." This is what Charles, the materialist, believes. Language is matter, and a lot coming from one mouth is the same as a lot coming from another. Language must be judged as pure extension, even as mass. Emilia, for once "almost shocked" by an idea of Charles's, insists on a self-evident ethical distinction between the two men:

the wordy constitutionalist Avellanos articulates a social ethic that cannot be equated by plain word count to claptrap like Holroyd's material evangelism. But while obviously her critical idealism pervades the entire novel, she is not coextensive with its dramatic meaning. When Charles as a producer sees words only as mass and extension, he resembles Conrad's own working conditions, as a producer of many words for a living, more than does Emilia.

These two positions regarding amassed language—the ethical, which holds that the altruistic content of verbal expansiveness can be real, and the materialist, which dismisses all expansiveness as the same sublimation of imperial force in "inclusive" prose rhythms—are irreconcilable and at the heart of the novel's tortured prose, of Conrad's quarrel with cumulative effect in the historical novel, and even with his own evolved techniques of *progression d'effet*, as described a little too preciously by Ford. Conrad often criticizes or mocks his own techniques for creating aesthetic "force." So the reader is meant to feel the amassing of prose in this novel itself, not simply as sublime energy, and not simply as historical "shit" (or excrementitious burden), but as the conflict between these. The prose-poetic question that the novel poses is: how are we to feel about the accumulation of language in any "great" historical or social novel whose physical mass as a big book is a weighty metaphor for populousness, even a demographic gesture? Is it potentially "beautiful," ethically high and sublime, socially inclusive, like a great constitution, potentially democratic and compassionate, as to Emilia and José; or is it always, even more violently than in the bleakness of late Dickens, some unconscious brand of "nationalist shit," the sublimated image of national greatness in the great massive novel? Thus when we scan *Nostromo* visually, or its amassed long paragraphs, and recall its temporal rhythms, we are presented with a question regarding massiveness itself.

Prose as the laborious production of masses of words is a recurrent theme in Conrad's letters, in which he often counts words in units of ten thousand, parentally scolding or praising himself for the month's yield. The parrot may come from Flaubert on banality, or may recall Melville's despair at writing as scrivening in his forced dialogue *Bartleby*—but it is also just a crude joke. Conrad's picture of himself as being compelled to write a lot, and his ability to register this strain and make it a prose rhythm, combine with his complex Polish sense of scale, and his very harsh sense of humor, to redefine the rhythmic ambition of the historical novel. To ignore his sadly "solemn mockery" of the ethical figures in the novel—even Emilia Gould, when she attends a birth of warm, fecal silver from the mine—is to sentimentalize his real case for them as persons with hopeful ideas. Leavis and Berthoud, who write brilliantly about the book in the tradition of moral criticism, nevertheless are a little too oblique or silent about this grosser laughter that has a different impact from high "irony." Consider this description of José Avellanos talking: "Then giving up the empty cup into his young friend's hand, extended with a smile, he continued to expatiate upon the patriotic nature of the San Tomé mine for the simple pleasure of talking fluently, it seemed, while his reclining body jerked backwards and forwards in a rocking-chair of the sort exported from the United States." This sentence imports the jerky physics of the rocking chair into its own syntax and shrieking rhymes in order to comment on Avellanos' dependent politics. The rhythmic form mocks the stated theme of fluency. The four *at*'s (expatiate, patriotic, nature) at the outset are monotonous, mechanical; the "it seemed" interrupts at just the wrong moment, after "fluently," for an effect of gross rhythmic farce; the image of the talking body of Avellanos sitting on a jerky machine indicates that he remains unconscious of the material base of his own eloquence; rest, unrest, arrest come together in false unison in the key motion of jerking; and the rocking-chair rhythm of the phrase "sort exported" shows us that Avellanos has an imported rhythm (rocking chairs being at this time a piece of furniture particularly associated with New England): his own rhetorical continuity and force are dependent. This is not to say that Conrad regards all parliamentary talk as just "superstructure"; but he does present most historical and political discourse as "jerkily" disconnected from historical reality. This "jerking" rhythm, with affectionate, almost Homeric satire about the tremors of the old, is associated throughout the novel with the speech and movements of Mitchell, Monygham, and Giorgio; it signifies both their broken physical courage and their various incomplete relations to the forced dialogues of social history. Avellanos, no matter how admirable in having survived torture, is a leisure-class figure in a rocking chair, somewhat cut off from material and social reality, whose speech, like the parrot's, derives from his "bottom," base, or seat.

Among other things, what Avellanos, like Mitchell, omits in his jerkiness is that labor is impressed, forced to work, imported, even enslaved. Impressment at the docks is left to Nostromo; he impresses laborers visually by his silver displays, and acts as a one-man press gang toward them, beating them to make them work. Such impressive "force" makes labor continuous. In discussing the "patriotic nature" of the mine, Avellanos also omits—as immediately afterward we are told Mrs. Gould knows—that "whole tribes of Indians had perished in the exploitation." Again, in this view of its supposed "nature," he omits the great joke, that Charles Gould himself owns the mine because it was originally *forced* on his father at a time when it was nonproductive; the mine itself has its origins in a grimly funny forced dialogue between the state and the Gould family. In all this the point is that Avellanos uses an unconscious oxymoron when he refers to "patriotic nature," just as Holroyd does more blatantly when he refers to the coming time for "proper interference" by North America in Sulaco. For Avellanos, the "deliciousness" of the rhetorical figure "patriotic nature" lies not only in its euphony but in its sublime combination of father and mother, patriotism and nature. But this is meant here to be an irrational synthesis: mines do not have patriotic identity. Speaking about property and nature, the two fall into similar contradictions. The argument that Conrad had a bad ear for English, and was himself trying to capture euphoniously the rhythms of the rocking chair, would, I think, be nonsense. His sense of the English verb is acute; *jerk* is the key verb for going on without achieved continuity throughout the novel. At the very least, the contrast between Avellanos' alleged fluency and the rhythms of the imported chair gives some credence to Charles' materialistic reduction of him. At the most, it implies that Avellanos, however sympathetic, is as much of a historical fool, out of touch with the real "continuity and force" of history, and of class relations, as is the more obviously ludicrous historian Mitchell. Avellanos is materially dependent on the United States for his rhythms; his speech is jerky because dependent systems of thought are by nature full of gaps.

To summarize what has to be a set of indicators rather than a complete description of this part of the novel's prose poetic: (1) *Nostromo* is a small big novel because its play with scale calls into question the spirit of amassing which it creates. It continually "contracts" the noisiness and expansiveness it also renders. (2) It can be helpful to understand the organization of the whole novel, as history and as the aesthetics of dialogue, by the term *filibuster*. The multiple dependent speakers threaten the parliamentary image of collective speech as much as the multiple fomenters of different revolutions in action in Latin America. (3) The issues of amassed prose and of proportion in dialogue are inextricably fused as both aesthetic and political in Conrad's work.

One main unstudied question about the poetics of *Nostromo* deserves close attention: the chime between the economy of "silver" in the narrative and the economy of "silence" in the dialogues. In a singularly precise way . . . the whole of *Nostromo* works to demonstrate that the two economies run parallel in any society, and that in this particular one "silence is silver," not golden. Silence, the reserve of dialogical power, resembles silver the reserve of political power, and both appear, when looked at closely, to be dependent, secondary currencies. They fluctuate in value in response to other currencies. Silver, for all its sometimes overworked visual recurrence in the book, has been carefully chosen by Conrad to displace gold as the "typical symbol" of value because it is less stable, and more dependent. In addition, as the lesser of the two "major" currencies, the smaller standard of value, silver had various meanings in the Americas at the turn of the century, and also, as we will see in a moment, makes a possible symbolic reference to Poland as a dependent nation. Silences likewise (at least the local silences in human dialogue, if not the natural silence of places like the Golfo Placido) are the lesser and more fluctuating part of social language; though sometimes silence in Conrad seems to be at the base of all dialogue, a reserve from which meaning is drawn, at least as often it seems by contrast dependent on and determined by the speeches surrounding it. He does not have a theory but a practice: his ability to exploit both these possibilities leads to much of the dramatic complexity of his writing. Throughout *Nostromo*, silver and silence become the linked defensive "possessions" of the various characters. The two elements are more meaningful together than alone: they indicate ironically that dependent persons who try to achieve autonomy have to do so through dependent, not absolute, means. This may be the most original feature of *Nostromo*, an extraordinary idea of linkage between the political economy and the dialogue economy that colonial people are forced to practice, formally registered by a polyphony between the dialogical and narrative forms of the novel. But to follow this prose chime— even to convince the reader that it is forcibly there—I will have to backtrack and discuss the way in which words are offered in the novel.

The geographical Sulaco, defended from the profane outside world, appears at the start as a natural temple of silence. The narrative, however, quickly dissolves this legendary, "dumb show" atmosphere (including the story of the gringos' silent death) to give a portrait of the progressive modernization of the country as "noise"—much as Decoud will later suggest, annoying Avellanos and Antonia by his own loud insistence, that colonial history is a progress of increasing noise. Though the opening folktale about gringos and their ghostly fate has often been taken to foreshadow the action, it is also one of those legends frequently found in Conrad, whose silent simplicity is at odds with novelistic realism. The dumb show is a legend of silence; the novel is a history of both silence and noise. Especially during the riot, part 1 sets up a contrast between nature as silence and history as noise. Between the absolute silence of the Golfo Placido and the total noise of anarchic riot, however, there is also music, which is here a kind of forced, or "strung up," order, and characters here are implicitly orchestrated as different political instruments. Mrs. Viola, for example, takes her name from her sonorous, perhaps pseudoprophetic "contralto," which has an ambiguous effect on Nostromo's future; and less clearly, Decoud's name suggests "unstrung" or "unthreaded," so that it is, as will be clear further on, part of an entire system of "musical bondage" and the political instrumentalization of persons—derived from the forcible tuning of strings—in the imagery.

For an understanding of the use of words, names, and noises, however, the companion book to the first part of *Nostromo* is probably again Cunninghame Graham's *Mogreb-el-Acksa*. That book is sprinkled with foreign words, and has a random exuberance of polyglossia or languages in contact. Graham presents himself as an ethnographer of speech, a collector of folk proverbs, and a *bête noire* to his contemporaries, reversing their moralisms into anti-moralisms of his own. In his witty protests he seems full of himself, where Conrad often seems, in direct contrast, empty of himself. As a result, what seems to be the common ground between them—ironic, detached criticism of a polyglot imperial world—is in fact the radical difference, because Graham finds it to be full, Conrad empty. Graham, for example, gives a waggish portrait of a vagabond as someone who "spoke almost every language in the world" and was therefore a "knave." Thus he seems to be debunking polyglossia. But at the same time Graham lets us know that he himself is the knave, the vagabond trickster, filling his book with clever insights. The book is filled with Spanish proverbs, jokes about the pretensions of philologists, and the entertainment of the mixed races of Morocco. Graham speaks in these heavily witty tones about naming: "How much there is in names; fancy a deity, accustomed to be prayed to as Allah by Arabs, suddenly addressed by an Armenian as Es Stuatz, it would be almost pitiable enough to make him turn an atheist upon himself." (The artfully assumed run-on speaking character of this syntax typified Graham's mobile style in the whole book.) "I feel convinced a rose by any other name does not smell sweet; and the word Allah is responsible for much of the reverence and the faith of those who worship him." He jokes, but he believes in the fullness of names. In spite of his apparent mockery of name superstition, as a stylist he creates a roving, rich, and exotic text full of interesting words and scenes. The book is a true travelogue.

Nostromo at first looks similar to *Mogreb-el-Acksa*. It presents us an American nation positioned roughly where Morocco is vis-à-vis Europe—"below"— and likewise "filled" with plural races. We get a medley of Italian, English, Spanish, American, American Indian, and Jewish figures. One impulse Conrad had in constructing the book was no doubt to fill it with these so that it would sell. The modern reader who sees Conrad as gloomy forgets to what extent the work had to be sold as full of swashbucklers and dark women. But of course at the same time he does subvert his own romance with bitterness and skepticism, and gives, unlike Graham, a feeling of contraction. The names that speckle his text in various languages are mostly empty, lacking in appropriateness, in property. They are not romantic but contractual, deliberately hollow, and often oxymoronic. Mrs. Viola, with her operatic faith in the force of speech, scoffs at Nostromo that his name is only a fool's contract: "He would take a name that is properly no word from them." But Nostromo's name, "taken from them," is a contract much like "Joseph Conrad," a contraction, and the word *proper* resonates emptily throughout the novel, most bitterly when Holroyd says his oxymoron, already quoted, about "the time for proper interference on our part." The littlest and ugliest of the islands is improperly named Hermosa—"beautiful"; the Rio Seco is the obvious oxymoronic place for Montero's great victory; the ubiquitous military guards are "serenos." From the beginning, steamship names from the Roman pantheon are inappropriate: "The *Juno* was known only for her comfortable cabin amidships, the *Saturn* for the geniality of her captain," and so on. What interests Conrad here is not the old boy's lament that words are losing their meaning. Conrad has a much larger intelligence of the transience of language and names in history. Though there is an obvious joke in the discrepancy between the Roman god's attributes and the individual boats and captains, Rome *itself* is appropriate to this context of modern imperial sailing. What interests him is that figures like Mrs. Viola, who believe "profoundly" in the individual propriety of names miss the larger force and continuity within changing language and history. A name that is improper for the individual, and that lacks appropriateness to his first character or being, may by that very emptiness be true to the force of history. "Nostromo," the name as renamed, as renown (compare the French *renommé*) is "taken from them" because fame necessarily has the structure of being renamed for others. Józef Korzeniowski himself altered his name so that it would have English currency. There is accurate comedy in the fact that the new *Saturn* is known for geniality. The fact that the original tones of names are "detonated" or "unthreaded" by history does not fill Conrad with conservative horror, or with the desire, like Graham, to be a wag. Names of historical persons *are* contracts. Mrs. Viola has a case when she points out that Nostromo is paid in words but is not even allowed his own name; but the fact that it is someone named Mrs. Viola who says this should lead us to suspect the sonority of the criticism as much as anything else.

Just as Decoud hears history in the changing noises of Sulaco, the reader is meant to hear the many little noises, splutters and renamings in the prose, and to organize them skeptically as signs of colonial history. Though it is risky to posit a "global" sense of names and words, it would be helpful to emphasize the frequent contractual emptiness of naming here. This is a kind of polyphony which is not "fullness" and not historical or social "plenitude." In Bakhtin's concept of novelistic diction as "heteroglossia" or "polyglossia" (plurality of dialects, languages, and ideologies), the novel in its truest generic examples shows forth the irreconcilable languages of different groups—classes, nationalities, and professions. These give the novel its unique sense of plenitude as surfeit, and its special powers to present a variety of consciousnesses. Bakhtin's work is great; yet the crude criticism could be leveled that, in spite of his desire to affirm "otherness," his work adds up, surprisingly enough, to an encomium on expansive nationalism. The novel, in all its exuberance, equals the various, large, cacophonous, tolerant, multivoiced nation—and the favorite examples will be national geniuses like Dickens and Dostoevsky— whose robust dialogics Bakhtin advocated partly as a protest against his own political situation. The relation of *Nostromo* to this pluralism of the historical novel is unusual to the point of being bizarrely antithetical. Conrad equally apprehends, but does not equally celebrate, what Bakhtin sees. The "heteroglossia" here, the polyphony of ideas, the diverse, irreconcilable languages have no exuberant flavor. Conrad imagined a more forced and negative "polyglossia," not exactly Babel, but a world in which the plurality of languages and ideas does not amount to a new plenitude. It only exists, marked by ironies, emptinesses, contractions, and contractualities of its own, rather than by glorious worldliness and freedom. That is, Conrad created, from his Polish-English contractual standpoint, a deliberately hollow and coercive international polyphony.

It is in this strangely ironic, oxymoronic, contractual, historically emptying context of naming in *Nostromo* that we have to ask the question, Why is the Gould mine a silver mine? Why choose silver as the ore and then name the owning family Gould? The false easy answers are two. One is that gold and silver are functionally identical here; the Gould family name indicates its position as source of value in Sulaco. The contrary, slightly less oversimplified reading would argue that this naming is a harsh oxymoron, almost on the order of Orwellian satire, which points mockingly to the relative instability and worthlessness of the novel's actual fetish of silver, as opposed to the family's illusory idealism in its search for a stable and perfect standard of value and of politics for Costaguana.

Neither reading is precise. Instead, silver in the novel has to be understood both in its relation to the book's dialogue forms and in its historical connotations. *Heart of Darkness* . . . "chimed" Ivory to Invoice, the economic standard of value to Marlow's obsession with an "in-voice," a powerful, idealist, standard-giving Kurtz. In that story the two fetishes equally required critique, but Marlow's effort to liberate himself from his idea of Kurtz's voice was a more difficult and prolonged "secondary" struggle, ending in the realization that forced dialogue, not freedom, is the form of Intention. *Nostromo* carries on, but in a more subtle and unforgettable way, this project of a chiming or parallelism between an economic currency—in Sulaco silver—and an illusory, pseudoliberating dialogical currency—in Sulaco no longer voice but silence. As often in Conrad, the alteration of a commonplace, as if both to rivet and revise the thinking of a large audience, is being undertaken without Flaubert's contempt or hilarity. According to convention, of course, "silence is golden." In the structure of *Nostromo*, "silence is silver." That is, both are secondary or dependent currencies, relatively unstable in comparison to the main currencies, language and gold.

Put the poetics of the parallelism between silence and silver aside for a moment, and consider the historical theme of silver. In the Americas at the time Conrad describes, bimetallism was a major popular issue; silver symbolized the increased distribution of wealth downward without forsaking the standards of capitalism. In the *Titanic* essays eight years later Conrad refers ironically to "nasty, cheap silver," parodying the voice of the superrich who might have to use it on a sea journey. One need not connect Charles Gould to William Jennings Bryan to see that Gould uses the idea of "cheap" silver as the more democratic and politicized of the two standards of value to half convince Emilia that his is an idealist capitalism, ultimately good for "the people." Silver will spread the wealth; when it is appropriated by Nostromo, the man of the people, as a secret hoard to which he is also in some sense entitled (actively and in dialogue, because no one has asked him about it), the political connotations are intentional: Nostromo has taken by covert silent force a form of popular wealth that was patronizingly given him before. And just as silver has a dependent but varying relation to gold—a restless relation—in its value, so silence, in any major work by Conrad, has exact but restless relations to what is being said. This restless shifting in the meanings of silences . . . was noticed by some of Conrad's earliest readers as an essential part of his ironic mastery and his involvement of the reader.

Thus we have broad historical and poetic uses of "silver" in this novel. Silver is (1) a secondary currency, raising the issue of dependence; (2) the currency in the Americas which theoretically, if not in fact, might open the field of wealth out from the aristocracy and oligarchy toward the people; (3) an analogy to silence itself, not only as the "natural reserve" but because it is secondary and dependent. Silver is the only weapon of Sulaco against the outside world; silence is the only weapon of dependent persons who are being made to speak. By this technique of chiming or parallelism between the political economy and the dialogue economy of resistance, Conrad can give form to his precise insight that dialogue forms are not the "free" part of social life, *or* of the novel, but complex expressions of other working relations and currencies. And he does this not in an abstract way but by showing how each of the major characters makes a *distinctive* personal synthesis of the two Sulacan defenses, silver and silence, in the struggle to achieve some kind of autonomy. The limit of these varied attempts to achieve independence via dependent means is the desperate plural story of the different persons in the novel.

Conrad would later write about the structure of *A Personal Record*: "In the purposely mingled resonance of this double strain a friend here and there will perhaps detect a subtle accord." "Silver and silence" is another subtle accord, giving a strange new unity to a work. One of the major actions of *Nostromo*—if by action we mean with Francis Fergusson the way the poetic writing leads the mind of the reader to make conscious connections among previously segregated categories of experience—is the play between dependent dialogical manners and dependent monetary currency. Through this action *Nostromo* departs significantly from Conrad's earlier sense of dialogue as primarily a "physics" toward the sense that dialogue is primarily a "political economy" practiced by dependent persons. Though here too there is a great deal of attention to the physical force of noise, to physically amassed language, to dialogue as a meeting of weights, the more economic and historical action of "silver as silence" allows Conrad to offer a representation of the linguistic economies of colonized persons, in which they discover parallel ways of using money and silence together.

The central compounder of silence and silver is of course Charles Gould. He prizes silver as the key to Costaguana's redemption from restless politics; he maintains various aloof silences with Holroyd, with the local bureaucrats, and with Hirsch (who wants to sell him dynamite and hides, but has trouble getting him to talk at all). Gould takes part in such "degrading" marketplace dialogue as little as possible. His stolid "character" *is* this resistive alloy of silver and silence; but his imperial stance eventually extends to the dialogue of his marriage, which had been intimate, or at least tender, at first. "It was," we are told in a scene clarifying that the marriage is dead, "as if the inspiration of their early years had left her heart to turn into a wall of silver bricks, erected by the silent work of evil spirits, between her and her husband." There is no question that in the portrait of Charles Gould, taciturnity is a fetish as recurrent and as crucial as silver, or that Conrad does whatever he can to make us hear the near-silent chime, even at the risk of seeming grossly allegorical. As in *The Secret Agent*, there seems to be no way for political people to draw a line between the dialogue economy with which they meet the world and the dialogue of their marriages. To simplify somewhat, the reader is meant to reason in this way: in the context of this whole inquisitorial society, silence is the most common mode of defense, from the Indios to Monygham. Gould—hence his name—seems to personify the proverb, or cliché, that silence is golden, but the whole effect is vaguely ridiculous, and in reality, he is in possession of silence and silver, a more ambiguous, less absolute, more comically mechanical power.

That the Gould-silver irony is being emphasized throughout the novel to point to a general condition of dependency is clear enough within the novel itself, but can perhaps be reinforced by a look at Adam Mickiewicz. Here is Napoleon in *Pan Tadeusz*: "Such were the amusements and disputes of those days in the quiet Lithuanian village, where the rest of the world was swimming in tears and blood, and while that man, the god of war, surrounded by a cloud of regiments, armed with a thousand cannon, harnessing in his chariot golden eagles besides those of silver, was flying from the deserts of Libya to the lofty Alps, casting thunderbolt on thunderbolt, at the Pyramids, at Tabor, Matengo, Ulm, and Austerlitz. Victory and Conquest ran before and after him." For our purposes, the footnote to the same translation is useful when it informs us that "the reference is *of course* [my italics] to the golden eagles of Napoleon joined with the silver eagles of Poland." Of course? Probably not for most of Conrad's audience, but probably for Conrad himself. Here a little effort can help us become "familiar" with—that is, factitiously informed about—his non-English historical perspective. Charles Gould has, in relation to Sulaco, and then to Holroyd, a paradoxical *imperium in imperio*, an empire within an empire. During the Napoleonic era, the emblematic alliance between gold and silver gave brief hope that Poland might repel the Russian empire by a French alliance. There is no space here to survey nineteenth-century Franco-Polish relations, but only to note that by the 1890s, they had fallen somewhat into the shadow of a French taste for things and novels Russian, which may be one reason why Conrad—unlike Mickiewicz and Juliusz Słowacki—chose England as his haven. The important point here is that gold and silver (Gould's silver mine) may be taken as an emblem of the unstable, unreliable, and often in the end disappointing alliance between a dependent nation and a great modernizing empire. Gould's silver alliance with the American golden boy Holroyd has *some* analogies to Poland's alliance with the golden power of Napoleon and its new world capitalism. It is not of course transparent symbolism—*Nostromo* is by no means "about" Poland's desire to secede from Russia—but the analogy helps us to feel Conrad's sense of "silver" as an ambiguous social force touched with dependency, weakness, and secondariness. The figure relies again on the reader's grasp of an uncertain "measure" and "disproportion" between two elements.

Silver has two nonmonetary meanings in the novel: it means "lesser" (like Poland) and it means "silence"; these together in turn mean the condition of dependency. To remain in Poland would have been to remain silent, or to have had to practice the arts of silent resistance. Mickiewicz, in the patriotic drama *Forefathers' Eve*, celebrates a Polish martyr who was messianically silent under interrogation but then was unable, after his release, to stop being silent with his friends and family. Conrad echoes this tragic fable when he shows how the necessary political silence invades and destroys the Gould marriage. But he was also skeptical of messianic or ineffable ideas of resistive silence in the first place. For him, silence, though sometimes admirable, is only *part* of the forced dialogue, not romantically transcendent. The misreading of Conrad that takes taciturnity in his work as a sign of transcendence must be critically dispelled. Only the early sea stories have something of this character, and even there not without irony. We might almost go to the opposite extreme and say that a major theme in the novels from *Nostromo* to *Victory* is a near-systematic critique of his own and his reader's "taste for silence" to show that it is often dangerously impractical and sadly deceived. Gould's English taciturnity, his practical English version of Polish messianic silence, is one of numerous examples: a strong political reserve, praised and admired to a degree, but also exposed as personally destructive. It kills his marriage, and is perhaps also a partial delusion of independence in the political realm: "Charles Gould assumed that if the appearance of listening to deplorable balderdash must form part of the price he had to pay for being left unmolested, the obligation of uttering balderdash pesonally was by no means included in the bargain. He drew the line there." His gentlemanly rule in dialogue is not unlike Whalley's: he will suffer cant politely but not lower himself to actually speak it. But in the perpetual stream of critical irony the sentence that ends with the emphatic word *there* sounds like mockery of his arbitrary choice as one made from vanity, snobbism, and class safety, not from real dignity or truth. It is of extreme importance that with Holroyd, Gould does relent, does not draw the line. Even his silences with Holroyd have less dignity, and are more compromised, than those he practices with bureaucrats or merchants; they mean that he suppresses frankness to keep the backing. In all this, the silence and silver of Charles Gould add up to a "strong character" not nearly as autonomous or regal as it seems. Gould cannot make himself the Golfo Placido incarnate; his silences are human and dialogized, not natural and infinite, however successfully he seems to transcend.

Gould's character and consciousness are outlined in three ironically related meanings of the word *mine* : (1) the personal pronoun—possession as silent self-possession; (2) the quarry itself—possession as material wealth, with emphasis on ore as buried and secret; (3) the final threat to detonate the mine, turning it into a "mine" in the third sense, found particularly in the nautical lexicon: a hidden explosive sometimes set off by acoustic force. At least some of this forced polysemy is implied when Decoud scoffs bitterly: "He and his mine"; "he has his mine in his head." It is a negative progress of meanings which need no paraphrase. The simplest, even most childish English word for the owning self is being redefined within the mode we are learning to recognize as forced dialogue. Ego is ultimately a property one can't refuse to have been given, and may be forced to define itself by a threat of self-destruction. This is why Charles Gould is not so much a great character as a great image of the tragic illusion in the idea that character is self-possession. "Mine" claims a self through an external object; this leads, logically, to the claim to the right to destroy the object. As in many places in Conrad's glossary, a word acquires its full meaning only when we perceive that identity has the unlikely structure of forced dialogue, involuntary relation. In addition, the polysemy of a word is not Gould's consciousness—the feeling throughout the novel that he embodies the ideas of "the mine," of strong secular identity as a logic of self-destructive pathos—implies that private identity paradoxically makes a last stand at the threat of self-destruction. Where Dickens ridicules the Coketown barons' threat to hurl their factories into the sea if the state intrudes, Gould's threat to detonate "his" mine, in a vast act of grotesque historical spite, though no less critically displayed as the logic of possessive identity, is no absurd bluff. And his attempt to make silence and silver the adequate sources of a locally strong personality is more than just stuffiness and archness. He expresses, through the logic of his class, one of the main themes of the novel—that the means, such as "property," by which dependent people must seek to establish independence are themselves dependent, and can become illusions of self-sufficiency, because all relation is in essence dependency, "destructive immersion." Only dependent instruments and compromising, coercive contracts are available.

The history of the Gould mine, called ironically a "Concession," and itself told as a forced dialogue, is one of the wittiest accounts of the origin of property in the English novel. "Concession" is a contractual speech act term used ironically here, since it was Gould Senior who conceded when he was forced by a political enemy to take on the mine as a tax burden, an unwanted, useless property. To own, for the Gould family, was originally to concede; property was not freedom but a forced relation. Later, Nostromo will become a more ambiguously forced owner of silver and silence in a similar concession of his best self to property. But the original outrage committed against Gould Senior, to *make him own* something, is very funny, with a sort of Balzacian acerbity about the idea that ownership is in essence free. The origin of this great family's wealth is a great crime against the family. English tradition usually associates ownership, like speech, with free choice. But here, to speak and to own are forced actions in which one must find a personality by choosing an answer from among limited options. This is how I would question, with more emphasis on circumstance and mutual force, Edward Said's thesis that Conrad's work in principle rejects "beginnings," and is concerned with tentative intentions rather than with origins. While this makes some sense in regard to Conrad's skepticism about authorship itself (though as already suggested he sometimes saw his writing as a forced contract), over and over, it seems to me, Conrad does present a clear notion of the forced origins of his various characters' lives in specific contracts they can't avoid. *Nostromo* as an action begins, comically, robustly, and primevally, when ownership of a useless mine is forced on Gould Senior; *The Secret Agent* begins when Verloc is forced, in dialogue with Vladimir, to produce terror; *Under Western Eyes* begins when Razumov is forced to talk with and shelter Haldin. Charles Gould's life, including his early study of mine engineering, is determined by the existence of the original Concession. He lives to reverse the status of the covenant that defeated his father, but though he then tries to forget the original involuntary character of the "mine" ownership, his life in fact has been defined by that coercion. Victory in forced dialogue is not the same as transcendence of its form.

This idea of ownership as forced possession, something inherited against one's will, like existence itself, both resembles and diverges from Harold Bloom's concept of poetic "influence." In the *Prelude* Wordsworth uses the term *inquisition* to describe his examination of himself for possible themes. As in Borges' reference to literature as "other inquisitions," the irony is infinite. Conrad, as his own work progressed, seems however to have turned, or to have tried to turn, partly away from the infinite ironic romance of self-inquisition (represented by the romantically compelled speaker Marlow) toward the representation, during the period of the political novels, of limited, external, crude forced dialogues in the world. There is the hint of a suspicion that it might be a bad defense, a bad infinity, to always internalize the format of coercion to speak as poetic will. Poetics, in Bloomian romanticism, may be the denial, by internalization, of the Oedipal order of forced dialogue in the outside world—the translation of inquisition into an inner feeling of compulsion to quarrel with a forebear or with oneself. In any case, Conrad turned from infinite self-inquisition to emphasize "objective" political scenes in which the enslaved, colonized, or dependent individual is made to speak, to own, to respond. In Bloom's signally moving personal terms, Gould's inheritance of the silver mine from his defeated father symbolizes Conrad's inheritance, from his own father and his "fathers," of Polish poetic dependency, Polish tragic "silence," Polish poetic minority in the greater world. And this is, to say the least, a viable reading. But Conrad's description of historical struggles for independence via dependent means is certainly also meant as a representation of actual political struggle by colonials against outside influences. This is one of the self-critical questions Conrad's later political novels direct, not always successfully, against his early work. He becomes convinced that the compulsion to speak does not always come from within, and that the political aspect of coercion to speak is at times disguised by inner agony.

Chronology

1857   Józef Teodor Konrad Korzeniowski born December 3, in Ber-
        dyczew, Poland, to Apollo Korzeniowski and Ewelina Bo-
        browska.

1862   Apollo Korzeniowski is exiled to Russia for his part in the
        Polish National Committee. His wife and son accompany him.

1865   Conrad's mother dies.

1869   Apollo Korzeniowski and son return to Cracow in February.
        Apollo dies on May 23.

1874   Conrad leaves Cracow for Marseilles, intending to become a
        sailor.

1875   Conrad is an apprentice aboard the *Mont Blanc*, bound for
        Martinique.

1877   Conrad is part owner of the *Tremolino*, which carries illegal
        arms to the Spanish pretender, Don Carlos.

1878   In February, after ending an unhappy love affair, Conrad at-
        tempts suicide by shooting himself. In June, he lands in En-
        gland. He serves as ordinary seaman on the *Mavis*.

1883   Becomes mate on the ship *Riversdale*.

1884   Is second mate on the *Narcissus*, bound from Bombay to Dun-
        kirk.

1886   Conrad becomes a naturalized British citizen.

1887   Is first mate on the *Highland Forest*.

1889   Begins writing *Almayer's Folly*.

1890	In May, Conrad leaves for the Congo as second in command of the S. S. *Roi de Belges*, later becoming commander.
1894	On January 14, he ends his sea career.
1895	Publishes *Almayer's Folly*. Writes *An Outcast of the Islands*. He is now living in London.
1896	Conrad marries Jessie George on March 28.
1897–1900	Writes *The Nigger of the "Narcissus," Heart of Darkness*, and *Lord Jim*.
1904	Completes *Nostromo*.
1905	Granted Civil List Pension. Travels in Europe for four months.
1907	Writes *The Secret Agent*.
1911–12	Writes *Under Western Eyes*, and *'Twixt Land and Sea*.
1914	Writes *Chance* and *Victory*. Conrad visits Poland in July, where he is caught when the Great War breaks out on August 4. He escapes and returns safely to England in November.
1916	Conrad's son, Borys, is fighting on the French front.
1917	Writes *The Shadow-Line*, and prefaces to an edition of his collected works.
1918	Armistice, November 11.
1919	Conrad writes *The Arrow of Gold*. He moves to Oswalds, Bishopsbourne, near Canterbury, where he spends his last years.
1920	Writes *The Rescue*.
1924	In May, Conrad declines a knighthood. After an illness, he dies of a heart attack on August 3. He is buried in Canterbury.
1925	The incomplete *Suspense* is published. *Tales of Hearsay* is published.
1926	*Last Essays* published.

Contributors

HAROLD BLOOM, Sterling Professor of the Humanities at Yale University, is the author of *The Anxiety of Influence, Poetry and Repression*, and many other volumes of literary criticism. His forthcoming study, *Freud: Transference and Authority*, attempts a full-scale reading of all of Freud's major writings. A MacArthur Prize Fellow, he is general editor of five series of literary criticism published by Chelsea House.

IAN WATT is Professor of English at Stanford University. His books include *The Rise of the Novel, Conrad in the Nineteenth Century*, and the forthcoming *Gothic and Comic: Two Variations on the Realistic Tradition*.

EDWARD W. SAID is Parr Professor of English and Comparative Literature at Columbia University. His books include *Joseph Conrad and the Fiction of Autobiography*, and several studies of the Middle East.

NORMAN N. HOLLAND is Richard J. Milbauer Professor of English at the University of Florida, Gainesville. His books include *The Shakespearean Imagination* and *The Dynamics of Literary Response*.

R. W. B. LEWIS is Neil Gray Professor of Rhetoric at Yale University. His books include *The American Adam* and a biography of Edith Wharton for which he won the Pulitzer Prize in 1976.

JOAN E. STEINER is Associate Professor of English at Drew University.

DANIEL MELNICK is Professor of English at Cleveland State University.

ADAM GILLON is Professor of English and Comparative Literature, Emeritus, at the State University of New York College at New Paltz, and Professor of English Literature at the University of Haifa, Israel. His books include *The Eternal Solitary: A Study of Joseph Conrad* and several books of poetry. He is the editor of *Joseph Conrad Today*.

RUTH NADELHAFT teaches at Bangor Community College, University of Maine at Orono.

J. HILLIS MILLER is Frederick W. Hilles Professor of English and Comparative Literature at Yale University. His books include *Charles Dickens: The World of His Novels*, *Poets of Reality*, and *The Form of Victorian Fiction*.

MARTIN PRICE is Sterling Professor of English at Yale University. His books include *To the Palace of Wisdom* and *Forms of Life: Character and Moral Imagination in the Novel*.

AARON FOGEL is Assistant Professor of English at Boston University. He is the author of *Coercion to Speak: Conrad's Poetics of Dialogue*.

Bibliography

Andreach, Robert. "The Two Narrators of 'Amy Foster.'" *Studies in Short Fiction* 2 (1965): 262–69.

Baines, Jocelyn. *Joseph Conrad: A Critical Biography.* New York: McGraw-Hill, 1960.

Barnett, Louise K. "'The Whole Circle of the Horizon': The Circumscribed Universe of 'The Secret Sharer.'" *Studies in the Humanities* 8, no. 2 (1981): 5–9.

Beach, Joseph Warren. "Impressionism: Conrad." In *The Twentieth-Century Novel: Studies in Technique*, 337–65. New York: Appleton-Century, 1932.

Berman, Jeffrey. *Joseph Conrad: Writing as Rescue.* New York: Astra Books, 1977.

Blackmur, R. P. *Eleven Essays in the European Novel.* New York: Harcourt, Brace & World, 1964.

Bradbrook, M. C. *Joseph Conrad: Poland's English Genius.* Cambridge: Cambridge University Press, 1941.

Brown, Robert. "Integrity and Self-Deception." *The Critical Review* 25 (1983): 115–31.

Chapple, J. A. V. "Conrad." In *The English Novel.* Select Bibliographical Guides, edited by A. E. Dyson. London: Oxford University Press, 1974.

Conradiana: A Journal of Joseph Conrad Studies, 1968–.

Cox, Roger L. "Conrad's *Nostromo* as Boatswain." *MLN* 74 (1959): 303–6.

Crews, Frederick. "The Power of Darkness." *Partisan Review* 34 (1967): 507–25.

Curle, Richard. *The Last Twelve Years of Joseph Conrad.* Garden City, N.Y.: Doubleday & Co., 1928.

Daleski, H. M. *Joseph Conrad: The Way of Dispossession.* London: Faber & Faber, 1977.

Dike, Donald A. "The Tempest of Axel Heyst." *Nineteenth-Century Fiction* 17 (1962): 96–113.

Ehrsam, T. G. *A Bibliography of Joseph Conrad.* Metuchen, N.J.: The Scarecrow Press, 1969.

Ellmann, Richard, and Charles Feidelson, eds. *The Modern Tradition.* New York: Oxford University Press, 1965.

Fogel, Aaron. *Coercion to Speak: Conrad's Poetics of Dialogue.* Cambridge: Harvard University Press, 1985.

Ford, Ford Madox. *Joseph Conrad: A Personal Remembrance.* Boston: Little, Brown & Co., 1924.

Galsworthy, John. "Reminiscences of Conrad." In *Castles in Spain and Other Screeds*, 99–126. New York: Charles Scribner's Sons, 1927.

Garnett, Edward. *Letters from Joseph Conrad, 1895–1924*. Indianapolis: Bobbs-Merrill, 1928.

Gekoski, R. A. *Conrad: The Moral World of the Novelist*. New York: Harper & Row, 1978.

Gillon, Adam. *The Eternal Solitary*. New York: Bookman Associates, 1960.

———. *Joseph Conrad*. Boston: Twayne Publishers, 1982.

———, and Ludwik Krzyzanowski, eds. *Joseph Conrad: Commemorative Essays*. New York: Astra Books, 1975.

Guerard, Albert J. *Conrad the Novelist*. Cambridge: Harvard University Press, 1958.

———. *Joseph Conrad*. New York: New Directions, 1947.

Harkness, Bruce, ed. *Conrad's "Heart of Darkness" and the Critics*. Belmont, Calif.: Wadsworth, 1960.

Hay, Eloise Knapp. "Joseph Conrad and Impressionism." *Journal of Aesthetics and Art Criticism* 34 (1975): 137–44.

———. *The Political Novels of Joseph Conrad*. Chicago: The University of Chicago Press, 1963.

Henricksen, Bruce. "The Heart of Darkness and the Gnostic Myth." *Mosaic* 11, no. 4 (1978): 35–44.

James, Henry. *Notes on Novelists*. New York: Charles Scribner's Sons, 1914.

Jean-Aubry, Gerard. *Joseph Conrad: Life and Letters*. London: W. Heinemann, 1927.

———. *The Sea Dreamer: A Definitive Biography of Joseph Conrad*, translated by Helen Sebba. Garden City, N.Y.: Doubleday & Co., 1957.

Johnson, Bruce M. *Conrad's Models of Mind*. Minneapolis: University of Minnesota Press, 1971.

Joseph Conrad Today: The Newsletter of the Joseph Conrad Society of America, 1975–.

Karl, Frederick R. *Joseph Conrad: The Three Lives*. New York: Farrar, Straus & Giroux, 1979.

———. *A Reader's Guide to Joseph Conrad*. Rev. ed. New York: Noonday Press, 1969.

———, ed. *Joseph Conrad: A Collection of Criticism*. New York: McGraw-Hill Book Co., 1975.

Kermode, Frank. "Secrets and Narrative Sequence." *Critical Inquiry* 7 (1980): 83–101.

Kirschner, Robert. *"Heart of Darkness": The Psychologist as Artist*. Edinburgh: Oliver & Boyd, 1968.

La Bossière, Camille R. *Joseph Conrad and the Science of Unknowing*. Fredericton, N.B., Canada: York Press, 1979.

Leavis, F. R. *The Great Tradition*. London: Chatto & Windus, 1948.

———. "Joseph Conrad." *Sewanee Review* 46 (1958): 179–200.

McLauchlin, Juliet. *Conrad: "Nostromo."* London: Edward Arnold, 1969.

———. "Conrad's 'Three Ages of Man': The 'Youth' Volume." *Polish Review* 20, nos. 2–3 (1975): 189–202.

Martz, Louis. *The Poetry of Meditation*. 2d ed. New Haven: Yale University Press, 1962.

Meyer, Bernard C. *Joseph Conrad: A Psychoanalytic Biography*. Princeton: Princeton University Press, 1967.

Miller, J. Hillis. *Poets of Reality: Six Twentieth-Century Writers*. Cambridge: Harvard University Press, 1965.

Moser, Thomas. *Joseph Conrad: Achievement and Decline*. Hamden, Conn.: Archon Books, 1957.

———, ed. *Lord Jim*. New York: W. W. Norton & Co., 1968.

Mudrick, Marvin, ed. *Conrad: A Collection of Critical Essays*. Englewood Cliffs, N.J.: Prentice-Hall, 1966.

Nettels, Elsa. *James and Conrad*. Athens: University of Georgia Press, 1977.

Palmer, John A. *Joseph Conrad's Fiction: A Study in Literary Growth*. Ithaca, N.Y.: Cornell University Press, 1968.

———, ed. *Twentieth-Century Interpretations of "The Nigger of the 'Narcissus.' "* Englewood Cliffs, N.J.: Prentice-Hall, 1969.

Rosenfield, Claire. *Paradise of Snakes: An Archetypal Analysis of Conrad's Political Novels*. Chicago: The University of Chicago Press, 1967.

Said, Edward W. *Joseph Conrad and the Fiction of Autobiography*. Cambridge: Harvard University Press, 1966.

Schwarz, Daniel R. "The Self-Deceiving Narrator of Conrad's 'Il Conde.' " *Studies in Short Fiction* 6 (1969): 187–93.

Sherry, Norman. *Conrad's Eastern World*. Cambridge: Cambridge University Press, 1966.

———, ed. *Conrad: The Critical Heritage*. London: Routledge & Kegan Paul, 1973.

———, ed. *Joseph Conrad: A Commemoration*. New York: Harper & Row, 1977.

Smith, J. Oates. "The Existential Comedy of Conrad's 'Youth.' " *Renascence* 18 (1963): 22–28.

Stallman, Robert W., ed. *The Art of Joseph Conrad: A Critical Symposium*. East Lansing: Michigan State University Press, 1960.

Tanner, Tony. "Nightmare and Complacency: Razumov and the Western Eye." *Critical Quarterly* 4 (1962): 197–214.

———, ed. *Conrad: "Lord Jim."* Great Neck, N.Y.: Barron's Educational Series, 1963.

Tennant, Roger. *Joseph Conrad: A Biography*. New York: Atheneum Publishers, 1981.

Thornburn, David. *Conrad's Romanticism*. New Haven: Yale University Press, 1974.

Tillyard, E. W. M. *"The Secret Agent* Reconsidered." *Essays in Criticism* 11 (1961): 309–18.

Van Ghent, Dorothy. *The English Novel: Form and Function*. New York: Harper & Brothers, 1961.

Verleun, Jan. *The Stone Horse: A Study of the Function of the Minor Characters in Conrad's "Nostromo."* Groningen, The Netherlands: Bouma's Boekhuis, 1978.

———. *"Patna" and Patusan Perspectives*. Groningen, The Netherlands: Bouma's Boekhuis, 1979.

Warren, Robert Penn. " 'The Great Mirage': Conrad and *Nostromo*." In *Selected Essays*, 31–58. New York: Vintage Books, 1966.

Watt, Ian. *Conrad in the Nineteenth Century*. Berkeley: University of California Press, 1979.

———. "Story and Idea in Conrad's 'The Shadow-Line.' " *Critical Quarterly* 2 (1960): 133–48.

———, ed. *"The Secret Agent": A Selection of Critical Essays*. London: Macmillan & Co., 1973.

Watts, Cedric. *Conrad's "Heart of Darkness": A Critical and Contextual Discussion*. Milan: Mursia International, 1977.

Whitehead, Lee M. "Recent Conrad Criticism." *Dalhousie Review* 61, no. 4 (1981–82): 743–49.

Wiley, Paul L. *Conrad's Measure of Man*. Madison: University of Wisconsin Press, 1954.

Wills, John Howard. "A Neglected Masterpiece: Conrad's 'Youth.' " *Texas Studies in Literature and Language* 4 (1963): 591–601.

Yelton, D. C. *Mimesis and Metaphor: An Inquiry into the Genesis and Scope of Conrad's Symbolic Imagery*. The Hague: Mouton, 1967.

Young, Vernon. "Joseph Conrad: Outline for a Reconsideration." *Hudson Review* 2 (1949): 5–19.

Zabel, Morton Dauwen. *Craft and Character in Modern Fiction*. New York: The Viking Press, 1957.

———, ed. "Introduction" to *The Portable Conrad*, 1–47. New York: The Viking Press, 1947.

Zuckerman, Jerome. "Contrapuntal Structure in Conrad's *Chance*." *Modern Fiction Studies* 10 (1964): 49–54.

Zyla, W. T., and W. M. Aycock, eds. *Joseph Conrad: Theory and World Fiction*. Lubbock: Texas Tech University, 1974.

Acknowledgments

"Conrad Criticism and *The Nigger of the 'Narcissus'*" by Ian Watt from *Nineteenth-Century Fiction* 12, no. 4 (March 1958), © 1958 by The Regents of the University of California. Reprinted by permission of The Regents.

"The Past and the Present: Conrad's Shorter Fiction" (originally entitled "The Past and the Present") by Edward W. Said from *Joseph Conrad and the Fiction of Autobiography* by Edward W. Said, © 1966 by the President and Fellows of Harvard College. Reprinted by permission of Harvard University Press.

"Style as Character: *The Secret Agent*" by Norman N. Holland from *Modern Fiction Studies* 12, no. 2 (Summer 1966), © 1966 by Purdue Research Foundation, West Lafayette, IN. Reprinted by permission.

"The Current of Conrad's *Victory*" by R. W. B. Lewis from *Twelve Original Essays on Great English Novels*, edited by Charles Shapiro, © 1966 by Wayne State University Press, 1977 by Charles Shapiro. Reprinted by permission.

"Impressionism and Symbolism in *Heart of Darkness*" by Ian Watt from *The Southern Review* 13, no. 1 (January 1977), © 1977 by Ian P. Watt. Reprinted by permission. Parts of this essay also appeared in *Conrad in the Nineteenth Century* by Ian Watt (University of California Press, 1980).

" 'The Secret Sharer': Complexities of the Doubling Relationship" (originally entitled "Conrad's 'The Secret Sharer': Complexities of the Doubling Relationship") by Joan E. Steiner from *Conradiana: A Journal of Joseph Conrad Studies* 12, no. 3 (1980), © 1980 by the Institute for Textual Studies, Department of English, Texas Tech University. Reprinted by permission.

"The Morality of Conrad's Imagination: *Heart of Darkness* and *Nostromo*" (originally entitled "The Morality of Conrad's Imagination") by Daniel Melnick from *Missouri Review* 5, no. 2 (Winter 1981–82), © 1982 by the Curators of the University of Missouri. Reprinted by permission.

"*Under Western Eyes, Chance*, and *Victory*" (originally entitled "The Desperate Shape of Betrayal: An Intimate Alliance of Contradictions" and "How to Love") by Adam Gillon from *Joseph Conrad* by Adam Gillon, © 1982 by Twayne Publishers, a division of G. K. Hall & Co., Boston. Reprinted by permission.

"Women as Moral and Political Alternatives in Conrad's Early Novels" by Ruth Nadelhaft from *Theory and Practice of Feminist Literary Criticism*, edited by Gabriela Mora and Karen S. Van Hooft, © 1982 by Bilingual Review/Press. All rights reserved. Reprinted by permission.

"*Lord Jim*: Repetition as Subversion of Organic Form" by J. Hillis Miller from *Fiction and Repetition: Seven English Novels* by J. Hillis Miller, © 1982 by J. Hillis Miller. Reprinted by permission of Harvard University Press.

"The Limits of Irony: *Lord Jim* and *Nostromo*" (originally entitled "Conrad: The Limits of Irony") by Martin Price from *Forms of Life: Character and Moral Imagination in the Novel* by Martin Price, © 1983 by Yale University. Reprinted by permission of Yale University Press.

"Silver and Silence: Dependent Currencies in *Nostromo*" by Aaron Fogel from *Coercion to Speak: Conrad's Poetics of Dialogue* by Aaron Fogel, © 1985 by the President and Fellows of Harvard College. Reprinted by permission of Harvard University Press.

Index

preface to, 138–39; Razumov's role in, 59, 129, 132–35, 136, 137–38, 226; *Secret Agent* compared to, 131, 136, 138, 139; stoicism discussed in, 137–38; Tekla's role in, 133, 134

Unwin, Fisher, 36
Ure, Peter, 186

Valéry, Paul, 88
Verlaine, Paul, 84, 87
Victory: as allegory, 71, 81; *Chance* compared to, 139, 140–41, 142; characters of, 65, 67–68, 69, 71, 78–79; concordance to, 149; Davidson's role in, 63, 65, 68, 72, 78, 148; death as theme in, 65, 72, 76, 81, 145–46; double in, 101; dramatic element in, 77, 78–79, 81; duplicity as theme in, 75–76, 80; ending of, 148–49; existentialism in, 63, 64, 65, 71, 72–73, 79, 148–49; fetishism and voyeurism in, 147; Heyst's role in, 59, 64, 66, 68, 69, 71–81, 143–45, 149; isolation as theme in, 64; Jones's role in, 59, 64, 65–66, 68, 69–70, 71–81, 140–41, 146, 147; Lena's role in, 64, 68, 69–70, 72–75, 78, 79, 80–81, 140, 143–44, 145, 147, 148, 149; as major novel, 4, 66; major themes of, 63–81, 129, 143–49; manifold vs. unitary truth in, 64, 70, 74; as melodrama, 143, 146, 148; Morrison's role in, 64, 70, 76–77, 143, 144; *Nostromo* compared to, 66–67, 70; as novel of ideas, 64–65; *Othello* compared to, 66, 67, 70, 145; Pedro's role in, 65, 68, 146; plot of, 67–68, 69, 70–71,

73, 74; preface to, 143; Ricardo's role in, 65, 68, 69, 70, 74, 75–76, 80, 140, 143, 144, 146, 147; Schomberg's role in, 70–71, 72, 78, 80, 143, 144; self-sacrifice as theme in, 73–74, 77, 144–45, 148; *Tempest* compared to, 146; as test of fiction, 68, 81; title of, 66, 148; unreality in, 143–44; visibility in, 78–79, 80; Wang's role in, 65, 68, 79, 146; writing of, 66, 67
Vida es Sueño, La (Calderón), 143
Villiers de L'Isle Adam, Auguste de, 97, 146
Virgil, 92
"Voyage, Le" (Baudelaire), 98

War and Peace (Tolstoy), 205, 206
Warren, Robert Penn, 115
Waste Land, The (Eliot), 33, 98
Watt, Ian, 176
Waverly (Scott), 205
Welles, Orson, 4
Wells, H. G., 32, 34, 86, 139
What Is to Be Done? (Chernyshevsky), 139
What Maisie Knew (James), 2
Wilson, Edmund, 83
Woolf, Virginia, 15, 85
Wordsworth, William, 27, 88, 226

Yeats, William Butler, 16, 88–89
Young, Vernon, 17–20
"Youth": evocation of the past in, 30–31, 32; Marlow's role in, 1–2, 30–32, 34; romance in, 31; sinking of *Judea* in, 1–2

Zola, Émile, 12